KRAV MAGA
EXTREME SURVIVAL

Active Shooter • Carjacking
Home Invasion • Predator Profiling

GERSHON BEN KEREN

Photography by COLIN O'REILLY

TUTTLE Publishing

Tokyo | Rutland, Vermont | Singapore

WARNING AND DISCLAIMER

Martial arts training can be dangerous—both to you and to others—if not practiced safely. Please note that the publisher and author of this book are NOT RESPONSIBLE in any manner whatsoever for any injury that may result from practicing the techniques and/or following the instructions given within. Always practice with a trained martial arts teacher. Since the physical activities described herein may be too strenuous in nature for some readers, it is also essential to consult your physician prior to training.

Published by Tuttle Publishing, an imprint of Periplus Editions (HK) Ltd.

www.tuttlepublishing.com

Copyright © 2018 Gershon Ben Keren

Library of Congress Control Number: 2018950083

ISBN 978-0-8048-5028-5

First edition
21 20 19 18   5 4 3 2 1

Printed in Hong Kong   1808EP

Distributed by:

North America, Latin America & Europe
Tuttle Publishing
364 Innovation Drive
North Clarendon, VT 05759-9436 U.S.A.
Tel: (802) 773-8930; Fax: (802) 773-6993
info@tuttlepublishing.com
www.tuttlepublishing.com

Asia Pacific
Berkeley Books Pte. Ltd.
61 Tai Seng Avenue #02-12
Singapore 534167
Tel: (65) 6280-1330; Fax: (65) 6280-6290
inquiries@periplus.com.sg
www.periplus.com

Japan
Tuttle Publishing
Yaekari Building, 3rd Floor
5-4-12 Osaki, Shinagawa-ku
Tokyo 141 0032
Tel: (81) 3 5437-0171; Fax: (81) 3 5437-0755
sales@tuttle.co.jp; www.tuttle.co.jp

Indonesia
PT Java Books Indonesia
JI. Rawa Gelam IV No. 9
Kawasan Industri Pulogadung
Jakarta 13930
Tel: (62) 21 4682-1088; Fax: (62) 21 461-0206
crm@periplus.co.id
www.periplus.com

CONTENTS

PART I: Active Killers & Mass Killings

PART II: Carjacking & Other Vehicular Crimes

PART III: Home Invasions

Dedication

The impact of a life isn't measured in years. There are those who may only be given a few years to make their mark but, in that short time, affect the lives of others to a degree that is disproportionate to the time their life was allotted: Ezra, was one of these. For Ezra, his fight against leukemia was a process that he engaged in even when he understood how great the odds stacked against him were and that a favorable outcome was not within his reach. He owned the phrase, "Never give up." In his 15 years, he was more the warrior than I have been in my lifetime.

It's one thing to be in a fight that lasts seconds or minutes and something else entirely to be in one that lasts days and months—a fight that each time you wake up starts again and when you go to sleep you do so knowing you will have to go through it when you awake. That takes a real fighting spirit. It is this spirit, more than anything else, which gives you the edge in a fight regardless of who or what the enemy is. It is good to have heroes, people who can inspire us to keep going and show us what can be overcome, not so that we can simply admire them but so that we can become like them. I'm not ashamed to have as one of my heroes a 15-year old boy who among many other things has taught me what it truly means to never give up.

Introduction

"The average person in a large urban area is safer walking on the street today than he or she would have been at almost any time in the past 30 years." —Brennan Center for Justice (2015)

Statistically, we are living in the safest times ever, with low and falling crime rates, overall—(obviously this may not apply to certain cities and specific locales). However, certain types of crime/violence, are on the rise. Active shooter incidents have been steadily growing year-on-year, since 2001 (when the FBI started recording them) from an average of 3 incidents between 2000 and 2001, to 20 between 2014 and 2015—a total of 40 incidents in a two-year period. Home invasions and carjackings are also more common now than they used to be, with certain cities seeing a disproportionate rise in these types of crime. Crime rates may be falling on the whole, but particular types of extreme violence are becoming more common.

There are a number of reasons for this, but one which we cannot ignore is the fact that past violent events can act as educators for future ones. Vehicular rammings, which were once largely confined to Yemen, the Arabian Peninsula and other parts of the Middle East, have recently been "exported" to Europe. The Columbine School shooting (1999), has inspired, empowered, and educated other students, to carry out similar/replica school and university shootings. Pat Sherrill, when he "went postal" in 1986 (in the incident that gave us the term), demonstrated to other disaffected and disgruntled employees, that they didn't have to play by or respect management's "rules," and could use a firearm to exact revenge, and experience a few moments of power. The statistics may show that we are living in the safest times; however, our risk of being involved in certain types of violence is on the increase, and if we are targeted for a carjacking or home invasion, or find ourselves in the midst of an active shooter incident, whether it is at our school, college, workplace, or even in a public space such as a shopping mall, these statistics will be irrelevant to us.

Extreme violence is on the increase, and we should be prepared to deal with it. This means educating ourselves, as to what it looks like, how it occurs, and what we can do when we find ourselves facing it. We need to take the lessons learned from previous incidents, and develop and improve on tactics and strategies that have already been proven effective. Dealing with violence is not about dogma, styles, or systems, but about understanding contexts, and responding appropriately—there is not a one size fits all solution to every situation, however attractive this idea/argument may be. Some of the solutions in this book may at first appear counter-intuitive, but then many extreme survival solutions are—it may not seem logical to charge an active shooter, but the Israelis, along with others, have shown that in certain instances/situations this is an effective survival tactic to use. Knowing when to do something, is often as important as knowing how—this book aims to teach both the when and the how of dealing with extreme violence.

Real world violence, occurs in real world environments. What works well when you have space and time, may not work well, when these are denied you, and unfortunately this is often the case with violence. Trying to apply an arm-bar in the confines of a car, when pinned down on the back seat, isn't impossible, but neither is it as easy as when in an unobstructed training facility—and there may be better, more appropriate responses/techniques when in a confined environment. Dealing with firearms and other weapons when seated, may see us having to employ tactics that don't rely on striking, as without leg, hip, and back mobility, our strikes may lack the power they require. This is reality, and we can't deny it. There is little point—other than satisfying our own egos—of trying to argue that reality should reflect the way we train, and not the other way around; e.g., we can all easily trap a knife that isn't being recoiled, and is left out there, for us to complete the technique, but no real-life assailant will attack us in this fashion; unlike our training partners, they want us to fail. Anyone who has experienced violence firsthand, will tell you that it is not a game.

Just as we should have realistic expectations about our attackers, and our environments, we should have realistic expectations about ourselves, and what we can hope to accomplish when under extreme stress and duress—some of us may well find out that we can raise our game, but most of us will default to the lowest level of our training; expecting more is unrealistic and dangerous. This is why it is important to have simple goals and methods, e.g., block the knife, trap it, restrict its movement, control the attacker, shut the attacker down, etc. Trying to do too many of these things at once, is in most cases expecting too much of ourselves, and would be completely unrealistic. Violent situations are normally best solved using a step-by-step approach, rather than by trying to do everything at once.

When we look at instances of extreme violence, such as active killer incidents, home invasions and carjackings, etc. we should look to assess our risk as pertains to these events. This will allow us to better prepare ourselves for dealing with them successfully.

Risk and Consequence

We all believe we know what the term "risk" means, but would likely have difficulty explaining it or describing it if called on to do so. When we look to define/assess risk, we will need to understand the three components that make it up, these are:

1. Assets
2. Threats
3. Vulnerabilities

An asset is anything that we value and want to protect (from a potential threat). This could include ourselves and our children, or possessions such as our house, car, or wallet, or even be something intangible such as information, etc. A threat is anything that may want to harm, or dispossess us of our assets. This could be a burglar who wants to break into our house to relieve us of our possessions (assets), a carjacker who wants to steal our car, or a sexual predator who wants to abduct our child. Vulnerabilities are those things which a threat can exploit, either inadvertently, or deliberately. A burglar may find a window inadvertently left open that they can exploit, or a large bush/tree in front of a window that they can hide behind as they force it open. The more vulnerabilities you have, the greater the risk. The more threats you have, the greater the risk. Risk is the interaction of assets, threats and vulnerabilities. When we make a risk assessment, we need to look at the assets we want to protect, assess the threats we may face, and explore the vulnerabilities that could be taken advantage of.

If you live in South Africa, one of the quickest ways to lower the risk of home invasions and carjackings is to move to another country, where the presence of such threats isn't so common. It's not normally in our power to eliminate threats, in order to reduce risk; most of our ability to limit and mitigate risk comes from addressing our vulnerabilities, and that is the focus of this book. As well as risk, there are consequences. We might be at much higher risk of being the victim of a mugging (there are more muggers and therefore a greater number of threats), but in most cases the consequences are low; i.e., we hand over our wallet, and lose some money, etc. An active shooter incident is less common, and there is less risk of us experiencing one, but if we do, the potential consequences are much higher. This book looks at "low risk/high consequence" scenarios, not the ones we are most likely to experience, but those which threaten our survival.

General Safety Precautions vs. Specific Safety Precautions

There are those people who will fixate on these extreme forms of violence because of their potential high consequences, and overlook the more common scenarios that they are likely to face, such as how to prevent and deal with social violence, how to handle a mugging incident, etc. What they often fail to realize, is that it is your general safety precautions, which will often allow you to prevent and identify the more specific and extreme ones; e.g., it is good situational awareness that will allow you to identify a team of carjackers who are working in your environment, or alert you to a car that is following you, etc. Good overall safety planning and procedures will allow you to prevent many more acts of aggression and violence directed towards you, than if you were to specifically focus on dealing with certain types.

The advice and information contained in this book, is not a substitute or a replacement for the self-protection and personal safety information that is contained in the first two books, *Krav Maga: Real World Solutions to Real World Violence* and *Krav Maga: Tactical Survival* but is instead intended as an extension to help you understand, identify and prevent becoming a victim, of these more specific and extreme forms of violence.

PART I

Active Killers & Mass Killings

We are all born with a natural aversion to killing. This is hard-wired into our DNA and is necessary for the success and survival of our species; otherwise we'd be wiping each other out over every disagreement and personal conflict. Even in extreme situations where our lives are threatened, most of us—unless conditioned in some way—will hesitate to kill; the survival instinct and strategy of our species overriding our own personal survival drive. For a person to overcome this aversion, and become acclimatized to using extreme violence, this instinct must be re-educated, retrained and redirected; through a set of experiences, circumstances and situations and/or a process of conscious training and learning. To do this, they must come to view killing as something which is not only justifiable, but much more importantly, something that is necessary. This re-education can occur organically (the bullied school kid, who goes on a shooting spree because they reach the conclusion that there is no other way of ending their torment and misery other than by punishing the institution they deem responsible for it), or it can be fabricated by others, as with the terrorist recruiter who reframes an individual's experiences, so that they come to want to align themselves with, and kill for, the group's cause, etc. To come to the conclusion that the only available option is the killing of others, and to action a plan that sees a person do just this, takes time and involves a process that has five phases/stages:

1. Fantasy Phase
2. Planning Phase
3. Preparation Phase
4. Approach Phase
5. Execution Phase

The Fantasy Phase is where the idea to kill is born and developed. There is a strong argument to be made that all violence—including mass killings (those where more than four people, excluding the perpetrator, are killed)—is a response to being disrespected in some way. A person may feel and believe that they are being disrespected because they belong to a particular ethnic or religious minority, or because they feel that the company they work for has treated them unfairly, or that the school and/or community they belong to hasn't recognized them in the way they would like them to, and feel they deserve, etc. This sense of disrespect may be real and genuine, such as in cases of bullying and actual harassment/persecution, along with the denying of rights, etc. or it can be imagined and "created," by rewriting incidents and experiences. Either way, this disrespect can lead to the hatred of the group, organization, institution, and/or community that the individual belongs to, and the overwhelming feeling that using lethal violence against them is both justified and necessary; perhaps to punish or take revenge, or to establish what they see as a greater good. This is not to justify the thinking of active killers, but to understand the "reasons" why an individual would drive a van or truck into a crowd, rampage through a school, shooting everyone they see, set off a suicide vest, detonate a bomb on a packed bus, or attack people waiting for a train with machetes and knives, etc.

Once the justification to kill is accepted, the fantasy regarding the means and methods to do this can be explored—and enjoyed; these thoughts of killing often lead to an emotional addiction, where the potential killer, keeps seeking the "highs" they experience when they fantasize about taking lives. In an active killer incident (the term active killer, encompasses active shooter incidents but can also be used to reference events where other weapons, such as knives, vehicles and explosives are used), there is one simple goal: to kill as many people as possible. The Columbine School shooting of 1999, that saw 13 killed, wasn't primarily intended as a shooting. Klebold and Harris had planned something much, much bigger. Their goal was to blow up the school canteen, and the library located above it, at a time when the projected casualty rate would be in the hundreds—with Klebold and Harris stationed outside, shooting those who tried to escape the carnage, before driving their cars filled with explosives into the school. It was only when their homemade propane tank bombs fail to detonate, that they revised their plans, and went on the shooting rampage. The fantasy may change and morph, but at some point, it will start to solidify, take shape, and become more definite. When this happens, the killer(s) will move to the Planning Phase.

The Planning Phase is where the meat is put on the bones of the fantasy, and precise details begin to be considered and planned—sometimes, accomplices are sought. In some instances, as in the attempted St. Andrew's School shooting of March 2009 (Drexel, PA), these would-be accomplices have ended up alerting authorities. Dates will be selected, and often these will have a certain significance; the Columbine School shooting was scheduled for April 19 (it took place on the 20th due to a delay in the supply of ammunition), the anniversary of the 1995 Oklahoma City Bombing, which in turn was timed to coincide with the anniversary of the botched government siege of the Waco Complex in 1993. The Columbine Massacre has itself become an inspiration for other school shooters and killers - Seung Hui Cho, who was responsible for the Virginia Tech Massacre in 2007, referred to Klebold and Harris as "martyrs." This is known as "Cultural Contagion"—where an event becomes contagious, prompting others to act in a similar way (this is why active killer/shooter incidents tend to be replicated and cluster—one study suggests that for every three mass shootings another is directly inspired). In many ways, Columbine has inspired many future killers, and acted as a model and blueprint for school shootings. Times of day, as well as dates, will also be chosen in this phase. Klebold and Harris timed their bombs to go off at 11:17 AM, during the school's first lunch sitting when they knew the school canteen would be at capacity. The Nice Truck attacker, chose to drive his 20-metric ton cargo truck through crowds gathered on the Promenade des Anglais at around 10:30 pm, just when the Bastille Day Fireworks Display that people had gathered to watch finished—this is when the crowd was judged to be at its largest.

During the Planning Phase, the killer may make notes, draw diagrams, and even discuss their ideas with others—they may also express their admiration for other active killers and research the incidents; looking for lessons to be learned, ways to increase their kill rates, and so surpass the deaths tolls of those who went before them—part of their fantasy might be to imagine the notoriety they will receive after the event (even if this is posthumous). Committing a mass killing is one way that a person who feels unjustly irrelevant and insignificant, may look to get the attention they deem they deserve. With recent generations becoming ever more narcissistic (fame is a goal in and of itself for many teenagers), mass-killings may become another way for these individuals, who feel they have been overlooked and strive to be noticed, to gain the attention they crave and believe they warrant. Elliot Rodger, who committed the 2014 shooting in Santa Barbara, made a chilling video the day before he went on his killing spree, where he stated, "I don't know why you girls aren't attracted to me, but I will punish you all for it," talking about a sorority that was one of his targets; this type of entitlement, is symptomatic of narcissism and those who suffer from narcissistic tendencies. The planning itself, may also fuel and direct the fantasy these individuals have built, and are developing. They may recognize some of the obstacles that are in their way, such as the difficulty of getting hold of materials to make explosives, and so reduce this part of their plan to a smaller component, or even ditch it altogether, and rework the fantasy. Once a plan has been developed, the Preparation Phase will begin. This is where the killer(s) starts physically preparing for their massacre.

Sometimes, the Preparation Phase can be as short as the time it takes to choose a crowded location, and drive towards it, such as with the Westminster Bridge Attack, in London, of March 2017. There may have been more preparation involved, such as the carrying out surveillance on the area, determining the best route to approach from, etc. but vehicular assaults/attacks can be successfully carried out with very little preparation—making them a type of mass killing which is likely to become ever more common, especially with the potential to kill and injure a lot of people; the Nice Truck Attack (July 2016) saw 86 people killed and 434 injured (by comparison, the deadliest mass shooting, which took place on the island of Utøya, Norway, in 2011, saw 77 people killed and a further 319 injured). The more sophisticated the plan, the more preparation time is required. Klebold and Harris, spent around 18 months, planning Columbine, acquiring materials for explosives, building prototype bombs, and experimenting with firearms, etc. During this time, the County Sheriff's Department understood the pair had been making pipe bombs and threatening students (Harris chronicled many of his plans, preparations and thoughts on his website) and had even applied for a warrant to search Harris's house—it was never executed. There were many people aware of the pair's dark thoughts and fantasies, and were aware of the activities they were engaged in, however almost everybody, through denying and discounting this information, failed to see their behaviors as warning signs.

A U.S. Secret Service report published in 2014, found that in 93% of the school shooter incidents they studied, the perpetrators had shown behavior that was judged concerning, prior to their attacks. In 81% of these cases, at least one other person—friends, schoolmates, family members—had knowledge of their plan, and in 59% of incidents, this was more than just one person. In most mass killings, there is somebody connected to the killer(s) who knows their plan—this is often true for acts of terrorism and workplace shootings, as well as school shootings. Many killers find it difficult not to "leak" their plans, possibly wanting to enjoy the admiration and fear of the event beforehand, or to receive some form of confirmation that others too believe they are justified in their actions. Sometimes a killer will inform certain people to stay away from the location they have chosen—a school, workplace, or similar—on a particular day; e.g., a 12-year old shooter, in Roswell, New Mexico, told friends and family members to stay away from school on the day of his intended shooting spree (January 14, 2014), Pat Sherrill warned a female coworker who had been kind to him, not to come to work the next day—the day he went on a shooting spree at the Edmond, Oklahoma Post Office where he worked (August 20th, 1986), killing 14. As Eric Harris and Dylan Klebold entered the Approach Phase of their plan, they came across Brooks Brown in the parking lot, a classmate who Harris told to, "go home."

The Approach Phase, is the lead up to the actual execution of the plan. Once the Preparation Phase has been completed, and the killer(s) has built their bombs, acquired weapons, stockpiled ammunition, hired a truck, possibly rented a hotel room near the location, etc. they can start to put their plan into action. There is a chance that a potential killer can get cold feet, and back out at this stage, however after the investment—both mental/emotional and physical—in the fantasy, planning, and preparation phases, it is unlikely that if they are already in the Approach Phase, they'll walk away from their target. As part of their Approach Phase, Klebold and Harris had planted a bomb three miles away from the school, in an area of parkland. The idea was that when this went off, it would divert emergency services, and keep them occupied, as the two bombs they'd planted in the school canteen were detonated. The Approach Phase can also see the killer(s), sending packages containing letters, videotapes, etc. as well as making phone calls to friends, family members and media agencies, explaining their reasons/motivations for the actions they are about to take. Often, the killer(s) will expect to die during the Execution Phase, and will want the world to know, rather than speculate, as to why they went on their killing rampage. Seung Hoi Cho, the Virginia Tech Killer, mailed a package to NBC News, before he went on his second killing spree at Norris Hall, and Klebold and Harris left a stash of documents, including a series of videotapes explaining their reasons (known as the "Basement Tapes"—as they were largely shot in Eric Harris's basement), so that the world would understand and remember them as rebel geniuses; rather than unpopular losers and outcasts, as their fellow classmates tended to see them.

Once the killer(s) has approached their target, and opened fire, driven up the curb onto the sidewalk, detonated their explosive device, etc. the Execution Phase has begun. For the targets, identification, prevention and avoidance are no longer options, and disengagement and engagement become the foremost survival strategies; that disengagement may be to a place where you can better protect yourself/stay hidden and/or exit the environment completely. It is easy to adopt a fatalistic attitude around mass killings, and conclude that there is little you can do to improve your survival odds—unless you are armed—however, people do survive these events, not simply by luck but by design, and survival solutions don't have to be complex or require great skill; e.g., in the Sandy Hook Massacre, six children took the opportunity to stop hiding and escape when the shooting stopped, recognizing that the killer Adam Lanza, was having to reload and/or clear a jam. Sometimes the simple reasoning of a child—when the gun stops firing it's because it can't shoot anymore, so run—beats the complex overthinking of adults. At Virginia Tech, students pressed a desk against a door to prevent Seung Hoi-Cho from entering; a simple solution that saved lives. Also, it's not always necessary to engage and disarm an active shooter to be a hero: at Sandy Hook, the school janitor ran through the corridors shouting that there was a gunman in the building, giving teachers time to evacuate and hide children. When faced with danger, however extreme, there are always things you can do to improve your odds of surviving, and saving others.

Active Killers with Knives

When we think about active killers, we tend to think about those individuals who arm themselves with rifles, carbines and other long-barrel weapons (most active shooters use handguns because they are more discrete, and can be hidden more easily than larger weapons), however, knives have also been used in mass and rampage killings. A knife is often easier to acquire than a firearm—especially in countries where guns are restricted, such as in UK, Australia, and many European countries—and doesn't require any background checks and/or training to be effective as a killing weapon. There are also active shooters who carry a knife as backup, for when they run out of ammunition, or to deal with someone who manages to get inside the range of their firearm, etc. In the 2015, Thalys Train Attack, committed by Ayoub El Khazzani, he used a box-cutter knife to try to fend off four passengers who attempted to subdue him—he had already shot one passenger with a 9mm Luger pistol, after they had tried to disarm him of his AKM Assault Rifle. Most active shooters have multiple weapons, and so in any attempt to disarm them of what appears to be their primary weapon, thoughts should be given to other weapons they may have about their person.

In most incidents of social violence, where knives are used, the attacker will attack at close range, and use their non-weapon hand/arm, to grab onto clothing, push against your throat, pull your head down and/or generally control and restrict your movement. In a mass killing where a knife is involved, the attacker will be much more concerned about attacking as many victims as possible, and so they are unlikely to spend a long period of time attacking each person, and instead move around, stabbing and cutting as many as they can—in the hope of having the highest kill rate. This may give you more time to recognize the threat and prepare for it, than you would normally have in a knife attack that targets you as an individual, and not as part of a group.

As soon as you register that there is danger in your environment, start to get to your feet—you are less vulnerable standing than sitting. Knives, unlike guns, don't make any noise so as you recognize the danger, inform others in your vicinity who might not be aware of the threat. You may also need to give those around you the instruction to run if they've become frozen in place.

Your initial goal should be to try to disengage, but if you haven't the time to make a safe exit, you will have to engage with your would-be killer. Unfortunately, the speed at which your attacker is moving may deny you the time and space to use a Glisha/sliding step that would add your bodyweight to the kick, in which case you should use the table behind you to support yourself, and help give you a stable base to kick from.

Holding onto the table, raise your knee high and begin to extend your leg towards your attacker. Due to the amount of forward momentum they have, and the fact that you will be fully supported by the table...

...they will absorb the full force of the kick and be pushed back quite dramatically. Make sure that you extend your hips with the kick, so that you are kicking not just with the leg, but with the body, as well.

Quickly recover by bringing the foot back down to the floor and judge whether your kick has bought you enough time to make your escape and exit the environment.

If your attacker recovers and makes another attack, once again, supported by the table, raise your knee and prepare to make a second kick.

Kick again to drive your attacker backward and create for yourself enough time/ distance to disengage safely.

It may be that although you have disrupted and damaged your attacker, they are positioned in such a way that they are blocking your disengagement points. If this is the case, you should look to arm yourself with some form of improvised weapon that you can use to protect yourself.

Against a knife or edged weapon, look for an object that resembles/is like a shield that you can use to block any further attacks. A chair can be brought up as a barrier to protect yourself.

When the attacker approaches, drive the legs forward into them. Angle the chair so that one leg is positioned in front of your attacker's groin and another in front of their face. Jab the chair out to force your attacker to hesitate and interrupt the momentum of the attack. Use this time and space to get your back to an exit, so you can move backward and exit while facing your attacker with the chair positioned between you. At some point when you have a clear exit opportunity, you may want to throw the chair at your attacker to distract them, and enable yourself to move away more freely.

The attack may happen at a closer range, where you don't have the space to keep your assailant back, and away from you. If they are moving fast, you may have to burst towards them in order to forcefully block, and take control of their knife hand/arm. Knife attacks involve multiple stabs/cuts, and so it is important that with any defense you make, you account for the recoil motion of the blade—trying to grab an edged weapon that is being recoiled, is extremely difficult to accomplish, and so you will need to utilize forward movement, and wrapping motions with your arms.

As you stand up, you may realize that there is no opportunity to disengage, no time to kick, and no room to make any form of lateral movement that might interrupt the rhythm of the assailant's attack. This is where "bursting" forward towards your attacker starts to become a good option. Start to raise your left hand up to meet your attacker's weapon arm—as you do this, move forward so that your blocking arm will have the weight of your body behind it.

When you make your block, try to have the bend at your elbow as close to a 90-degree angle as possible. You aren't looking to deflect the movement of your attacker's weapon arm or change its direction but to actively stop it. You should look to intercept it before the knife has gotten any real momentum; e.g., before it starts travelling downwards. The added benefit of meeting it at this point is that you are stopping the blade a good distance away from your head, face, and upper-torso (the normal targets of an ice-pick style attack.

If you have confidence in your striking abilities, you could try a simultaneous punch as you block in order to move your attacker away from you. However, in a real-life situation punching a small target such as the head with power when surprised is extremely difficult. It is generally advisable to look to control the weapon arm and take all movement of the knife away before attempting to soften up/shut down your attacker with strikes.

To get control of the weapon arm, start to reach over your attacker's arm with your blocking arm making sure that you are still travelling forward, towards your attacker, so that you can beat the recoil of the knife. Keep wrapping your arm over and around your assailant's weapon arm to prevent them from recoiling it and making another attack.

As you do this, grab onto their shoulder and start pulling yourself forward so that you are close to them and can have a very "deep" control of their arm. You should think of yourself as diving and clambering over their shoulder and arm. Once you have dealt with the initial recoil movement of the knife, start to pull their arm down so that you can trap it under your armpit.

Once you have their arm secured, take a step forward, and behind them to take their balance—you can position your forearm under their chin to direct them backward. By taking their balance, and controlling their movement you will take their attention away from the weapon, and put them in a disadvantaged position.

Once you have the weapon secured, start to deliver lower body strikes such as knees and shin kicks towards the groin and the upper legs/quadriceps. You can use your grip on the attacker's clothing with your left hand to pull them down and into the attacks. You should continue to move them around as you make these attacks to further distress and disorientate them.

Once you feel/believe that your assailant has experienced enough shock and pain that they aren't thinking too much about the knife, run your arm down theirs, keeping it pressed into your side, until you are able to grab hold of the wrist. At this point, you should still be pulling the weapon arm into you so that its movement is severely restricted.

When you are ready to perform the disarm, push the knife away from you, rotating the arm, so that the blade points upwards. As you do this, deliver a knee strike...

...so that your attacker's focus is drawn to this and they don't try to pull their weapon away. Once your attacker's arm has been completely rotated and the knife is pointed upwards...

...quickly pull their arm down, and in, in a circular motion. The pull should be fast, with the aim of taking your attacker off balance. You should step back/around as you do this, adding power to the arm movement and moving your body out of the path of the knife—this body movement will also add power to your pull, and help take your attacker off balance. If at this point they pull back, and twist their arm to try to retain their weapon, you have several options—one of which is to release your grip, and look to arm yourself with a chair or other improvised weapon; another would be to try to keep control of your grip on their arm, and follow its movement back, striking your assailant as you move in.

The circular swing used to move your attacker's arm, should take their balance, and feed the hand holding the knife, to your free hand.

Press firmly on the back of their hand, along the knuckles, using the heel of your palm to open their hand up. If they have a strong grip, rather than pressing, you can make a palm strike against their knuckles.

If you do this, be aware that the knife may be knocked out of their hand due to the force of the strike. Reach around their fingers with your own, and scrape the knife from their grip.

You can now use the knife as a weapon with which to protect yourself, cutting and stabbing your assailant, and any other attackers who may be present. If you are going to have weapon disarming as one of your core competencies and skills, it would be useful to gain some training and knowledge in how to use them. There is a danger to disarming somebody of a knife, when you are not proficient in its use, as you may find yourself hesitating to use it if your attacker— or any others in the environment— continues to fight, even though they are now unarmed.

Weapon disarming can be extremely difficult when you're not able to control your attacker's body movement, so there are times when it may be more effective to bring them down first, so that you can press them into the ground. You can also use the ground as a large striking surface that is harder than any of your body's striking tools and so big that it never misses its target. When people see the ground rising up to hit them, basic instincts such as trying to prevent their fall, come into play, taking their focus away from the knife, and killing you.

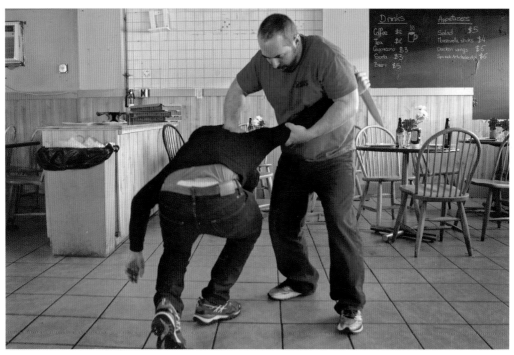

After blocking and securing the weapon arm, deliver some knee strikes to your attacker's groin/stomach, so that they naturally pull their hips back, to defend this area. This will mean that their head will be forward, past their shoulders and hips, and that they'll be off balance. Take advantage of this by rapidly pulling them forward and down, using their clothing to control their movement.

Use your right hand—the one that is grabbing their clothing—to direct them towards the ground. Make sure you still have their weapon arm pinned close to your body, so that it's not free to move. As you pull them to the ground, smashing their face into the floor as you go...

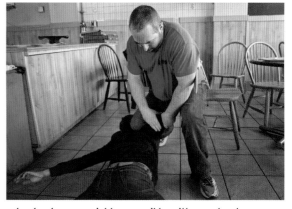

...try to stay as upright as possible, with your head over your shoulders, and your shoulders over your hips. You shouldn't let this compromise your own balance and stability. Once you have them on the ground, put your right knee onto their spine, and pin them down. You should drive all your weight into them to keep them pinned.

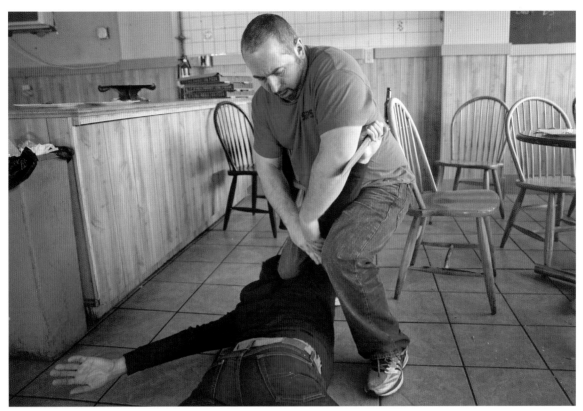

Push in with your left knee/thigh, so that your attacker's weapon arm is trapped between both legs. Keep control of your attacker's arm with your hands until you have the arm squeezed and secured between your legs and it is unable to move.

Once the arm is immobilized between your legs, you can release your grip on it, and transition your hands to a position from which you can disarm. One hand should secure the wrist and the other should push down on the back of the hand–on the knuckle line–to open it up. Once the hand is open, reach in, and scrape the knife out of your attacker's grip. Once you have disarmed them, disengage to a place of safety. In most legal contexts, stomping your attacker's head when they are on the ground is deemed an excessive use of force. However, in an attack where your life is clearly at risk, and where it is reasonable to assume that your attacker may have another weapon, doing whatever is necessary to nullify their attack is justified.

Another good reason to take the attacker to ground, while remaining on your feet, is that many terror attacks where knives are utilized involve more than one attacker; e.g., Kunming Train Station Attack (March 2014, China), Kehilat Bnei Torah Synagogue Attack (November 2014, Jerusalem, Israel), Guangzho Mass Stabbing (May 2014, China). In these situations, you should look to angle yourself, and move the attacker you are controlling, so that as you drag them to ground, you are positioning them to be between yourself and any other attackers.

Dealing with Recoil

One of the biggest issues when dealing with a knife attack—whether it's a mass killing, terror attack, or incident of social violence, etc.—is the recoil of the knife. In a real-life knife attack, repeated stabs and cuts will be made, and the knife will be pulled back after each one. In order to control your attacker's weapon arm, you will need to be able to deal with their recoil. It isn't enough to just stop the blade, you must be able to "chase" it, and restrict its movement as it is pulled back. This means committing your movement forward, rather than backing away. This remains true whether you are dealing with an "ice-pick" style attack, as described above, or a shanking attack, as described below.

To be successful, your defense will need to occur at the earliest opportunity; i.e., you need to be moving forward, as your attacker pulls the knife back, for their initial/first attack. As soon as you identify this movement, you should start to throw yourself/dive towards your attacker's weapon arm. This involves having the awareness to recognize the pre-violence indicators that precede such attacks, and putting yourself in a position from which you can deal with them. When caught by surprise, you will only be able to react to the attack, and in all likelihood, this means that your assailant will be able to make several cuts and stabs before you are in a position to respond.

You must be fully committed to intercepting the weapon arm at the earliest opportunity. By throwing yourself forward and making a 360-Block with your forearm, you should be able to stop the knife before it gathers any real momentum—in the photo, the knife is being blocked before it has even passed beyond the attacker's hip. You will also restrict the distance that it can be pulled back from, meaning that when you chase the arm as it recoils, you will have to travel less distance with each block,— improving your chances of controlling it. By attacking the weapon arm in this way, you will also be disrupting your attacker's rhythm, as they will have been expecting their knife to travel much further forward (into your body) before pulling it back.

As your attacker starts to recoil/pull the knife back, you should continue your forward movement, initially pushing their weapon arm back with your block i.e. drive it back, rather than chase it. Once you have taken over control of their arm's movement, slip your blocking hand under it, so that you can pull it to your chest as you continue to move in. Rather than bend the forearm at the elbow, which is a large movement that could see the knife redirected up towards your face, initially snake the hand around your attacker's forearm, only bending the hand at the wrist.

Continue to travel forward, stepping out to the side, so that you can deliver a knee strike into your attacker.

From this position, you can either attempt a disarm, and/or drag them down towards the ground, as shown with the ice-pick style attack; your left arm will control the weapon, while your right pulls them towards the ground. The most important take-away from this sequence is how imperative it is to keep moving forward, taking away the recoil distance of the knife as it is pulled back.

If you are taken completely off guard by a knife attack, your chances of bursting forward to meet the attack will be extremely limited. It may be that you can only react and try to block for the first few cuts and stabs, as your attacker moves in on you, repeatedly cutting and stabbing, before you can get yourself into a position from which you can make a successful attempt to control/attack your assailant. This is the reality of a knife attack, and you shouldn't have unrealistic expectations around what you can hope to achieve, when caught by surprise. This is why it's important to recognize the pre-violence indicators to such an attack, and be able to control range and distance, so that you can make an effective defense and counter-response.

If there is an active killer armed with a knife targeting a group you are part of—as one of a number of customers in a restaurant for example — there may be no sounds to alert you of the danger, as the knife will be silent, and not everyone will scream or shout as they are cut and/or stabbed. This is one of the ways that mass stabbings differ from mass shootings. In an active shooter incident, you will probably be first alerted to the presence of danger, by the sounds of the shooting—unless the killer(s) is directly in your eye-line. When a knife-wielding killer first targets others in the group, identifying the movement of the killer(s) as they attack, is probably going to act as your first pre-violence indicator. If you are able to get to an exit safely, you should do so—if possible, you should try to slow down your attacker's route to you by moving tables and chairs (or other obstacles) into their path, as you escape. Even moving behind a table as they attack will buy you some time to check your escape routes and assess the situation.

If the assailant has targeted you as the initial victim of the group, there are several signals that may identify them as a would-be attacker (these indicators also hold true for knife attacks, in which you are targeted as the single victim). Many attackers will "target-glance," making repeated glances at the person they are looking to assault. They may well move their position, between glances/looks, checking to see if their target has noticed them, and whether they have selected the best potential victim (according to their agenda), in the group. Human predators are no different in this regard to animal predators, such as sharks, who also spend a long time looking at their prey from a variety of angles before they attack. These glances will be brief, but if you notice somebody who is moving about, and/or repeatedly looking at you, it would be worth considering why they have an interest in you.

Scanning is another behavior that predators will engage in. Not only will an attacker want to check their victim out, they will also want to check that their environment is conducive to an assault; e.g., that there isn't a law enforcement presence nearby, that there aren't third parties who may be able to assist the victim, and—depending on the nature of the attack—that escape routes they've identified are still open and available to them. If an attacker knows an area to have a prevalence of CCTV (Closed Circuit Television) cameras, they may even look up as well as around, in order to identify whether their actions will be captured or not, and whether security personnel will be able to be quickly dispatched to the scene, etc. Even if they have carried out detailed surveillance of an area, and know where the cameras are located, they will often still look up, to check and re-check the angles and blind-spots, of the cameras they'd previously identified.

Picking up on Target-Glancing and Scanning, should be part of your overall Situational Awareness (SA), as is identifying a predatory individual's Synchronization of Movement (SOM) with you. For an assailant to attack you, they will first need to put themselves in a position from which they can make their attack, which involves them moving towards you, or having you move to them—such as waiting for you in a place that they know you are heading to. A more detailed description of Synchronization of Movement, is contained in "*Krav Maga: Real World Solutions to Real World Violence*" (pp. 61–62).

Knife attackers rarely make single attacks, and if you are caught off guard, with an attacker who is extremely close to you, your natural reactions will take over. While these will help you defend yourself against the initial attack, they will not assist you in either controlling the weapon, or attacking your assailant. When a swinging attack directed to your groin/stomach area catches you by surprise, your instinctive reaction will be to pull your hips back, in an attempt to protect the target area, and initially bring your arms in, to protect your body...

...before throwing them out to try to intercept the knife. This will allow the knife to travel much further forward—and recoil further backward—than if you'd been able to dive in to meet it. As part of the movement of pulling the hips back, your feet will have been thrown backward.

When caught by complete surprise, there is a danger of extending the arms too far, to try and push away, or grab the knife hand - two things which aren't possible in a dynamic attack. There is also the danger that as you try and grab with your fingers, you open and expose them to being cut/slashed - this is one of the reasons why you want to try and keep your fingers close together when you make your 360-Block.

Before you have time to recover to a position from which you could attempt to gain control of the weapon arm, your attacker will likely have pulled the knife back and started to make the next attack. You should think of the blade as moving like the needle of a sewing machine, making quick, repetitive stabs.

As you instinctually move back again to block, you may well find yourself backing into a wall, or other piece of furniture, or into another person or group. In reality, you will run out of space, very, very quickly, as most environments are cluttered with objects or crowded with people. With the speed of the attacker moving towards you, and the fast, repetitive nature of the stabs, it will take all of your efforts just to block the knife and protect yourself, if you are caught by surprise.

With your room to maneuver gone, and your attacker closing the distance, and having had the time to recover from your initial movement away, you may now be in a position—both mentally and physically—to try to control the knife In situations where you are caught off-guard by an attack, it is unlikely that you will be able to control or attack your assailant in the initial assault. You will likely have to deal with a few attacks before you are able to get yourself into a position from which you can actively try to deal with the knife.

Second and Third Phase Attacks

Although the initial phase of a knife attack may see an assailant repeat their first attack several times; e.g., they keep shanking the knife towards the same target, they are probably not going to keep to the same pattern, especially if you are successfully blocking their attacks. At some point, they are going to change targets, especially in a frenzied attack in which they are trying to kill you; the greater the number of puncture wounds they can deliver, the quicker you will bleed out. This is one of the reasons why it is so important to try to gain control of their weapon arm in the very first moments of the assault. Dealing with an attacker who is changing target areas between making their stabs and cuts, is an extremely difficult proposition to deal with, however if you have not been able to secure the weapon arm—which is a distinct possibility, given the nature of real world knife-attacks—then this will be the situation that you will soon find yourself in.

Your attacker may have backed you into a corner, as they ran at you, repeatedly shanking their knife. If taken by complete surprise, you will most likely have only been able to back away from the attack, and gotten an arm out to block the knife—under pressure from the sheer intensity and ferocity of the attack, this is how you will have found yourself reacting.

Your attacker, having been unable to find a way through your defense, will likely change the attack, not only changing the level of the attack, but the side and direction, as well. This movement of the knife is extremely difficult to identify and work out, and is one of the reasons you should keep your other arm up, guarding your neck, when you defend low knife shanks. If your arm is not already in this position when an attacker decides to make a circular stabbing motion to your throat, your chances of making a successful block are slim.

As they bring the knife around, make a high 360-block, to intercept their stab. You will want your forearm to be at a 90-degree angle to your upper arm, so that the knife is stopped, rather than deflected—which might be the effect if the angle was greater. Having your arm in this position also means that you will have the full length of the upper arm between your shoulder and the knife, to stop it from travelling into your neck.

As you make the block, dive forward, so that you are in a good position to be able to deal with the pull-back/recoil of the knife. No attacker will leave the knife out there, for you to control, instead they will pull it rapidly back, so that they can quickly make another attack. By diving forward, you will put yourself in a position from which you will have a chance of catching their arm, as the knife is pulled back.

As you dive forward, bring your blocking arm over your attacker's weapon arm. Aim as high up the arm as possible, as this will be the slowest moving part, and therefore the easiest to catch (with the knife and wrist being the fastest).

Wrap your arm around your attacker's weapon arm as tightly as you can, securing it under your armpit. With your other arm, reach around and grab the back of your attacker's t-shirt, sweater, jacket, etc. Often when there is sweat and blood involved, clothing will give you better purchase than trying to control a limb or a body part, which may be slippery.

While controlling your attacker and their arm, start to throw knee strikes into their body, and upper legs. Because you will have a good control of them, you will be able to move them about and re-position them so that if there are other attackers in the environment, you can use them as a shield/barrier with which to protect yourself. Be aware that spending time striking an attacker is delaying you in disarming or turning the knife on them, and if they are highly adrenalized they may not even register the pain your attacks should be causing them.

When you are ready to use their knife against them, bring your left arm under their armpit, and secure it, so that you now have one arm over theirs and another one under it.

Once you have the weapon arm secured with your left arm, slide your right hand down towards their wrist, and take hold of it.

Turn their knife towards them, as you slide your other arm down to their elbow joint, pinning it to your chest.

With their forearm clasped against your body, drive up with your hips as you lean back, to thrust the knife into their side.

In a real-life situation where there is sweat and blood—possibly both yours and your attacker's—trying to perform a disarm can be extremely tricky. At the point where you disarm, the control of the weapon arm that you started off with is often compromised by having to change grip. It's also worth noting that your attacker will hold on to their weapon for dear life, believing that their own chances of survival will be compromised if they end up losing it to you. In a terror attack, they may even wrap duct tape, or similar, around the knife handle and their grip, as the London Bridge attackers had, (June 2017) so there is no chance of them dropping it or being disarmed. Someone who takes this action is most likely expecting to die during the attack, as they will not be in any position to comply with the demands of armed police and/or security forces, if they are instructed to drop their weapon. Actions such as this can alert you to the intentions and commitment of an attacker.

Depending on the situation, you may believe your best survival chance, would be to disarm your attacker, and use the knife to incapacitate them, and any other assailants who may be in the environment. If you are going to use the knife against your attacker(s), think about attacking the tendons and ligaments of the joints, as these will mechanically shut down your attacker's limbs, potentially disabling them more quickly than a cut or stab wound that they would need to bleed out from. After you have blocked/trapped the arms and delivered several knee strikes...

...step behind your attacker, and with your left hand, grab their clothing and pull them backward so that their balance is compromised. From here, you could deliver shin kicks to your attacker's groin, as their wide stance makes them extremely vulnerable to such attacks. You are also in a good position to reap/kick out one of their legs from under them.

As you pull your attacker back, load some of their weight onto the leg you are going to attack (in this case, their right), and then take it out from under them ...

...with a Minor-Outer-Reap (Ko-Soto-Gari), that drags their supporting leg, so that they start to fall. Make sure that you keep a good grip on their weapon arm, as they descend.

Guide their descent, lowering yourself as they fall, so you are able to keep control of their weapon arm. Still keep it firmly trapped under your armpit.

Once you have directed your attacker's fall, release your left hand from their clothing, and move it to the wrist of their weapon arm—sliding it under your other arm, so that the weapon isn't given any room to move.

Instead of just grabbing the wrist, you should pull it towards you, so that it is also pinned to your body. Once this has been accomplished, you can release the grip you had on your attacker's arm, and position your hand over theirs. If at any point when they are on the ground they resist, or you end up needing to disengage from them—because other attackers are coming towards you—you can stomp and kick your assailant's head so that they are no longer a threat/danger to you (due to the severity of the situation, you should not be concerned that this may be deemed as excessive force).

Rather than simply pushing on their hand, make a palm strike that drives into the back of their hand around the knuckle line. The force of this strike should open your attacker's hand up...

...so that you can reach into their grip and scrape the knife out of it. You will now be able to use the weapon to disable your attacker's arm, or as a means of improving your odds against any other assailants who may be in the environment.

It is important when you are dealing with a series of repetitive stabs, not to become fixated and hypnotized by the weapon. When under extreme stress and duress, you will suffer from tunnel vision, and everything will seem to be smaller than it is. This means that if an attacker suddenly changes from a low attack to a high one, it is unlikely you will pick up on this. If you are watching/tracking the knife, you will find that it will suddenly disappear from your window of sight, and you will need to search for it again, if you are to be able to block this new attack. Instead, you should watch the arm, rather than the knife, so that when it moves to make the new attack, your eyes will naturally follow it, allowing you to successfully make the block.

Rather than switch direction, your assailant may change their attack so that they are bringing the knife high towards your neck and back, on the same side.

Your attacker's dynamic and aggressive forward movement may mean that you are forced backward with all your attention taken up with simply making effective blocks. This is the issue when you are caught off guard and find yourself simply reacting to an attack. By understanding the pre-violence indicators that accompany knife attacks, such as scanning, target-glancing, and Synchronization of Movement, you may find that you have an opportunity to disengage from the environment completely before the attack is launched or at the least prepare yourself for the assault that is about to take place.

After a few repeated shanks, your attacker may swing their knife in a wide loop, towards your neck. If you have been watching the movement of the arm, rather than fixating on the knife, this wide swing will trigger your natural flinch reflex and your left arm will come up to protect yourself. Using the "flinch" to start your block, extend your forearm by moving it out, in a vertical position, to stop the knife, rather than just chopping at your attacker's arm.

Just as you would with the ice-pick style attack, start to dive forward, throwing both your blocking arm, and your second arm, over your attacker's weapon arm, as they begin to recoil the knife. Don't try to grab the arm with your hand as it will be moving too fast when recoiled. There is also a good chance that there will be blood and sweat involved in a knife attack, making the arm too slippery to grab. These things combined make it next to impossible to control the limb by grabbing it.

Pull yourself over their arm, as you pull it into you, to secure it under your right armpit. Try to get as high up the arm as possible.

From this position, you can begin to soften them up, using lower body combatives, such as knee strikes to the upper legs, groin and stomach. When you make your strikes, move your attacker around so some of their focus is directed to their footwork and staying on their feet.

Keeping a tight grip on your attacker's weapon arm, bring your right arm under their upper arm/triceps...

...to grasp it firmly to you with an under-hook. You should now have one arm under, and one over their weapon arm, squeezing it tightly to you. If necessary, you can continue to throw knee strikes and shin kicks at your attacker.

Make sure when you hook under their triceps/upper arm, that your elbow is positioned out, against your assailant's chest. This position will prevent them from being able to move around you to take your back.

If the elbow was down then it would be possible for your attacker to start moving and reaching behind you, putting you in a disadvantaged position.

When you are ready, slide your left arm down your attacker's weapon arm, and grip their wrist. From here, you should rotate their arm in towards them, so that the knife is now pointed at your attacker.

Slide your under-hook down your attacker's arm until it is positioned under their elbow, and start to secure the knife to where your belt buckle would be.

Hug your attacker's forearm to your body, and point their knife towards them. If you want to secure their arm even more tightly, grab your own clothing, with your right hand, and rotate your wrist upwards to "scoop" the elbow joint—this is a similar motion to the way in which you would perform a Rear-Strangle Attack; i.e., you wouldn't simply pull your wrist back into your attacker's throat, you would scoop your wrist inwards and upwards as you pulled back.

Keeping your attacker's forearm squeezed against your body, explosively push your hips forward, so that the knife can be driven into them. Pushing your hips forward in this fashion, will also see your upper torso pulled back somewhat, which in turn will pull your attacker onto the knife.

Your attacker may not swing the knife wildly, but instead cut/stab in a much tighter arc. If this happens, it is unlikely that your flinch reflex will be stimulated, as the knife won't cross your peripheral vision—it will already be travelling inside it. If this happens, you will need to make the block with the right arm, rather than the left; even if your flinch reflex was triggered, you probably wouldn't have the time to block with this arm, as the change in distance from the low shank, to the high stab, will be very short.

Although the attacker may begin by repeatedly shanking, you should assume that at some point, the angle/direction of the attack will change (if you're unable to control the weapon arm, or shut the attacker down). This is why it is critical that although the left arm is dealing with the shank here, the right arm is positioned to deal with high attacks (when it's unable to be effectively used for striking).

With the right arm raised, even if a high attack comes to the left side, you will only need to turn the torso slightly, to make the block. With such a tight, circular attack, it is extremely unlikely that you will be able to get your left arm up in time to stop it.

As your attacker pulls back the knife, recoiling it in order to make another attack, shoot your left arm under your attacker's weapon arm, and as you dive forward...

...hook your hand around to take hold of it. Pull yourself to the arm, while at the same time pulling the arm to you.

As you gain control of the weapon arm, bring your right hand to the back of your assailant's upper arm/triceps, and start to rotate their arm, so that the blade of the knife starts to point towards the ground.

If your block intercepts your attacker's weapon arm nearer to the elbow than the wrist (and in a dynamic, ever-changing confrontation, just making the block is an accomplishment), slide your left hand/arm down towards your attacker's wrist, making sure to keep the arm pinned squarely to your chest as you do so. It is much easier to keep control of your attacker's lower arm, than to try to control the arm closer to their body—where they will be much stronger.

Keeping the arm hugged tightly to your chest, throw knee strikes into your attacker's lower body—you can also throw them around, taking their balance, to further disorientate them. When you are ready to perform the disarm...

...take your right hand off the back of the weapon arm, and move it to your assailant's hand. This is also why you will need to slide your left hand/arm closer to the wrist, as you'd probably not have had the reach to get to their hand in this position, if you had trapped the arm higher up.

Reach over the back of their hand, along the knuckle line, and pull so as to release their grip on the knife.

Keep pulling with your index, middle and ring fingers, on the back of their hand, and use your little/pinky finger to take hold of the handle of the knife, and pull it out, as your other fingers continue to open the hand up.

Once you have the knife in your grasp, make a long, continuous cut, along, around, and down your attacker's arm, severing as much muscle, tendon and ligament as you can. Your goal is not to punish (in a survival situation, what happens to the attacker in the moment is irrelevant — your job Is to stop them attacking you) but to render their weapon arm inoperable. Afterwards, back away, scanning for any other threats/dangers.

Although knives lack the mass killing power of a rifle or pistol, they are sometimes chosen for other advantages they have over firearms. They are much smaller and easy to conceal—and a ceramic knife will not be picked up by a metal detector; smuggling a knife into a restricted area is an easier proposition than trying to get a gun in. As security starts to tighten up around crowded locations, to prevent shootings and bombings, those looking to engage in mass/group-killings will look for ways to bypass and circumvent these measures, and this may mean that mass knife attacks start to become more common. In terms of access to weapons, knives are one of the least restricted weapons available. This means that anyone who wishes to engage in a killing spree with a knife, will be able to easily acquire the means to do so. Between 2015 and 2016, there occurred in Israel what became known as the "Intifada of the Individuals," where Palestinians conducted over 166 stabbings and 89 attempted stabbings (along with 47 Vehicular Rammings), using what they had at hand; knives and cars—there were nearly 3 times as many knife and vehicle attacks as there were shootings during this time.

Another advantage that knives have over firearms, is the lack of training needed to use them. While firearms aren't technically difficult to operate, they can jam and malfunction — especially in the hands of an inexperienced individual—and some technical knowledge is required in order to rectify these issues. A shooter will also need to know how to change magazines, and be able to perform these actions under a certain level of stress and duress. No training or experience is necessary to use a knife (plus it won't jam or run out of ammunition), just a level of emotion, that will allow you to kill somebody at close range, possibly in contact with their body (knife attackers will often grab, push, or pull their victim to them in the fight). Where the person behind the trigger of a firearm can be somewhat removed from the killing, those using knives are experiencing it up close and personal. The practical aspect of this is that after subduing, or disarming, a shooter of their firearm, they may respond submissively (as has happened in a number of incidents), whereas a knife attacker, due to the emotional state they are in, is much more likely to keep fighting.

Vehicular Rammings

As security measures tighten, killers who are unable to acquire and/or make explosive devices, or get a hold of firearms, will look to other methods of killing, such as knives and cars—sometimes using the two together. From the perspective of a terrorist organization, the fact that such "weapons" are freely available, means that they don't have to offer any practical or financial assistance to somebody who is sympathetic to their cause, and can instead play the role of inspirer and influencer; something that they can do remotely, over the internet. In this communication age, it is rare that any terrorist is in fact a true "lone wolf," who acts as a self-contained unit. Groups may also use previous events to provide inspiration to those they are grooming, and the simplicity of a Vehicle Ramming and the relatively high casualty rates that result from such attacks, gives the new "recruit" an obtainable means of bringing success to the cause.

While there is little that you can do to stop a 7.5-metric ton truck that is hurtling towards you, if we can understand how targets are selected, we can raise our awareness when we are in such locations, or avoid them altogether, if we are in a city/country where there are heightened tensions and/or civil unrest.

Speed, Funneling, and Potential Casualties

The faster a vehicle is travelling, the greater the impact will be when it hits into a crowd—and the greater the death-toll. This means that the vehicle needs a stretch of straight roadway, with an absence of curves and bends, which it would have to slow down for. The Promenade des Anglais in Nice, where Mohamed Lahouaiej-Bouhlel drove a 19-metric ton truck at high speed (around 60 mph) into a crowd, is an almost straight stretch of road that follows the city's coastline. This enabled him to reach this relatively high speed. Khalid Masood, was able to get his car up to 76 mph as he drove over Westminster Bridge (bridges by nature tend to be straight), killing 4 pedestrians, and injuring another 49. The heavier the vehicle, and the greater the speed it can reach, the greater the number of potential casualties (the Nice Truck Attack of 2016, killed 86, and injured 458 others) and while the truck was moving at a slightly slower speed than the car on Westminster Bridge, the weight of it contributed to a much higher death toll.

This also makes traffic and road congestion, factors in target selection, including the time of day when such attacks occur. A heavily trafficked road means that it will be difficult for a vehicle to get up the necessary speed to achieve a high casualty rate, and may make it difficult for the killer to maneuver their car/truck onto the pavement/sidewalk or other pedestrian area they are targeting. High curbs, and parked cars, will also limit an attacker's ability to access crowds on the sidewalk/pavement, and so when we find ourselves in such areas, we shouldn't be overly concerned about these types of attackers. This doesn't mean we should switch off completely, but that we will be more likely to face other threats and dangers.

Funnels are something that many criminals use; e.g., a pickpocket will use an escalator as a "funnel,") to slow down and restrict the movement of potential targets. A bridge is another type of funnel, where people can become trapped and blocked in on either side, and have little chance/room to escape. When Masood chose his location, he did so knowing people would be trapped in the funnel of the bridge as he drove down it. Obviously, it is impossible to avoid walking over bridges; however, if we can make sure that we are walking with our eyes towards oncoming traffic, we will have a better chance of identifying a ramming attack than if the car/truck were to approach us from the rear. Anytime we find ourselves approaching a funnel, we should up our awareness, and look to pass through it as quickly as possible.

Mass killers want casualties; the more the better. This means that the larger a crowd, the greater the potential kill-rate. The Nice Truck Attack took place on Bastille Day, and targeted the large number of sightseers who had gone to watch the fireworks—the attacker chose a long stretch of crowded road on which he could get up to a high speed, and that acted as a funnel, trapping people and restricting their movement. On December 19, 2016 a truck was driven into a Christmas Market in Berlin at 8 pm, at a time when there were large crowds gathered, for the nighttime shopping. Two years previously, a killer had driven a van into another Christmas Market in the French city of Nantes—the attack came a day after a similar attack in Dijon. Events attract crowds and crowded events attract mass-killers. There are of course things that the authorities or those planning events, such as festivals, markets and other public gatherings can do, such as temporarily putting concrete blocks around the perimeters and/or the approach to such locations, and/or by redirecting traffic in such a way that a killer would find it difficult to get up the necessary speed to make such an attack, etc. Even if the authorities take these precautions and preventative measures, we should still follow our own personal safety protocols regarding Vehicular Rammings.

It is likely that the driver will survive the first phase of their attack, and once over (because their car/van/truck is no longer drivable, or they have run out of space/room to maneuver it, etc.), begin a second phase of killing using another means such as a knife, gun, or other weapon (an exception to this would be a vehicular ramming that is intended to breach a building and detonate a bomb, in which the driver would likely be killed such as in the Glasgow Airport Attack of 2007). In many instances, the weapon of choice used after the ramming will be a knife (e.g., Ohio State University 2016, Haoman Nightclub Attack, Tel Aviv 2011, etc.) A vehicle in these cases was used due to the variety of restrictions that the killer faced in using a firearm—such as their inability to acquire/use one and/or a lack of available ammunition. In countries that have implemented an almost complete firearm ban such as the UK in 1997, there are still many weapons in circulation; however—because there is basically no legal gun ownership and no supporting firearms industry—ammunition is not as readily available as it is in other countries where private ownership is legal such as in the U.S.

Active Shooters

If a stranger attacks a group you are among, there will be little chance of you predicting it, whereas if you have some sort of relationship with your attacker, such as them being a work colleague, a school friend, or somebody you go to school with, then there may be signals that they give off, that can warn you of their intentions and plans. While this section will look at strategies of engagement and disengagement where active shooters are concerned, it will also look at predictive measures that may allow you to notice the changes in the individuals you work alongside, or go to school with, and alert the relevant authorities and individuals to your fears and concerns. The greatest enabler of any violent incident, whether it directly involves you or not, is the denial and discounting of the potential threat. If you believe that violence can't and won't happen to you, and you excuse and reason away all the obvious warning signs—that your gut feeling says you should take seriously—then you are giving up the opportunity to possibly prevent or avoid it.

Some Common Misconceptions Concerning Active Shooter Incidents

Most of our information concerning active shooter incidents comes from the media, and the media covers those events which they deem newsworthy—this means we often remain uniformed about those shootings which don't contain newsworthy elements; e.g., the victim count isn't particularly high, the story behind the shooting is complicated, and/or the victims aren't individuals you'd be particularly sympathetic to, or they come from a community/background which the agency doesn't feel represents the demographic of their readership/viewership. This means we can be left with a very distorted view of what real-life active shooter incidents look like, and because of this, the solutions we intend to use, may not necessarily be the most effective ones.

Many people, when they think about active shooter incidents, think of the shooter as being armed with a long-barrel rifle or gun, whereas in reality, most involve handguns, such as revolvers and pistols—these are much easier to conceal and smuggle into schools, workplaces, and other areas (some of which may actively restrict the presence of firearms). When long-barrel weapons are used, in many instances they are attached/fixed to a sling. This makes weapon disarming a very difficult proposition.

Long Barrel Weapons with Slings

Most active shooter incidents involving adults in the U.S., are carried out by a single shooter, who is white, male, and middle-aged. However, there are situations that involve a second shooter—most commonly in school shootings. On December 2, 2015, Syed Rizwan Farook and Tashfeen Malik (his wife), went on a mass shooting at a workplace Christmas party, where they killed 14, and injured another 24. There have also been occasions in mass shootings where the shooters have taken hostages, and/or rounded up people as they've tried to escape and take them to a location for execution—Bataclan Theatre Shooting, Paris 2015, Lindt Café Siege, Sydney 2014, etc.

A shooter coming through the front of a restaurant may send a group fleeing through the kitchen. If a second shooter is involved, they may enter through this second exit, to prevent an exodus of potential targets. When taken hostage as part of a group, you may find that there is a period of time during which you will want to comply with the demands of the hostage-takers, to improve the chances of survival for both yourself and the other prisoners—until you can better position yourself to act.

Having stopped you exiting, the shooter may have you turn around, with the gun to your back, so as to move you to where the main group is being held hostage.

Working off the same premise you would in any violent situation—that you shouldn't allow an attacker to move you from one location to another—you may decide that your only effective solution at this point is a physical one. Furthermore, if you are forced to kneel (with the group that you are being moved to), your chances of making an effective defense will decrease. While you should try to act before you are placed in a kneeling position, any solution you choose in this situation will have to take into account that there are other people in front of the gun.

Turning, drop your hand down so you can bring it up and under the gun. You should initially use your shoulder to turn the gun away from you and those who are in front of you/the weapon. There are other rear weapon disarms that you could have selected if you were on your own, but when there is a crowd in front of you, it would be irresponsible to put them in the line of fire, as you make your defense. With a weapon that has a short barrel, is compact, and is attached to a sling/harness, most of your effort will have to go to controlling the attacker, rather than the gun; i.e., there is not much actual gun to control, and its movement will be restricted by the sling.

As you move around your assailant to take their back, lift your arm up, to move the barrel of the gun so that it is pointed in the air. Your assailant will now have to fight against your shoulder, and your arm, in order to bring their weapon down and across, if they want to shoot you and those with you. Stay tight to your attacker, and make sure you remain behind the muzzle of the gun. The UZI SMG (Submachine Gun), has been used in a number of mass shootings, including the 1999 Los Angeles Jewish Community Center shooting, and the 1984 San Ysidro, California, shooting that saw 21 killed at a local McDonald's restaurant. It is therefore appropriate to train for the possibility of a short-barreled, slung rifle.

Keep moving the gun upwards using your left arm, with the intention of smashing it into the shooter's face, as you move behind them and their weapon, aiming to grab hold of their right shoulder with your right hand.

In this position, continue to lift your arm up, pressing the weapon into the shooter's face and start to drag them directly backward so that their balance is compromised, and their attention is taken away from trying to control the gun.

Now that you are almost behind the attacker, reach to their weapon with your right hand and start to slide your left hand under it...

...taking control of it. Try not to grab the barrel itself, as this will be extremely hot if the gun has been repeatedly fired. Keep pulling them backward, so that they are off balance. If their focus is on staying balanced, and on keeping their feet beneath them as they move back, it is unlikely that they will be thinking about reaching for a second weapon - more than likely they will try and hang on to the weapon at their neck, in order to support them. If their hands do move down to their pockets or waistband, quickly take them to the ground, by dragging them down, and turn them onto their front - from here you can look to better control them and prevent them from drawing another weapon.

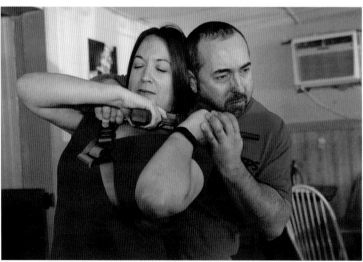

Pull the weapon into your attacker's throat, so that you start to strangle them with it. Their initial and natural reaction to this, will be to try and pull the gun away from their throat to relieve the pressure. Drive your right shoulder into the back of their head, to increase the pressure on their throat. Continue to pull them backward so that their balance is compromised and their thoughts are concentrated on trying to relieve the pressure on their throat, and staying on their feet. If you feel/see them going for a secondary weapon, rapidly take them to ground and/or shout for assistance from those around you—one way you can cause a serious amount of trauma to your attacker's neck, is to have somebody lift their legs up.

As soon as you start to attack the second gunman, it is likely that the primary shooter, will start to open fire on those who are kneeling in the group. With nothing to lose...

...they should collectively charge, staying low, and getting under the weapon. Using sheer weight of numbers, they should drive the shooter back, denying them the space to re-train their weapon. The group should then use concussive strikes to incapacitate the shooter further.

Active shooter incidents involving multiple assailants are extremely rare; a 2014 FBI report, found that of the 160 active shooter incidents in the U.S. that they studied between 2000 and 2013, only 2 involved multiple shooters. It's also worth noting that on the occasions where there have been multiple shooters, most of these involved the shooters staying together, rather than splitting up—there are of course exceptions to this, such as the Bataclan shootings in Paris, where a group with some degree of training, coordinated their attack on the theater to take place from a number of directions. However, most shooters lack the training to split up and coordinate an attack, without the fear of possibly shooting each other. Often, they will also require the moral support of their partner(s). In some instances, such as Columbine, there is also the need/desire to perform for each other.

Another common misconception that many people apply when coming up with solutions to active shooter incidents is that the shooter only has one weapon; i.e., if you disarm them of this, they will be deprived of the means to kill. In the 2015 Thalys Train Attack, the shooter's primary weapon was an assault rifle, but he had both a pistol and a knife on him, as backups. When James Eagan Holmes went on his shooting spree in a movie theater in Aurora, Colorado (July 2012), he equipped himself with a Smith & Wesson M&P15 rifle, a Remington 870 Express Tactical Shotgun, and a Glock 22 handgun—he also had two tear gas grenades that he used. active shooters rarely have just one weapon. One of the reasons for this is that they recognize that there are times when they are vulnerable, such as when they have to reload, or if their weapon jams — which happens quite frequently in incidents when the shooter has little experience of weapons use, has a poorly maintained—or even "overly" maintained, such as being over-lubricated—weapon and/or has fired a high number of rounds; e.g., there can be a build-up of gunk that interferes with the weapon's firing pin, the barrel heating up can cause the bullets' casings to expand so they don't get ejected cleanly, etc. Guns are mechanical machines, that can and often do malfunction, especially when overworked, and poorly operated—something that can happen to even an experienced shooter when they find themselves working under stress and duress.

One way that some active shooters, including James Eagan Holmes, try to reduce the number of reloads that they must make in order to keep killing, is to use high-capacity magazines—Holmes used a 100-round drum magazine for his Smith & Wesson M&P15 rifle.

While in theory drum magazines, and similar, seem a good way to be able to keep continuously firing, without having to interrupt a shooting spree to reload, they are not always that reliable—Holmes' gun jammed after firing 65 rounds. The reason for this is that drum magazines use fairly complex spring mechanisms, which will often fail to feed the gun, especially if it is fired rapidly, or if the mechanism has not been wound tightly enough— you can see in the photograph, the clockwork-style handle that must be turned so that the spring-mechanism has enough tension on it to push bullets from the magazine, into the gun's chamber.

In certain cases, depending on how the shooter is using their sling, you may be able to use it to control and incapacitate them. While the sling gives the shooter many advantages—such as allowing them to change weapons and reload easily — and can be seen as a hindrance to someone trying to control and/or disarm the weapon, it can also be viewed as a potential "noose" around the killer's neck.

When you initially attempt to disarm a shooter of their weapon (and the various ways to do this will be detailed later), you may not be aware that it is on a sling or harness—especially if you have always trained long-gun disarms, without your partner using one—and it may only be as you start to try and take the weapon away from the attacker, that you realize you aren't able to.

As soon as you realize that you can't make the disarm, smash the weapon repeatedly into your assailant's face. Your initial disarming motion should have weakened their grip on the weapon, so they will not be in a strong position to resist, as you drive the rifle into them. Each time you strike, recoil the weapon fully back, so that your attacker is rapidly pulled forward and their balance compromised. Delivering concussive strikes with the gun may be enough to incapacitate your attacker; however, if it is not, or you are concerned that they may be thinking of drawing a second weapon, you may need to control them and put them in a position from which they will be unable to further assault you.

Instead of continuing to smash the gun into their face, drive the barrel alongside their neck, and behind their head.

This will wrap the sling around their neck, and allow you a certain degree of control of your assailant's head.

If you rotate the weapon slightly, and move further around, you may be able to exert a choke using the sling; however, there are many variables at play in such a situation—including the amount of slack in the sling—so relying on the application of an effective choke would be a mistake. It is much more reliable, to use the sling to control, rather than choke, but if opportunities for the latter present themselves, they should be taken. If you can apply a strangulation/choke, your attacker's natural instincts to free their airway, will see them try to pull on the sling to relieve the pressure. while they are engaged in this activity, they won't be reaching for a second weapon.

Position the end of the barrel on to the back of your attacker's neck and drive them towards the ground. As your assailant falls forward, they will instinctively put their hands out to break their fall—this natural response will override any thoughts they might have of trying to go for a secondary weapon.

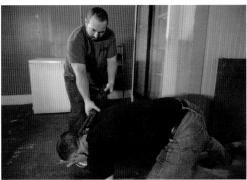

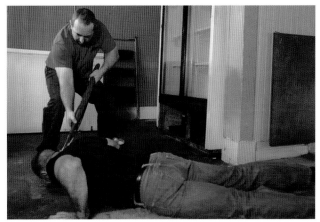

Control your attacker, by pressing the weapon into the back of their neck.

Once you have the shooter controlled, you can use stomp and soccer kicks against their head and/or look to use the weapon against them. In this case, you are dealing with an individual who wants to see you dead, and may well have a second weapon on them, so it is essential to incapacitate them, so that they can't continue with their rampage.

Run, Hide, Fight—Three Options for Dealing with Active Shooters/Killers

One common methodology/framework for deciding what course of action should be taken in an active shooter incident, can be summed up as: run, hide, or fight. These are not necessarily listed in preferential order, i.e., that you should first try to run, then to hide, then to fight, but should instead be situationally based; what option is appropriate for the situation you find yourself in? When Naturalistic Decision Making (NDM), is applied to these options, you will be able to reach a decision, and act upon it extremely quickly. NDM, sees you select the first effective option, rather than compare options for the best one (which is what Rationalistic Decision Making would see you do); comparison takes time, and requires a certain amount of mental bandwidth. If you suddenly find yourself face-to-face with an active shooter, you will not be able to hide, so you will have two choices: to run/disengage, or engage—there really isn't an option of talking your way out, etc. You must choose not which is the best option, but which one will be effective; e.g., if you are some distance from them, engagement might not be effective, as you'll be too far away to attempt to control them, or their weapon. If this is the case, running/disengaging will be the only effective option left to you; if the shooter is changing the magazine on their rifle and seems preoccupied with the task, you may now have the time to engage, and if this is the first effective solution you come to, you should decide and act upon it, without comparing whether running is actually a better solution—in the time it will take you to make this comparison, your attacker will have reloaded, and you may find that both options have vanished.

Gunshots are extremely loud, and if heard in close proximity, will trigger your flinch/startle reflex; something that is designed to alert you to danger. You should accept as reality, rather than deny or discount, the noise you have heard.

Running/Disengaging

Gunshots are loud, especially in buildings where the sound will echo and be amplified. You might confuse a slamming door with a gunshot, but you wouldn't confuse a shot with a slamming door—there is no mistaking the volume of gunfire. The times when people have confused and/or explained away gunfire in active shooter incidents, it has normally been because they believed the noise came from somebody letting off fireworks in the building; e.g., Craig Scott, who was in the library during the Columbine School Shooting, later said on realizing that he heard the shot which killed his sister Rachel, "I thought it was a prank—that some seniors brought fireworks to school." Gunshots are loud, very, very loud—there is a reason that shooters on a range, wear ear protection. It takes a fair amount of denial, and discounting (which is a natural response to danger) to explain gunshots away as something else, but people do—employees at the Standard Gravure plant (Kentucky, 1989), explained away the sounds from Joseph Thomas Wesbecker's AK-47S (a Chinese derivative of the AK-47 Assault Rifle) as some-

The quicker you can start acting—and action starts with moving—the more likely you will be to survive an active shooter incident.

one setting off firecrackers. The question is: which is more likely in an office-building or school? Firecrackers or gunshots? It would be nicer and easier to think fireworks—which is why so many people discount the gunshots they hear to be this—but in today's world, it is much more likely to be gunfire.

A good decision-making tool that can help us quickly decide whether the noise we are hearing is gunshots or something else, such as fireworks, is the problem-solving principle of Occam's Razor. This states that when considering alternatives, the one that requires the fewest number of assumptions should be selected. If we consider the arguments and assumptions you would have to make in order to decide that somebody was setting fireworks off in your building, you'd have to make several. The first would be to question, why? Is it likely that an office-worker would be setting fireworks off as a prank? How many assumptions would you have to make, to explain to yourself that the explosive sounds you were hearing, were part of a prank involving fireworks in your building? What would be the point of a prank that involved fireworks, and would it be worth the risk of an employee losing their job over it? Many assumptions would have to be made, to conclude that what you were hearing was in fact fireworks. Compare this with how many assumptions would have to be made, if you were to consider that what you were hearing was the sound of repeated gunshots, as a disgruntled employee (or ex-employee), took revenge on management and coworkers by engaging in an active shooter incident. Nothing really sounds like a gunshot, and you would have to make a lot of assumptions to reach the conclusion that you are hearing something different.

If the sounds are at some distance, you will have one of two choices: to run, or to hide. If you can ascertain the direction from which the shots are coming, and know a route out of the building (or area) you are in, that won't require you to pass by the shooter, then running/disengaging might be an effective option and solution.

Many school shootings start and take place in libraries and cafeterias, as the shooter(s) can be sure that there will be a large number of students there, either studying or eating. They may time their shooting for when the greatest number of students and staff are gathered in these places, ensuring them a high kill-rate, at the start of their rampage. If you are in the same room as a shooter, it will be obvious where the shots are coming from; however, if you are outdoors or are in a very large space, you may in fact identify the echo of the shot, rather than the shot itself. In these situations, it may be worth getting low and behind something before ascertaining the direction in which you should run.

There is often a temptation to initially put as much distance between yourself and the shooter as possible, but there are times when you may want to consider taking stock of your situation, and trying to work out what is actually happening, rather than just blindly running. There is a difference between running from danger and running to safety—and it is always better to do the latter. Running short distances, between objects that can offer you cover and/or concealment (cover refers to an object that can stop a bullet, while concealment hides you from view), may be a safer option than just running, especially if spending a long time in the open will give the shooter a chance to identify you and pick you off.

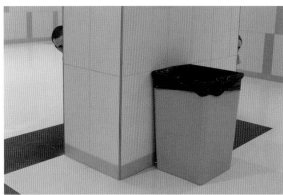

Once behind something that can offer you cover/ concealment, you may want to try to assess your situation. To safely observe what is going on in your environment, and reduce the risk of getting shot, stay low (below the natural eye-line of the shooter—they will be looking primarily at head/torso height), and only use one eye to look at what is going on around you—this will offer the smallest target possible.

When you are disengaging as part of a group, or in a pair, and the environment, and situation permit it, don't run together or as a group. Instead, stagger your run, so that the shooter, is denied a large mass of people/targets to shoot at. You are much more likely to be shot as part of a large mass of people they can indiscriminately shoot at, than as an individual, who presents a single moving target that they will have to take the time to aim at—and have the marksmanship skills to hit.

If you run as part of a staggered group or pair, have your partner or a member of the group who has run before you, and has taken cover, watch your back while you make your run. This will allow you to concentrate all of your efforts on running as fast as you can, rather than having to repeatedly look behind you, to check for the presence of the shooter(s).

Don't run down the center of a corridor where your shape/silhouette will stand out. Instead, run close to the wall where you won't stand out as much. Don't waste time and energy zig-zagging.

If you are in a group or pair, try to take cover behind different objects so that you will provide a divided target for the shooter. The more individual and smaller targets a shooter must choose between, the more you will slow them down, as they will have to decide where and whom to shoot at—with a smaller target, they will also be more likely to miss.

In an active shooter incident, there is a tendency to panic, and look for instructions from others. This is why many people didn't leave their desks when terrorists flew two planes into the World Trade Center Towers, in New York on 9/11. They were waiting for fire marshals/wardens to tell them what to do. There is a tendency to follow the "crowd," even if the crowd doesn't know what it is doing. We may also find ourselves being drawn to the crowd because we believe that there is safety in numbers—this can be true when we attempt to engage/fight the attacker and/or work as a team to barricade ourselves in a room, etc. However, when we are looking to disengage, being part of a crowd may pose some serious dangers.

We may feel safer running as part of a group. However, in doing so, and adding our number to it, we provide a much larger target for the shooter to aim at. In such a situation, it would be almost impossible for them not to hit someone, if they pointed the weapon in the general direction of the group. Running in a large crowd will also mean that getting out through the doorway will be a relatively time-consuming process, as each member of the group will end up getting in the way of the others. It could even be, if the doors open inwards, that the weight of people pressing against the doors prevent them from opening, at all. All of these factors will allow the shooter time to increase the number of casualties, of which you could be one.

If a space/room has multiple exits—and most public spaces require different points of egress as part of the fire regulations/code—then rather than running with the crowd towards one, and getting jammed up, the group should scatter in multiple directions, towards different exits. This means that the shooter will have to decide which individuals to shoot at—this decision-making process will take time, and even a small amount of time will allow those that are targeted to get farther away, and increase their survival chances. The shooter will also have to take longer aiming, than they would if they just had to point their gun in the general direction of the group.

When disengaging, the group should try to create as much confusion for the assailant as possible. We can take lessons from the natural world as to how flocks of birds and herds of animals reduce the number of casualties when they flee from a predator. Both birds and fish take advantage of the "Predator Confusion Effect." When a member of the group identifies a predator, who is about to attack—such as a cat attacking a flock of birds on the ground—they warn the others through movement and/or sound, and the flock/shoal scatters in a multitude of directions. This movement is intended to confuse the attacker by being generally overwhelming, and confusing them as to which individual they should select and target. The aim is that in the decision-making process, all members of the group put enough distance between them and the predator, that they are safe. Human groups/crowds can employ the same strategy against human predators, or individuals can peel away from the group, to increase their own survival chances.

Animals also understand how not to stand out and how to camouflage themselves, and blend in with their surroundings. While it would be ridiculous to suggest that you choose the colors you wear to blend into the building colors, or décor of your workplace or school, etc. it is worth recognizing if the clothes you are wearing will make you stand out, in the environment you are in. The military understand the benefits of camouflage, and use it to make soldiers, vehicles and the like, less obvious targets.

Even though the person in the blue jeans and grey shirt is running in the open, their clothing (grey shirt and dark jeans) causes them to blend in with their surroundings, much better than the individuals running along the wall who stand out in their respective red and blue t-shirts. One way that those wearing the bright t-shirts could lower their profile and visibility would be to take them off, as their skin/flesh tones would better blend in with the color of their background. When you are dealing with extreme situations, anything that can help increase your survival chances is something you should be looking to do.

Secondary Exits and Cover and Concealment

There is a Chinese proverb that says, "A sly rabbit will have three openings to its den"—When it comes to escaping active shooter incidents, this idiom can be taken almost literally: you need to have more than one escape route, as they may have been blocked and/or chained shut by the active shooter—a tactic believed to have been used by the Virginia Tech shooter who wanted to stop people escaping from Norris Hall and make it difficult for the security forces to get in (the chains were administered two days before the actual shooting).

Fire escapes are obvious secondary exits, and mentally noting where these are, and your quickest route(s) to them, could mean the difference between life and death, in a real-life incident. A good habit to get into when you start a job in a new building, is to familiarize yourself with the locations of the different fire escapes, so you will have an idea of where to head in the event of an active shooter incident, as well as a fire. If there is a shopping mall (or other public space) that you regularly frequent, gain an understanding of the different escape routes that may be open to you, such as which shops have a loading dock behind them, and where the entrance from the main shop to the warehouse that backs onto them is located. During the Westgate Shopping Mall attack, Nairobi, Kenya in 2013, many people found themselves trapped in the mall, some due to not knowing possible escape routes that were available to them—there were 67 fatalities, and 175 injured, in an attack/siege that lasted 3 days.

Most people in a restaurant will head for the main exit in the event of an active shooter incident, as it is the most obvious point of egress. If there is a secondary exit that you know leads out of the building—such as the kitchen—and it is not being blocked by the crowd, look to use it. Being part of a smaller group will make you a less attractive proposition, than a large crowd, where the potential kill-rate would be much higher. This doesn't mean that a shooter won't follow you and chase you down, but they will probably target the larger group first, giving you time to make distance.

Keep moving through the kitchen, looking for doors that lead to the outside of the building. A restaurant kitchen will have to have at least two exits in order to meet the fire code, and so you can be sure that one door will open onto a yard or receiving dock, etc.

If you have children or other dependents, be prepared to help them over, under, and around obstacles.

You will be safer running along walls, rather than into the open; however, if you believe you can get to objects in the environment that can offer you cover or concealment, such as parked cars in the parking lot, it may be worth taking the risk of running to them.

There is a difference between cover and concealment. Standing behind a car door might conceal you from the shooter, but if they were to fire shots into the car, most rounds would go through the door and may hit you. If you are positioned behind one of the front wheels, you will have the engine block—which can stop bullets—between you and the shooter, providing you cover.

Hiding, Barricading, and Lockdowns

One effective option that may be available to you is "hiding" and barricading, to prevent the shooter gaining access to you. This is a practice that has been proven effective in saving lives on a number of occasions. Barricading can be extremely simple: in room 205 of Norris Hall, students shoved a table against the door to stop Virginia Tech shooter, Seung-Hui Cho, from entering. In 2016, at the University of California, Los Angeles (UCLA), former Ph.D. student, Mainak Sarkar, went on a killing spree in an engineering building. He was largely unsuccessful in gaining access to students, as they secured

A belt, electrical cable, or similar wrapped around a hydraulic door closer will prevent the door from being opened fully and prevent a shooter from accessing a room.

the outward opening doors, with belts and electrical cables, to prevent them from opening—sometimes holding onto the belts and cables that were wrapped around door the handles, and sometimes tying them to permanent fixtures in the room.

It is probable in both cases that the shooters would have been able to get into these rooms if they were determined to, and had enough time—Cho managed to force the door being barricaded with the table open 6-7 inches but quickly gave up as the task became more difficult. Most shooters are looking to kill as many people as possible, and so are on the lookout for easy targets spending time trying to break into a room takes away from time they could be killing. Even if a barricade simply slows down an attacker from entering a room, it is likely they will move on, looking for rooms which are easier to enter. In the UCLA shooting, students communicated using cell phones to warn fellow classmates of what was happening, advising them to barricade themselves in as well—in the end no students were killed in Sarkar's shooting spree.

Barricades can also be reinforced by the people in the room—at UCLA, students wrapped belts and electrical cords around door handles and pulled them tight. In

Room 205 of Norris Hall, students got on the floor (under the gunman's sight lines), and pushed on the table they were using to block the door with their feet to help reinforce it. A filing cabinet pushed across a door will easily be moved aside on its own; however, if people were to lean against it, and add their weight to it, there's a good chance that a shooter/killer will not be able to move it; and if there are potentially easier rooms to gain access to, they will likely move on in the hope of finding easier and more accessible victims. From the moment they start shooting, an active killer will know that they have only a limited time before law enforcement or security personnel arrive, and so they will look for the easiest and most accessible victims—many shooters will kill themselves when they hear the sirens of the emergency vehicles, preferring to take their own life rather than have it taken by armed personnel; many killers want a narrative that sees them in complete control throughout the incident.

Barricades may be used to create time in order to make an escape, through another exit; e.g., putting a chair under a door handle, will not hold for long, but it might give those inside a room, enough time to escape through a window, or exit to an adjoining room, that leads to a route out of the building, etc. Anything that slows down a shooter's rampage is likely to in some way, save lives.

The Failure of the Traditional School Lockdown

When Patti Nielson, came back from investigating the "explosions" in the hallway outside the library at Columbine High School, having been shot at in the process, she immediately instigated a "lockdown" in the library, and called 911—the transcript, and recording of the conversation between her and the dispatcher, is available from a number of sources (there is no actual video footage of what went on, and that which can be found online involves actors playing the part of Dylan Klebold and Eric Harris).

The traditional school "lockdown," which is still extremely prevalent in the US, involves the teacher turning all the lights off in the room and then hiding under the classroom/library tables with the students, while waiting for law enforcement to turn up and engage with the shooter(s). The procedure is a good example of how safety protocols that protect you from one threat, can make you vulnerable to another; e.g., if a woman walks home late at night with a friend, she reduces the risk of being targeted for a sexual assault, but may increase the risk of being targeted by a mugger (there are now two purses to steal, rather than one). The idea of getting under tables, as a means of dealing with active shooter incidents comes in part from schools in Los Angeles that found this to be an effective strategy when dealing with drive-by shootings, where shooters sprayed bullets into classrooms, hoping to kill rival gang members. When such a threat is outside of the school, getting low and hiding is a good strategy, but when the killer is inside the building, it is a dangerously flawed idea—it makes students effectively sitting ducks for the shooter(s).

Those in the Columbine Library, had an escape route, as well as time to escape. It took Klebold and Harris, four minutes and 10 seconds, to enter the library, from the time Patti Nielsen first made the 911 call. In that time, there is a good chance that all 52 students, and 4 staff members could have exited the library—not through the main doors that opened onto the hallway, but through the room where the periodicals were stored, an adjoining office, or the AV room. However, rather than trying to evacuate the library, Nielson, following procedure—which the 911 dispatcher encouraged her to do—instigated a "lockdown," instructing students to hide under the desks.

Klebold and Harris, knew the lockdown procedure, and upon first entering the room, instructed everybody to "Get up!"—this instruction can be heard on the despatcher's recording of her conversation with Patti Nielson. When nobody stood up, Eric Harris said, "Fine, I'll start shooting anyway!"

It is hard to imagine what it must be like to watch from under a desk a shooter walking up and down a library, shooting your fellow students and wondering when your turn will come. This strategy of hiding and waiting for the inevitable is fatalistic, disempowering, and goes against all our survival instincts, and yet it is still the preferred strategy for dealing with active shooters in most U.S. schools.

Klebold and Harris then preceded to walk around the library, shooting under the desks, knowing that this is where everyone would be hiding. The two reloaded their weapons together offering a break in the shooting; however, nobody was in a position to take advantage of the opportunity to engage or get away, because they were stuck, hiding under the desks. In all, Harris and Klebold killed 10 people in the library, and wounded 12 more. Few students ran, or tried to tackle the shooters, even when they might have had the opportunity (the shooters reloaded their weapons twice); everybody was following a lockdown procedure that was designed to protect them from a threat that was outside the school, instead of one that was inside. Neither Patti Nielsen nor the Dispatcher, should be blamed for what happened in the library; they were following a strategy that they'd been instructed to implement.

The flaws in the traditional lockdown procedure are numerous and obvious. It goes against all of our natural fight and flight instincts. Students whose survival instincts kicked in and wanted to evacuate and run, were told by Patti Nielson to "stay down," and the dispatcher reinforced this by telling her that the police were on the way and she just needed to keep the students down, hidden under the desks. When we look at strategies for dealing with active shooters, they should work with our instincts, not against them. If evacuation isn't an option, then doors, windows, and every other access point should be blocked and barricaded to deny the shooter entry and, if it's necessary, to hide. This should be done in a way that doesn't compromise the ability to engage physically with the shooter, if this becomes a survival option.

Hiding under a desk isn't really "hiding" when a desk offers little concealment and the shooter knows that this is where you'll be. With most active shooter incidents ending before the police have time to respond, some form of action is required from those who are being targeted, whether that involves running/evacuating, barricading a room, and/or engaging/fighting the shooter.

Engaging and Fighting the Shooter(s)

The quicker an active shooter incident can be over, the fewer the casualties, not simply because the shooter has less time to kill, but because the faster the emergency services and medics can attend to the injured, the more lives will be saved. In the Pulse Nightclub shooting (Orlando, Florida, 2016), the shooter, Omar Mateen, shot and killed 49 people, and injured 58 more. A major reason that the number of casualties was so high, was the fact that Mateen was engaged in a 3-hour stand-off with the police; many people who might have lived had they been treated sooner, bled out and died during this time. Dying from a gunshot wound isn't inevitable; however, your chances of survival are reduced the longer you are denied medical treatment. Had Mateen been stopped in the first few seconds of his rampage, fewer people would have been shot, and more of those with life-threatening injuries could have been treated quickly, and possibly saved.

Convergence Tactics or "Swarming"

Our best chance of surviving an active shooter incident is by working as a team with those around us. This can involve communicating to others that there is a shooter present, either by shouting out this information, or by texting and calling others—such as in the UCLA shooting incident—to let them know that a shooter is in the building, etc. We can also engage/fight with the shooter as part of a group; something that is known as "swarming." Swarming is a convergence tactic that sees individuals converging/swarming in on an attacker from multiple directions in order to confuse, distract, and overwhelm them. This tactic was originated and "organically" evolved in Israel for dealing with terrorist shooters (civilians learned it was better to deny a shooter time and space by moving towards them, rather than moving away) and became effective enough that the Palestinian terrorist organizations started using suicide bombers instead—where the response of people running towards the killer would result in a higher death toll.

Swarming is most successful if members of a group, such as those attending a school or who work together, etc., know that this is a strategy they should implement when evacuating and barricading aren't options. Though training for this as a group is ideal, individuals have been able to inspire groups they were in—who hadn't received any training—to assist them when they've tackled a shooter. Others may well come to our assistance when they recognize that their survival is dependent on the success of our actions.

A school shooter may choose a library to initiate their killing spree as there is likely to be a large number of potential victims. As soon as you recognize gunfire, you will need to respond. Charge towards the gunman, shouting commands to those around you such as "follow me." If the group you are in has been trained in the merits of swarming, they should be moving to assist you. They should recognize that without an option to evacuate, engaging with the shooter, rather than being a static target, will increase their survival odds.

The more people that can charge the shooter the better, and if they can run at the shooter from different directions, the group is more likely to be successful in subduing them. If the shooter has to choose moving targets closing in on them from multiple directions, they are more likely to get caught in a moment of indecision before they select one. This is similar to the Predator Confusion Effect described earlier. When you run, stay low, under the shooter's natural sight-lines.

Most active shooters won't have access to fully-automatic weapons that would allow them to simply hold the trigger down and move their weapon, spraying the crowd—if they are using a semi-automatic weapon, they will have to make a trigger pull for each shot they make, severely reducing their ability to shoot at multiple targets. The first person to reach the shooter should aim to get "under" the weapon and lift it so the barrel is pointing upwards. At 10-15 yards, the first person should be reaching the killer in the matter of a few seconds. This will allow the shooter time to make only two or three badly-aimed shots.

As more people in the group reach the attacker, they should "swarm" them so that the shooter is overwhelmed by the sheer number of people who are now attacking them and restricting their movement.

If the shooter has their weapon attached to them via a sling or harness, it will be extremely difficult to disarm them. If it isn't, you can try to wrest it from their grip. If they have only let off a few shots, the barrel should be cool enough to grab; if the weapon has been fired many times, it will be too hot and you will need to control it around the lower hand-guard. Either way, the group should look to attack the shooter, punching, kicking, and hitting them with objects at hand, delivering enough concussive force to incapacitate them (they may well have a second weapon, such as a handgun on them).

The group using their weight of numbers should start to drive the attacker back so that their focus is on staying upright and on their feet. With the weapon pointed up, no one in the group should be in the line of fire.

Swarming has been proven to be an effective tactic in limiting the number of casualties of the group that the shooter is targeting. A shooter, unlike most criminals, wants time and distance; they will want to control the movement of the group, pick targets, and kill without pressure. Swarming puts the shooter under immediate pressure, quickly reducing the time and distance they have to select targets and make accurate shots. It is likely that some in the group will be shot; however, the overall number of casualties is likely to be much be lower than if the shooter was allowed to go on a prolonged shooting spree, and medics will be able to get to and treat those who have been injured once the shooter is neutralized, hopefully saving more lives.

Like all solutions to such acts of violence, swarming comes with no guarantees, but it has been shown to work on a number of occasions, such as in 2007, when a group of military reservists rushed a shooter at the New York-New York Casino in Las Vegas, and in 2009, when a gunman who had assassinated a church pastor at Maryville Baptist Church in Illinois, was subdued by members of the congregation. There are also ways to improve the success rates of swarming, and reduce the number of victims shot.

When Kip Kinkel opened fire in the Thurston High School cafeteria in 1998, the magazine of his rifle contained a total of 48 bullets (he'd already fired two shots in the patio area outside, killing one student and injuring another). After he emptied it, killing another and injuring 24 more, he needed to reload. One of those he injured, Jacob Ryker, took this cessation in the shooting to lead a charge, which saw Kinkel taken down and wrestled to the ground. Even as he was being dragged to the ground and pinned down, he managed to draw a Glock 19 that he had in his waistband and get one shot off, hitting Ryker and further injuring him (he also had a .22LR Ruger MK II pistol, and two hunting knives on him). Kinkel was disarmed and then pinned down and restrained until the police arrived. In total, 7 students were involved in the "swarm," that subdued him.

There are times that while you are evacuating, you may need to temporarily hide/conceal yourself. If you need to do this, don't compromise your ability to engage and tackle the shooter, i.e., by hiding under a desk or table, which would restrict your ability to move. As the shooter advances towards you, shooting at anyone they see move, get yourself prepared to tackle and swarm them. Make sure you have all sound notifications on your phone turned off as you don't want to alert the shooter to your location prematurely.

If the shooting stops suddenly, despite there still being available targets for the shooter to aim at, it may be that they are in the process of reloading their rifle and are attempting to change the magazine. Unless the shooter is highly trained, this will be a relatively slow task for them to perform and even if they have some tactical training, you should have the time to reach them and tackle them before the weapon is operational again, particularly as charging them at this stage will put them under pressure.

As they perform the magazine change, start to rush towards them; shout and encourage those who are in the environment to join you in attempting to subdue the shooter. Keep low as you run towards them as the shooter won't be as quick to spot you if you are below their natural sight-lines.

Your group should try to get control of both the weapon and the shooter...

...and get under the gun to bring it up and towards your attacker; if you have control of it and can use it as an impact weapon, smash it repeatedly into the shooter's face. Those with you should drive them back as you do this so that they become overwhelmed and confused as to who and what they should be responding to.

Shout for assistance, telling those around you that you have control of the weapon; the last to arrive will probably be those who hung back, waiting to see whether those initially swarming the attacker would be successful. If they know that the gun is now being controlled and the risk to their safety is lower, they will be more likely to join in and assist you.

Tackling the shooter when they've run out of ammunition/were engaged in a magazine change has been successful in a number of incidents, e.g., Jim D. Adkisson, was tackled by church members when he paused to reload his shotgun in the Knoxville, Tennessee, church shooting of 2008; in the Hudson Valley Mall shooting of 2005, the gunman, Robert Bonelli dropped his rifle as he tried to change magazines, giving those nearby an opportunity to subdue him. This is not the only time that a shooter has dropped things when reloading. In the 2011 attempted assassination of Gabrielle Giffords, where the shooter (Jared Lee Loughner) dropped the new magazine as he was trying to reload, a bystander picked it up, and the gathered crowd swarmed the shooter. Recognizing an opportunity to act is a key survival skill, as the "when" is often more important than the "what" and "how" of the solution you attempt to put in place.

Creating Environments That Improve the Success Rate of Swarming and Tackling

Many modern buildings—especially office buildings—are constructed largely out of glass including interior walls, and rooms. This makes it extremely difficult to create successful barricades as the shooter can simply shatter the glass by firing into it. This may mean that trying to block/barricade the door just isn't an effective method of preventing a shooter access to you and others who may be in your room/office. This may force you, and those with you, to engage with the attacker if evacuation isn't an option. It could also be that you lack the time to build a successful barricade and should instead prepare the room/space you are in for engagement.

There may not be the time to build an effective barrier or barricade and, with the large glass panel next to the door, it is questionable how effective this strategy would be in keeping a shooter out of the room pictured; in saying this, if a barrier could slow the shooter down enough, they may give up and look for a more accessible group of victims. Even though it is unlikely that a barricade would prevent entry in this situation, those inside the room can set things up, so that they can improve the likelihood of successfully engaging with the attacker.

One thing that can be done is to up-end a table and/or create a barrier directly in front of the door. This should be set roughly at the distance where the muzzle of the gun or rifle they are holding would knock into it as they enter. If the shooter is under emotional stress and duress, they will be suffering from tunnel-vision and will actively have to turn/swivel their head to see around this obstacle. This alone won't end the event but in extreme situations, survival is often accomplished by gaining a millisecond of an advantage here, and a millisecond of an advantage there.

The lights in the room should be turned off (in the photo sequence that follows, they are turned on for demonstration purposes). This is so that the attacker's eyes will need to adjust to the dark before they are able to see clearly. The darker you can make the room the longer this process will take. The group should position themselves to one side of the room so that when the gunman is tackled and moved, there will be no one in their line of fire. Those in the group should put their hand on the shoulder of the person in front so that they can feel where they are and move with them when the person at the front of the group initiates the charge.

There should be a small group, armed with a collection of missiles, such as bags, books, staplers, etc., who are ready to throw them, when the shooter commits themselves to stepping into the room. The group waiting to charge should be positioned close to the wall—outside of the gunman's peripheral vision, and low, below their natural sight-lines; i.e., they will normally look along the barrel, into the distance, with their eyes at head height/level.

As the gunman steps into the room the "missiles" should be thrown at them. We are born with a natural flinch/startle reflex, and when objects cross our peripheral vision, we have a tendency to bring our arms up to protect ourselves, whether we are holding something or not. At the same time, the assailant's eyes will be adjusting to the dark, while having to process that their movement and sight is blocked by the upturned tables/desks in front of them. As this happens, the group waiting along the wall should initiate their charge, and attempt to tackle the shooter.

Human beings process information sequentially, and if that processing is interrupted by a new bit of information we must take on board—process, and decide what to do with—and then we are hit with another piece of information and another, another, and another, etc., we will quickly become overwhelmed, and hesitate. Decisiveness is largely what determines survival, and if we can cause the shooter to hesitate, we will improve the chances of our tackle being successful.

The job of the first person in the group is to charge into the gunman, and start moving them across the room, slamming into them and taking their balance. They should not initially try to grab the weapon, as this may stimulate the attacker's natural grab/snatch reflex, which will see them automatically pull back on their weapon to try and retain it. This would turn the struggle into a one-on-one engagement, and the group's numerical advantage would be lost—this is the one strength that the group has; i.e., working as a team, and this should be utilized to the full. The group should follow each other, adding their weight to the charge.

The second person in the group, should look to try and get control of the weapon—not necessarily to make a disarm, but to make sure that it is directed away from the group. They should have felt the first person move and initiate the charge, as they had their hand on their shoulder. The group will need to move fast as one unit, driving the attacker across the room.

Depending on the size of the room, the shooter may end up being slammed into a wall, before they are taken to ground. The group should press into them, preventing as much movement as possible, so that they are unable to fight back or try to reach for another weapon, be it a gun or a knife.

Drive the attacker to the ground, wresting their weapon away from them. Keep driving and pressing them down.

Rain blows and kicks down onto them, and if you do use their rifle as a weapon, use it as a cold, impact one, to deliver concussive force to your attacker (making sure that the barrel is never pointing at a member of the group). This is not a time to measure your force, your attacker needs to be conclusively shut down so that they are unable—in any way shape or form—to continue their rampage.

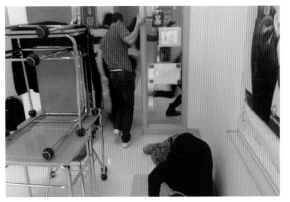

If law enforcement is closeby, you may decide to keep the assailant pinned down, and wait for the police to secure them; however, you may also wish to evacuate the room and disengage as quickly as possible (especially if you have reason to believe that there may be a second shooter in the building).

While you could attempt to converge on an attacker from multiple directions, in an ambush setting, trying to communicate the moment of attack between different groups/individuals, while maintaining the element of surprise, would be extremely difficult, especially if you only have a few moments to prepare everyone. There would also be a risk of bringing people into the field of fire, if they were spread out around the room, and then started to move in on the assailant. It is much safer and more effective to have everybody positioned in one group, if you have the time to do so, so that they can all move as one unit.

There may be an occasion when you are caught in a similar position, but in which you are the only person in the room, and will have to engage with the attacker on your own. In such a situation, you may be better to try to control the weapon, rather than the attacker—as you will not have the advantage of weight of numbers. When trying to control long-barrel weapons that have been fired repeatedly, don't attempt to grab onto the barrel of the gun. The size of rounds used in semi-automatic rifles such as the AK-47, are much larger than those used in handguns, and so heat the barrel up to higher temperatures much more quickly.

It may be that when you attempt to evacuate you take a wrong turn or realize that the distance you will have to cover to complete the evacuation is too great and the shooter would have a clear and easy shot at you. In this case, it may be in your best survival interest to conceal yourself and engage the shooter, using the element of surprise to your advantage.

Pressing yourself flat against the wall, just behind the corner where your attacker would only be able to see you if they turned the corner, wait until you see the barrel of the gun pass by. In this situation, it's likely that the shooter will be concentrating on following the main group and will be more focused on what is going on to their left, where the group evacuated to, than to their right. Even if this was not the case, you will still have the element of surprise on your side.

As the barrel of the gun passes by, start to dive out...

...with one hand positioned under the gun (the right hand) and one over (the left hand). Don't try to grab the barrel—after firing a number of rounds, it will be red-hot and you probably won't be able to hold onto it. If the shooter is looking down the barrel of the gun and has tunnel vision they will only see your arm movement at the last moment.Part of what will help you get a "deep" control of the weapon is the fact that the shooter will be moving forward as you approach them from the side so you should end up grasping the gun, around the lower hand guard/fore grip, rather than the barrel.

Pull yourself to the gun and the gun to your chest, wrapping it up and hugging it to your body. If it is pulled in tight to you, your body might well block the ejection port meaning the spent casings can't be ejected. If this was to happen when the shooter went to fire the gun again they would find it to be jammed. Even if you don't jam it, having your body this close to the ejection port will mean that the hot casings will be less likely to hit you in the face.

Pulling the rifle to you with your right hand and locking it to your body, start to turn outwards using the power of your body to wrest the rifle from your attacker's grasp.

Once your assailant has lost control of the weapon with their right hand...

...step back as you continue your turn to pull it away from them completely.

Continue to turn and transfer the weapon into your hands so you can repeatedly strike your aggressor with it.

Aim for large targets like the body first so you make sure that you hit something and then turn your focus to smaller targets such as the face/head.

In most active shooter incidents, handguns/short-barrel weapons are used—or at least carried as a backup weapon in case a rifle should fail to function, or run out of ammunition, etc. If you find yourself in a similar situation, and instead of the barrel of a rifle passing by, it's a handgun, you can use a similar tactic to perform a disarm.

In this scenario, the shooter is armed with a short-barrelled weapon. It could be that this is their primary weapon, or it could be a backup, that they've resorted to after their rifle jammed or became non-operational. They may even have the skillset and knowledge to clear a jam, but believe it will take time away from killing, so instead use another weapon they have about their person so that their rampage can go on, uninterrupted.

As the shooter's weapon passes by you, dive/jump out to grab it. Your right hand should grab the gun with an underhand grip, and your left should grab the nearest wrist to you, using an overhand grip—if you are dealing with a right-handed shooter, and approaching them from the same side, you will now have control of both their weapon and the hand/arm that is controlling it. If you were to approach your assailant from the other side, you would have control of the weapon, and the shooter's supporting hand/arm (this will still give you enough control to make an effective disarm).

Whenever you enact a solution to a violent situation, you must be prepared for the various ways your aggressor could respond: psychologically and emotionally, as well as physically. One concern you should have when disarming, is that your attacker may be able to retain their weapon, pulling it away from you and back to them; possibly putting you back in the line of fire. To prevent this possibility, roll your elbow over the shooter's arm and hug/squeeze their arm, against your body and under your armpit.

If they now try to pull their weapon back they will pull your elbow into their chest, allowing you to stay behind the weapon. With the arm secured, you can now begin the disarm.

Start to turn the firearm towards your attacker in a tight arc.

Use the barrel as a lever to loosen your assailant's grip on the weapon.

As you turn the weapon, pivot your body so that it isn't just your arm/hand that is doing the work of moving the gun.

As the attacker's grip loosens, step/fall back allowing your bodyweight to pull the gun from their grasp.

Once you have control of it, use the gun as an impact weapon making sure that you don't muzzle yourself in the process. Although it is safe to assume that their weapon is operational—their intention was to use it to kill whereas with a mugger or similar criminal, their weapon may be more for show than to be used—in the disarming process it may have jammed—particularly if the shooter pulled the trigger while you had the slide secured. Rather than wasting time clearing a jam, you are better to start attacking your assailant using the gun as a strong impact weapon, to prevent them from trying to continue their assault.

Tactical Breathing and Negating Some of the Adverse Effects of Stress

It is important to manage your stress levels in a violent situation, and especially so when your survival depends on you being able to think clearly, and act decisively. One of the ways we can deal with some of the negative side-effects of extreme stress and duress, is through Tactical Breathing (sometimes referred to as Combat Breathing). By controlling our breathing, we can regulate our heart rate, which in turn controls the amount and rate of oxygenated blood, that is sent to our body and our brain, along with any hormones, such as adrenaline, that are being carried by that blood. Regular, deep breathing also activates the hypothalamus, which is connected to the Pituitary Gland in the brain, and stimulates it to send out neuro-hormones that can counter many of the stress-inducing hormones, contained in adrenaline. While we want to make use, and take advantage, of the effects of adrenaline—such as increased physical performance and increased pain tolerance—we don't want it to take over control of us, so that we panic and end up running to get away from a threat/danger, in situations where we should really be biding our time, such as by hiding, and choosing the opportunity when we may be better engaging with our assailant; e.g., when we see the barrel of the gun go past us, etc. By controlling our breathing and regulating our physiological responses to stress, we can make sure that we have our foot on the adrenal gas pedal so we can control it, and not allow it to control us.

Tactical Breathing works best when you have the time to think about controlling your breathing. It is important that it isn't prioritized over certain survival instincts; e.g., if you see a shooter at the end of a corridor, your body will want to run away, and in situations where this is a viable option, that is exactly what you should be doing. If you run into a room, and can lock the door and start barricading, for example, this would be the time to engage in Tactical Breathing.

The process is very, very simple, and extremely effective. It comprises of three parts:

1) Breathe in through your nose for a count of 1-2-3-4
2) Hold for a count of 1-2-3-4
3) Breathe out through your nose for a count of 1-2-3-4

Keep repeating this, until you start to feel that you are gaining control of yourself, and repeat the process, when you start to feel overwhelmed again. It is also good to be able to recognize your own body-language as a means of determining if you are in a state of emotional stress and duress; e.g., if you have hunched your shoulders up, so that they are close to your ears, you are in a high state of fear, and it would be good to start practicing Tactical Breathing—this is useful for any stressful situation you find yourself in, and not just active shooter incidents.

One serious symptom of stress, when adrenalized, is suffering from tunnel-vision. Our Survival/Fear system, will narrow our field of vision, in an attempt to focus on whatever the immediate danger or threat is, and to keep us from getting distracted by what is going on around us. There is a lot of sense to this, especially if we are dealing with an aggressor who we have to engage with; in the midst of a violent confrontation, we want to be focusing on the danger we have identified, and not reacting to other movements around us, which may not pose an immediate threat to our safety. While there are obvious benefits to this, and it may be a good survival response in the majority of violent incidents, when the start of the confrontation sees us directly facing our aggressor, it may also put us at a disadvantage when we don't know exactly where the threat is coming from, and need a greater field of vision to be able to pick up on the movement of one or more attackers, at the earliest opportunity.

The other issue with tunnel-vision is that as we start to become more visually focused, we will start to suffer from auditory exclusion, i.e., our senses aren't really able to multi-task, so we're not able to see and hear well at the same time—we can basically do one or the other. If we are hiding, waiting to engage with an attacker, we will probably hear them before we see them, so being visually-focused in this case is not a good state for us to be in. One way, along with Tactical Breathing, to deal with these adverse responses, is to scan (this will also help us get a better appreciation of our surroundings). This involves swiveling our head, and looking around us—as we do this, we should try to focus on objects at different depths and distances. As our eyes focus and refocus, our field of vision will open up; and now that we're not too visually focused, we'll get some of our auditory senses back—rounding out our abilities to identify danger. You will also improve your ability to hear/listen by keeping your mouth open rather then closed—so if you identify a sound, it is worth interrupting your Tactical Breathing to do this, to try and identify what the sound is, and its relevance to your survival.

Times When the Barrel of the Gun May Be Handled

Weaponry has changed over the years. In the 1930's and early 40's, most infantry carried a bolt-action rifle, rather than an assault rifle that was capable of selective fire, including semi- and fully-automatic. While the barrel of a bolt-action rifle will heat up, it will not do so at the same rate as an assault rifle; e.g., the barrel of an AK-47 semi-automatic, is too hot to handle after 20 or so rounds have been fired. While controlling a 1930's/40's rifle (which is when Imi Lichtenfeld, and those teaching KAPAP—Krav Panim A Panim—were developing long-barrel disarms), by the barrel may have been possible, attempting to do so with a modern assault rifle that has been fired several times, is virtually impossible; and because of this, certain controls and disarms have had to change and be adapted to reflect this new reality. This goes to demonstrate the ever-evolving nature that typifies the Krav Maga approach.

There are those occasions though when it is safe and possible to grab the barrel—which can be good, because if you are in front of the weapon, it will be the closest thing for you to grab, allowing you a quick control of the weapon. If you know that the gun has yet to be fired, or has only fired a few shots, then you should be able to hold the barrel, as it won't have heated up yet. To know this for sure you must not only hear at most one or two shots, but you must also see the shooter draw their weapon, so you will know the gun hasn't been fired multiple times elsewhere, before the killer reaches you.

Sometimes there are warning signs to an attack such as a person entering a location with a large bag stretched at both ends or putting in earplugs (a shooter knows how loud the repeated fire of their weapon will be). There may even be the opportunity to hear/recognize the sound of a charging handle being pulled to pull the first bullet into the chamber.

If you didn't pick up on any warning signs, it may be only as the shooter stands up and points the weapon that the realization hits you that they are intending to shoot you and everybody else in the restaurant. Those with you may be in a state of shock, discounting the danger as a prank or similar. At this stage, the shooter may have fired their first shot at the person who was immediately in front of their sight-lines, but as you start to get up they are likely to pick up on your movement and turn to train the gun on you.

As they sweep the gun towards you, bring your left hand out to grab the barrel—in this situation, it is known that the weapon has only fired once. It is important to note that even in the U.S., fully automatic weapons are difficult for most people to get access to. If this was a fully-automatic weapon, the shooter could depress the trigger, and as long as they held it down—and until it ran out of ammunition—the gun would keep firing. In semi-automatic mode, the shooter must pull and release the trigger for every shot they make. While this may not slow down the process of firing much, it does create "spaces" between each shot.

The further in on the barrel you can grab the better—and if the shooter is moving towards you they will help facilitate this. Immediately push the barrel up, attempting to get under the gun. With your other hand, start to reach for the stock.

Push forward and up with your left hand, and pull back and down with your right in a circular motion.

If the rifle has a pistol grip, your attacker will find it almost impossible to hold onto it as the rifle's rotation will put pressure on their grip and wrist—especially as you will have the leverage advantage of the weapon to assist you.

Pull the weapon away from your attacker—depending on your proximity to them, you may end up dragging the barrel of the gun down their face, as you do this. If, as you pull the weapon away, you are met with the resistance of a sling, drive the gun repeatedly into your attacker's face before possibly using the sling to control their neck and head.

Pull the rifle back...

...and ram it into your attacker's body. First, aim for a large target area, that is difficult to miss, and then...

...aim for the head.

After you have struck your assailant so that they are sufficiently stunned/incapacitated, and will not have the chance to pull another weapon, disengage to safety.

Issues with Playing Dead

Where violent incidents are concerned, many people want simple answers; e.g., whenever X happens, do Y, etc. However, violence involves the interaction of individuals, within the context of a situation, and what may work in one incident, may not in others. This may be for no real/discernible reason or logic. In some active shooter incidents, pretending to be dead has worked for people, in others it has not. The reasons it works in some situations and not others aren't clear—it could be down to simple carelessness on the part of the shooter, as they fail to notice another potential victim. It could be that they simply don't care enough about killing that individual (some shooters, will spare certain individuals as they go about their rampage), or that they feel their time could be better spent moving on to target larger groups, etc. They may even want to leave a survivor/witness, who can report on the death and carnage they caused, making their crime seem more real, and less abstract, i.e., causing it to have more impact. At the end of the day, we can only speculate. However, playing dead is a risky tactic, and not one to be advised, even if on occasion it has been showed to work; in the Virginia Tech Massacre, Cho returned to the fallen bodies he'd previously shot and shot each one in the head, to make sure that his victims were dead; though one intended victim played dead and survived the incident. Although no solution to violence comes with a 100% guarantee, playing dead is an extremely unpredictable strategy, with such high-stakes consequences, that it is highly inadvisable.

Exiting After an Active Shooter Incident

Even if you manage to successfully disarm a shooter and disengage, you should keep in mind that you will still be involved in an active shooter incident. This is something that often gets left out of self-defense training. For example, once a technique such as a gun disarm has been performed, the training scenario ends without considering all the things that could potentially follow, e.g., the attacker trying to get his gun back, the attacker pulling a knife and attacking, how you disengage safely from the environment, etc. This is the danger of technique-centric training at the expense of scenario-based training. One issue you may face is that you could be identified as the shooter by law enforcement. In the wake of Columbine, where the police waited an extremely long time to enter the school, until after both Klebold and Harris had committed suicide and the rampage was over—though they weren't aware of this—the general policy is for the first officer at the scene to attempt to identify and engage with the shooter. This could see you encountering law enforcement, relatively quickly, and if you can manage to not be holding a firearm when you do come face to face with an officer, there will be less chance of you being mistaken for the shooter.

We may think that law enforcement officers have received the type and level of training, that means that they're impervious to the effects of stress and duress. In an extreme situation, such as an active shooter incident, they will be coping better than an untrained individual, but this doesn't mean that they won't be affected at all. We may be unable to imagine that could appear to be a threat; however, to an officer just turning up on the scene, who may have limited information about the incident, anyone could be the source of the violence. Whenever we deal with a law enforcement officer, we should consider how things may look from their perspective, and obey any commands they give us.

If you need to take the weapon with you, find a container to put it in. You will want to clearly demonstrate to those around you that you are not an immediate threat. You should hug the container to your chest so that your arms are occupied and it is clear that you can't easily access the gun; i.e., you would have to put the container down, reach in and pull the weapon out, etc. Those with you should hold their hands high and keep them up. You should follow the instructions that law enforcement officers give you to the letter, without hesitation. You shouldn't be surprised if you are treated somewhat roughly, as they may be trying to evacuate the area quickly, and also check that the shooter hasn't tried to sneak out, by blending in as part of the group.

One way you can assist law enforcement and potentially save lives, is with information about the situation; e.g., has the shooter taken hostages, where are they located if they have, is there just one shooter or many, did you see any explosive devices, etc. If you can provide information about what the shooter was wearing, and what part of the building they were last in, this may enable the security forces to end the incident quickly—and the shorter the event, the more lives are likely to be saved, as medics will be able to treat the injured that much sooner.

Killers are getting more adept at achieving higher kill-rates in the shortest possible time (the "Stopwatch of Death" model/equation, that divides number of attempted killings by number of minutes, has shown that since Columbine, where there averaged out to be one killing per 8 minutes, other killers have become much more "efficient"), and so ending these incidents as quickly as possible, is of the utmost importance. One thing that can help shorten this timeline is good and accurate information that SWAT teams and other agencies can use.

Active Killers and Explosive Devices

When we think about what happened in the Columbine School Library, we might at first envisage a scene, where the two shooters, wandered around an otherwise normal library, picking off targets, etc. This wasn't the case; the library was filled with smoke, the fire alarm was ringing, and the sprinkler system had been triggered. This is because Klebold and Harris had let off a number of pipe bombs and other explosive devices—in fact, their original plan had been to blow up the school cafeteria with two propane tank bombs, not go on a shooting spree; that only took place once they realized the bombs had failed to detonate—there is a lot of speculation as to why the detonation mechanism failed, as it worked successfully on their diversionary bomb, and the circuitry required was relatively simple; however, the fact that the two main bombs didn't go off, demonstrates the unreliable nature of homemade explosive devices—unless constructed by a trained individual. Shooting and stabbing, is a much more predictable method of killing, yet there are still those shooters who have used explosives—and the threat of explosive devices—as part of their active shooter rampage killings, and those who have engaged in bombing campaigns (London Nail Bomber, April 1999).

A bomb or explosive device is basically a fast-burning material, confined in an enclosed container; e.g., if you were to take a regular firework, open it up, spread the black powder into a pile, and then light it with a match, the powder would burn extremely quickly, but because the gases that are created can expand unhindered, there would be no blast—packed tightly together in a container with no opening, this release of energy in a confined space, will cause an explosion, breaking the container apart and fragmenting it. An explosive device has two ways of killing: via the concussive force of the blast itself and/or through the fragments of the container (and/or objects such as nails that are attached to it), that are propelled by the blast. When we look at surviving a blast—such as from somebody throwing a nail/pipe bomb or similar at us—we need to mitigate these two things: the concussive force of the blast, and the fragmentation it creates.

Hand Grenade Attacks

Violence can be both general and also very specific; e.g., in one country or region, machete attacks may be extremely common, and in others almost non-existent. In one city, such as Chicago, there may be a serious problem with gun crime, and in another U.S. city like Boston, only a minor one. Sweden has a problem with hand grenades—in 2015, the city of Malmo experienced 30 grenade attacks in August alone. Sweden is not the only country that has suffered grenade attacks in recent years. In 2012, there was a series of gun and grenade attacks across Merseyside in the UK, and in September of the same year, two female police officers were killed in a gun and grenade attack in Manchester, while investigating a burglary. There have also been several foiled terrorist attacks in the US, where grenades were involved; e.g., Derrick Shareef—2006, Ahmed Ferhani & Mohamed Mamdouh—2011, Abu Khalid Abdul Latif & Walli Mujahidh—2011, etc.

There are two steps that have to be completed in order for a hand grenade to be detonated: the pin needs to be pulled out, and the handle/spoon needs to be released.

The pin keeps the spoon locked in place. Once this safety pin is removed, the spoon would be released and fly off under pressure, as the striker spring unwinds...

...unless the person throwing the grenade holds the spoon/lever down manually.

The striker spring pushes against the lever/spoon—you can see in the photograph that if pressure on the lever starts to be released, the striker spring will begin to push the handle/spoon away.

Once the pressure on the spoon/lever is released, the striker pin will unwind, propelling the spoon away, and allowing the striker to hit the primer, which will explode, lighting the fuse—the delay—which burns down to the detonator and detonates the charge. The resulting explosion will create both concussive force, and fragmentation, as the grenade's outer shell is blown away.

Your best defense against any explosive device is distance; the further away you are, the weaker the concussive force of the blast will be, and the fewer fragments will reach you—these may in fact be decelerating if and when they do hit you, decreasing the risk and extent of possible injuries. The concussive killing force of a grenade may be as little as a 2-meter radius, around the detonation point; however, fragments can be propelled significantly further, with the extent of the injuries being determined by the targets they hit. It is worth noting that there are different grenades which are designed with an emphasis on producing either concussive force, or fragmentation; e.g., the M67 is a fragmentation grenade, which is judged to have an effective killing radius of 5 meters—however, depending where you are in the blast pattern, you may be able to survive at a closer range. This is because the blast-pattern isn't linear, and in fact rises, the further away from the grenade you are, making it possible to get under the blast, and the fragmentation, if you are able to stay low to the ground.

Disarming an Assailant Armed with a Hand Grenade

A shooter may take a multi-phased approach to killing; e.g., they may first conduct a vehicular ramming outside of a building, before using the car to ram the entryway and gain access; they may then go on a shooting spree, and either when they run out of ammunition—or when they hear the arrival of law enforcement—look to commit suicide by means of a hand grenade, killing everyone in the environment around them.

You may find yourself, at some point in the rampage, positioned behind the attacker—who is threatening a group with a hand grenade. From where you are, you may have no idea if the pin has been pulled, and whether it is only the pressure of the shooter's thumb on the spoon/handle that is stopping the striker from hitting the primer.

While the killer is distracted, come up behind them, and with your left hand grab their wrist. With your right, aim the heel of your palm at their knuckle line.

Push down so that you can bring your weight to bear on your assailant's hand that is gripping the grenade—this should also have the effect of breaking their posture/frame.

Push down and buckle your attacker's legs so that they start to fall towards the ground. As you do this, push on their knuckles to open up their grip, and "scrape" your hand around, to take hold of the grenade. If you can secure the spoon as you do this, then you can prevent the grenade from detonating; however, this is highly unlikely, and so you should work to the assumption that you will now have a live grenade in your hand.

The delay time varies between different grenades; e.g., the M67 fragmentation grenade has a 4-5 second delay/fuse, whereas the Soviet/Russian F1 grenade, has a delay of 3.5–4 seconds etc. Some have an initial delay, but will detonate on impact (RGN), if they hit something (like the ground). That said, it is dangerous to rely too heavily on the specified delay time, as the fuse can be affected by the conditions in which it is stored, and over time, etc. It is unlikely that those grenades that find their way into civilian hands have been looked after in an optimal way. In reality, you may only have a couple of seconds to act, once the striker has hit the primer.

If you know that the corridor behind you is clear, throw the grenade in an underhand fashion, and low to the ground, so that the blast pattern is directed upwards, rather than downwards (which may happen if the grenade is thrown high)

Your goal is to get low—under the blast—as quickly as possible, so dive rather than run or roll; either of which would see your body become a large target area for the blast and fragmentation. Remember, you may be working with an old and badly stored grenade, and so offering as little of your body as a target, at the earliest opportunity, should be your goal.

Lie close to the floor, with your legs crossed, so that the insides of your legs are not exposed, and the soles of your shoes/sneakers are directed towards the blast— making the closest part of you the smallest target for any fragmentation. Put your hands over your ears and open your mouth, so that when the concussive blast hits you, air can be driven out of your mouth, rather than against your lungs, likely bursting them; you want the blast to "deflate" you rather than be met with any resistance.

The method for taking the grenade out of the attacker's hand is described below—this is the same method that has been used for disarming knives throughout the book.

Secure your assailant's wrist with your left hand, putting your right hand over theirs. You will want your hand to cover theirs so that you'll be able to apply pressure to the back of their knuckles and open up their grip.

As you push on the back of their hand/knuckles, their hand will begin to open and their grip on the grenade will weaken/lessen...

...allowing you to slide/scrape your hand around, and take control of the grenade.

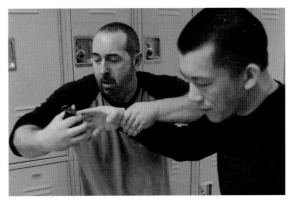

Once you have hold of it, pull it away from your attacker's hand. If you have a space/area to throw it safely, get rid of it as quickly as possible.

Blast Patterns

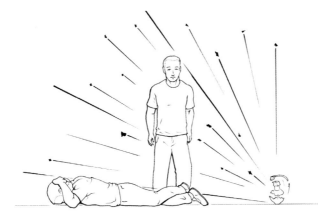

When a grenade on the ground detonates, the blast pattern, including both the concussive force of the explosion and the fragments of the grenade, are pushed outwards and up. By diving and getting low, it may be possible to get under the blast, or at least limit your exposure to it. By crossing your legs, you will offer the soles of your shoes, and the outside of your legs, as the closest target areas to the blast—with your head farthest away, it may even be possible for this part of your body to be under the blast completely. If you are caught standing or, rolling, where your body is high, you will be hit with the full force of the blast, as well as the fragments of the grenade.

Nothing in reality is as simple as it looks in a book or a video. Stress, nerves, sweat and blood, can make controlling a knife, a gun, or a grenade, much more difficult than, in one sense, it should be. Just as active shooters have been known to drop their weapons, or magazines as they reloaded, so might you drop the grenade, as you disarm your assailant. If this happens, it is unlikely that you will have the time to bend down and pick it up to throw.

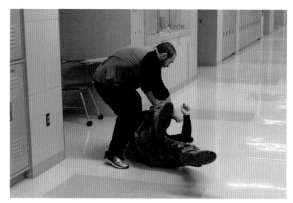

As you make the disarm, the grenade may come loose, and fall out of your, and the attacker's hand. Trying to chase after it would see you move closer to it, when it is distance, where grenades are concerned, that improves your survival chances. Having missed the opportunity to throw the grenade away, and put distance between you and it, you should now aim to use your attacker's body to absorb the blast. You would likewise try to employ this strategy, if throwing the grenade away might put others at risk.

Pull your attacker's arm up, so that it is straight. In doing this, you will be turning them onto their side. If your left foot isn't positioned past your attacker's head, move it there as you pull up on their arm.

Bring your knee and shin up, against their extended arm, and put pressure on the arm, to start turning them over and onto the grenade. Do this with impact, and think of it more as a strike than a push; striking is done in an instance, whereas pushing takes time.

Once their weight has been shifted so that they are falling onto the grenade, start to bring your foot back to the ground, and then...

...start to dive to the ground so that you make distance, and remain low, under the blast. Diving, also means that you are getting your head, and upper body, low towards the ground faster than your legs and feet, meaning that your brain and vital organs, will be moved away from the blast as quickly as possible.

Using the assailant's body to suppress the blast of the grenade, may also be a tactic you want to employ, if you are in a confined space, where there isn't the opportunity to make distance and/or there are others around, who may also not be able to escape the blast radius. In such an instance, as you disarm your attacker, you would roll your attacker over, and place the grenade under them - be aware that this is a time-consuming action and should only be employed if the situation dictates it.

Workplace Violence and Active Shooters

Workplace violence can take many forms, from bullying and physical harassment, to flare-ups over perceived supervisory and management mistreatment, etc. It can involve individuals and external groups, such as animal rights activists/organizations, which target the employees and facilities of companies that engage in animal testing. Doctors and those who work at abortion clinics, are also at risk from violent activist groups. It is not only the type of company, but the specific work that you do, which can increase your risk of experiencing violence in the workplace; e.g., if you are a nurse who works in the emergency room of a hospital, or a social worker who handles at-risk clients, you are more likely to be assaulted than the managers and administrators who work in your building. Most workplace violence is low-level, and rarely fatal; however, in the case of the "lethal employee"—the coworker who feels they need to take revenge on their managers, their supervisors, and the company as a whole—this is not the case.

While there is a natural focus on school shootings, due to the fact that children are targeted, businesses —both open (such as restaurants, shops and similar) and closed to the public (such as private offices, warehouses, factories, etc.)—remain the most common locations for active shooter incidents—between 2000 and 2013, 27.5% of all active shooter incidents in the U.S. took place in businesses open to the public, and a further 14.4%, took place in those that were closed to the public; i.e., 41.9% of all active shooter incidents took place in the workplace—this doesn't include government, military, and hospital buildings, etc.

The Lethal Employee

The media likes to present simple stories. When a gun-obsessed employee, whose nickname was "Rocky," went on a killing spree armed with an AK-47, four other firearms, and a bayonet, at the Standard Gravure Print Works in Kentucky (1989), the media quickly created a profile of the shooter—47-year old Joseph T. Wesbecker—as an angry, macho, testosterone-fueled killer. While this came to be world's view of Wesbecker, it's an extremely misleading portrayal of the man behind the killings. Had the media dug deeper, they'd have realized the nickname "Rocky" was an ironic one, ascribed by Wesbecker by his work colleagues, after he was beaten up by a woman he'd been hitting on, in a bar (his nickname prior to this incident was, "little doughboy"). Although he did feel a lot of anger towards a company—and more specifically the supervisors and managers—that he believed had discriminated against him (and there was evidence that this was the case), he was a far different character to the one that the media initially portrayed him as.

If we look a bit closer at Joseph T. Wesbecker's transformation from a model employee, to a desperate killer who took revenge on the company (and his coworkers) he'd once been proud to work for, it can provide us with a chilling education as to why—and how—some employees can turn into lethal ones.

Disrespect

Almost all acts of violence ultimately come down to issues of respect, and the Standard Gravure shooting was no different. One of his victims—and coworkers—Michael Campbell, who survived the shooting spree, allegedly stated, "Everybody understood where he (Wesbecker) was coming from. His only problem was that he shot the wrong people." The work culture at Standard Gravure was a toxic one, where management had all but obliterated the unions, and were looking to reduce the workforce, cut costs, and possibly even relocate the Print Works out of state, to Pennsylvania. Many of the workforce felt betrayed and cheated, especially when the company was sold in 1986, with $10 million taken from the work's pension fund in order to secure the deal. This forced many to work double shifts, with no contract, and no pay increases. The new owners/management may have felt that they were in full and total control of the print plant, but that was only if the employees, agreed to play by the rules, and Wesbecker was coming to the conclusion, that these weren't fair and respectful enough to be abided by.

In 1987, Wesbecker filed a discrimination complaint against the company, which stated that they were forcing him to do stressful jobs, such as working on "the folder" (he'd been complaining to supervisors about this since 1980), that affected his mental health (they eventually reached a settlement with him, but denied that he'd been discriminated against). Wesbecker blamed Standard Gravure, not just for his own deteriorating mental health, but for his older son's scoliosis (curvature of the spine), and the fact that his other son was compelled to expose himself in public. He was convinced that the inhalation of fumes from the solvents he worked with on the folder, had altered his genetic code, and that his sons' conditions were a direct result of this. He was beginning to develop "theories" about his situation, that took all responsibility away from him for his personal problems, and directed them at the company. He was starting to develop a "bad guy" that he could direct his anger towards—not unlike Mark O. Barton, who conducted a spree killing at two Atlanta day trading firms in 1999, and left a note stating that he was killing those who had, "greedily sought my destruction." When an employee starts to blame a company, business, organization, and/or enterprise for their personal problems, and failures, this should be taken as a warning signal, that they may be planning to exact revenge.

Wesbecker had no support from his Union, his coworkers had no desire to relieve him of the job on the folder, and management flatly refused to recognize his mental health issues. Wesbecker was running out of options, and couldn't imagine a future for himself—some, when they reach this point, commit suicide, others look for revenge—homicide and suicide are closer bedfellows than we like to think. In August of 1988, he took medical leave, citing stress. When he came back in February 1989, instead of finding him less stressful work, management put him on disability and slashed his pay; something they planned to do again in October of that year. Wesbecker, the once-proud worker, who felt he'd been a loyal employee, couldn't understand why he was being treated this way. On disability, he now had the time to cultivate his anger, and sense of injustice, and fantasize about taking revenge on those who, as he saw it, had treated him with contempt and disrespect. Wesbecker felt he had nothing left in his life and without a support system behind him to help encourage him about his future—his second marriage had ended in 1984, after he'd found out that his wife had been sleeping with his co-workers—he saw little point to his existence, other than taking revenge. Cultivating anger to the point where one is ready to engage in mass murder takes time, and Wesbecker had plenty of that.

Wesbecker felt that the management of Standard Gravure, especially President Michael Shea, needed to start paying for what they'd done to the company he had given 20 years to, and on September 14, 1989, he took matters into his own hands. As he saw it, his supervisor, needed to pay for the way he'd disrespected and discriminated against Wesbecker, his coworkers needed to pay for sleeping with his wife, and the company needed to be shut down for good. Wesbecker literally and figuratively started at the top, riding the elevator with his Polytech AK-47S, to the executive reception area on the 3rd floor, and opening fire on the receptionists who worked there as soon as the doors opened. He then moved around the offices on the 3rd floor, shooting, before walking down to the lower floors and the pressroom, shooting anyone he could find—excluding John Tingle, who he told to get away (active killers may well spare individuals, either for personal reasons, or to demonstrate their ability to control life and death). His killing spree ended in the breakroom, before he walked back to the pressroom and shot himself. In all, he killed eight and wounded a further twelve.

Although the Standard Gravure shooting was not the first U.S. workplace shooting, and perhaps not as infamous as Pat Sherrill's rampage at the Edmond Post Office three years previously (which gave us the term, "going postal"), it was the first incident that really caused coworkers to think about whether the person who they had worked alongside for many years, had any lethal intentions towards them. Like many active shooters, those committing acts of workplace violence are often inspired by others; Wesbecker became obsessed by Sherrill's shooting rampage (a clear warning sign) while he was on disability. There were other warning signs, but they occurred over a long period of time; Wesbecker didn't "snap," he slowly simmered, and many of his actions and behaviors became normalized to his coworkers and management, and thus many were discounted, that should have been cause for concern/alarm.

The Lethal Employee and the Need for Revenge

In most workplace mass killings, the shooter searches out individuals. Wesbecker started his killing spree, on the 3rd floor, where management were located, and later in the rampage, went looking for one of his supervisors who had put him on the folder. Pat Sherrill, when he went on his rampage at the Edmonton Post Office, searched for the supervisors who had conducted his latest disciplinary hearing, the day before, and Richard Farley headed for the office of Laura Black—an ex-coworker he'd been stalking for several years—when he shot up his old workplace, ESL Incorporated in Sunnyvale, California (1988). Michael McDermott, who is responsible for the Wakefield Massacre of 2000, when asked where he was going, as he walked along a corridor with an AK-47 slung over his shoulder, shouted back, "Human Resources"—he blamed them for his poor financial situation as they had started to withhold money from his paycheck at the request of the IRS and had refused to give him a cash advance a week before Christmas. Although the shooting was planned and premeditated, the trigger event seems to have been a phone call from a Chrysler representative, the day after Christmas when he was at work, informing him that they were repossessing his car; that was when he went and got his guns, which he had already hidden at work.

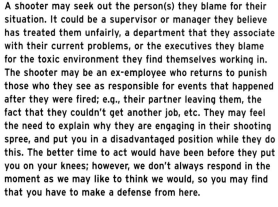

A shooter may seek out the person(s) they blame for their situation. It could be a supervisor or manager they believe has treated them unfairly, a department that they associate with their current problems, or the executives they blame for the toxic environment they find themselves working in. The shooter may be an ex-employee who returns to punish those who they see as responsible for events that happened after they were fired; e.g., their partner leaving them, the fact that they couldn't get another job, etc. They may feel the need to explain why they are engaging in their shooting spree, and put you in a disadvantaged position while they do this. The better time to act would have been before they put you on your knees; however, we don't always respond in the moment as we may like to think we would, so you may find that you have to make a defense from here.

As the shooter talks, try to engage them in conversation, as while they are processing what you are saying, their focus will slip away from the gun. There is really only one eventual outcome to this situation, so you will need to enact a physical response. With your left hand, grab the gun as close to the trigger-guard as possible, while at the same time swaying to the left, pulling your head out of the line of fire. This swaying action will also put weight onto your left leg, allowing you to free your right leg, and begin to stand up. Grab the back of the firearm where the hammer is located, with your right hand.

As you move the gun away, start to turn it upwards, bending your attacker's wrist; this will make it harder for them to pull back and retain the weapon. (In the photo, the right hand can be seen coming to take control of the weapon, at the back of the barrel, where the hammer is located). If the shooter pulls the trigger (and the gun is a semi-automatic), while you are holding the slide, the spent casing will not be able to be ejected, and as a result, a new bullet won't be cycled into the chamber. With the gun jammed in this way, it will not be operational, until the jam has been cleared.

With your hand cupped around the back of the gun, and the barrel pointed upwards—compromising your attacker's wrist and ability to pull back—and over your right shoulder, start to pull yourself up, towards your attacker. If they start to pull back in order to retain the weapon, their action will assist you in getting to your feet. You should have been able to get your right leg up and under you, at almost the same time. Make sure that you turn/angle the gun upwards as you move it away from you. The time to attempt to make this control is while you have the shooter engaged in conversation. This way, their focus will be on what either you or they are saying, rather than on the gun.

Twist the gun so that the barrel turns towards your attacker, and pull it away. Use this same pulling action to help get your left foot forward and behind the weapon—this will assist you in pulling the weapon past you. This strong pulling action will also compromise your attacker's balance, pulling them forward, as the gun is ripped from their grasp—with the barrel acting as a strong lever to turn the weapon in their hand. If their finger is on the trigger, it will probably be broken or dislocated as it will get caught on the trigger-guard (if there is one) as the gun is rotated. Depending on the make and model, there is a chance that pressure on the trigger may have caused the gun to fire (if it wasn't already jammed); a tight grip on the slide will stop the gun from cycling and if it wasn't jammed before, it will be now.

With your left leg forward and your right leg back, you will be in a good position to make a snap kick to the groin. It is necessary to keep your attacker's focus away from any secondary weapons that they may have about their person, and start to shut down their ability to continue with their attack.

If the gun is jammed, you will not have time to clear it and use it as a "hot" weapon; instead, you must use it as a "cold" one to deliver concussive force to your assailant. At some point, you will want to regrip the gun, so that the barrel points towards your assailant. This will allow you to use the strongest part of the weapon—the barrel—to jab and slash with. You may also want to think about clearing the jam, if you have the time and space to do so, so that you have a weapon in your hand that can deliver lethal force. It is safe to assume—unlike a mugging or similar—that the weapon is loaded and operable, because the shooter only had one use for it, and that was to kill, unlike a mugger who may be using it simply as a tool to intimidate.

You may find yourself in a similar position, but facing a shooter with a long-barrel weapon. It can't be stressed enough, that allowing yourself to be put in a kneeling or other compromising position, where your abilities to fight back are limited, should be avoided — especially when the position you are being put in, has an inevitability to it; e.g., it is one associated with execution. In almost all situations and scenarios, you will have more survival options from standing than from kneeling.

One of the advantages that you will have when dealing with someone armed with a long-barrel weapon, is that they will need more space and time to retain and position it than they will with a handgun. With the stock of the rifle positioned against their chest/ shoulder, they won't be able to simply pull the weapon back, to move it away from you, and will in most instances need to take a step back away from you, to prevent you from controlling their weapon. Their ability to do this may be compromised by objects in the environment, such as office dividers and desks, etc.

Quickly strike the barrel of the rifle, to your right, and up, with your left hand. Being on your knees means that you will already be under the barrel. At the same time, lean your head to the left (out of the line of fire), so that you have a body defense as well as a hand defense.

As you do this, step up with your left leg, and reach as far forward with your right arm as you can—keep your left hand up, to help prevent the shooter from retraining their weapon onto you. The majority of your defense from here is to move forward, getting yourself behind the muzzle of the gun.

The shooter may step back to try to keep you from securing their weapon; if they do, follow their movement, keeping your head to the side, out of the line of fire. Your goal is to get behind the weapon as quickly as possible—if you can do this before your assailant pulls the weapon back, you will increase your survival chances. This method—of knocking away with one hand, and clasping with the other arm – will be familiar to anyone who has done traditional martial arts weapon defenses, against certain types of spears—where the goal is to get behind the spear's point and prevent the person wielding it from pulling it back.

With your right hand, wrap it around the front of the weapon, and with your left, grab to the rear, where the stock is located. In reality, your assailant pulling the weapon back may assist you in your effort to stand up, and get to your feet. Once up, hug the weapon to your chest.

Keeping the weapon secured to your body...

...pull your left shoulder back, and drive your right forward, as you turn away from your attacker. Start to step back with your left foot, to assist this turning action, and add your bodyweight to the rotation of your torso.

Rip the gun away from your attacker's grasp, and either use it as a "cold" weapon to strike and hit your attacker with and/or...

...move away and use it as it was intended. Because your attacker's goal was to kill, rather than intimidate or force you to acquiesce to a demand, you can be fairly sure that the weapon is operable, and loaded—if the shooter had run out of ammunition before they had confronted you, they would likely have changed the magazine.

In an active shooter incident, you must be prepared to use lethal force. As with any violent incident, you must enter the confrontation, prepared to use, at the very least, the same level of violence that your assailant intends to. This means that if somebody is ready, prepared, and willing to kill you, you must be psychologically and emotionally prepared to do the same. Just because you have disarmed a shooter (in any situation), doesn't mean that the incident ends there. In an active shooter incident, it is likely that they will have a second weapon and will be prepared to use it. Also, most shooters in these situations are prepared to die, and so may decide to charge/tackle you, even if they don't have a second weapon.

Most active shooters don't expect to come away from the incident alive—either planning to commit suicide, or expecting to be killed by law enforcement. Most active shooters are suicidal, but suicidal with the need for revenge, suffering from both depression and anger. While we should have sympathy for those who suffer from depression, we should not have sympathy for the anger that active killers possess, nor should we accept it as a justification for their actions. We do, however, need to understand the complex and often contradictory profiles of such individuals, if we are to identify them in the workplace, and predict/prevent such extreme actions of violence.

Profiling and Predicting the Lethal Employee

Few employees were surprised that there was a workplace shooting at Standard Gravure. The surprise was that the shooter was Wesbecker; i.e., there were much angrier, more aggressive employees who their coworkers believed would be more likely and capable to commit such a crime. A police officer who was at the Standard Gravure massacre, and who talked to employees immediately after the shooting spree reported that they, "named three or four other workers before Wesbecker who they thought might have been capable of doing that." In most active shooter incidents where we have some form of relationship with the shooter, we are often likely to discount them as killers, even when the warning signs are evident; e.g., no one could imagine Klebold and Harris as killers even though there were many warning signs over a period of time.

Five warning signals that should be taken into consideration, in terms of predicting workplace shootings, and identifying potential shooters are as follows:

1. The Blaming of Others
2. Extreme Frustration
3. Weapons Fetishes
4. Vocalization of Violent Intent
5. Depression, Anxiety & Mental Health Issues

Wesbecker, like most shooters, blamed others for his situation, rather than himself; in the shooter's mind, they are the victim. Wesbecker, believed that Standard Gravure, was to blame for his two sons' physical and emotional problems. This turned into something of an obsession for Wesbecker. When a complaint becomes an obsession, there are few positive directions in which this can head. When someone starts to fixate on something, it usually ends in a confrontation—and in Wesbecker's case, it was a fatal one. Michael McDermott (Wakefield Massacre, 2000), saw Edgewater Technologies as being responsible for his financial problems—by withholding taxes he owed, from his paycheck—rather than acknowledging his own financial mismanagement. Richard Farley, blamed ESL Incorporated, for "forcing" Laura Black (the woman he was stalking), to take out a restraining order against him, and for firing him several years previously. When an individual identifies the company—or certain individuals in it—as the reason for their under-achievement, lack of recognition/respect, relationship failures, etc. this should be taken as a serious warning signal. Unfortunately, in the case of Standard Gravure, almost all of Wesbecker's coworkers became desensitized to his blame-shifting; sometimes because they had their own complaints that trumped his, and other times because they simply became accustomed to it—it was yesterday's news.

Wesbecker was frustrated. He'd brought his complaints to supervisors and management. He'd provided a doctor's note stating that he should have been relieved his duties on the folder. He'd had his union representatives bring up his complaint. Finally, seven years after bringing his initial concern/request to supervisors about not having to work on the machine, he brought a discrimination suit against the company, which they settled. However, he still had to work on the folder. Wesbecker was trying to change his situation and was meeting opposition at every turn. As he looked at his alternatives within Standard Gravure, he found he had none, but to continue doing what management wanted him to do. His one recourse was to leave but by now he was so committed to his frustration, that he didn't see this as an option. When an employee becomes so invested in their frustrations, that they don't consider walking away to be a solution, then a confrontation is inevitable. Often, management and supervisors feel that to give in to an employee's frustration is to give them too much power. There may be times when this is the case, but there are also times when it can be an effective strategy, for both increasing productivity and for avoiding a showdown—which in the case of Wesbecker, was a showdown that management lost. Sometimes, it is better to be effective than to be right.

It may be that after engaging in a short rampage, the shooter will look for managers and supervisors and round them up, together in a room, so that they can explain their actions and why they have engaged in the shooting spree, before executing the hostages. As you walk, lean back slightly into the barrel of the gun so that the shooter puts forward pressure on it and it is under a certain degree of tension.

As you are about to take a step forward with your left foot, spin towards your attacker instead, stepping around. Drop your right arm down as you turn. Your goal should be to turn and step deep into your attacker—don't try to immediately control the weapon, but instead look to control your assailant's weapon arm, as they may well try to pull it back in order to retain the gun.

Reach your arm up high, under their weapon arm, as you step in, close to your attacker.

Now start to pull their weapon arm to your chest. As you do this, bring your left arm over your attacker's weapon arm—in certain cases, depending on arm length and how deep you've come, you may be able to make an elbow strike, as you step in towards the shooter. Your turn and step should have seen you move deep in towards your attacker, with your right arm reaching high on your assailant's arm, to deal with any pull-back of the weapon.

If you remain in this position, you will find it difficult to make the actual disarm; because you will have come in deep, anticipating your assailant's possible retention/pull-back of the weapon. In this position, you may be too far away from the firearm to reach over and take hold of it.

To remedy this, slide your left hand down, keeping pressure on your attacker's weapon arm, to secure your assailant's wrist to your body. This will also prevent the shooter from moving the wrist to relieve the pressure, as you turn the barrel of the gun in their hand—away from your body. Securing the gun in this way will also prevent the shooter from trying to move it, and aim it at other people, who may be behind you, or at your side. Even if there are people around you, your first action should still be to turn and step in deep, to deal with any attempts your attacker may make to retain their weapon.

Turn the gun away from you, so that this rotation opens up your attacker's grip. If they manage to keep hold of the gun, as you turn, rapidly turn it back towards you—ensuring that you don't muzzle yourself—and then quickly turn it the other way, again to loosen their grip. You can also throw knee strikes from here to take the shooter's attention away from the weapon.

Once released, use the weapon as an impact weapon to strike concussively, in an attempt to render your assailant unconscious.

A disgruntled employee, who blames others, and is frustrated at their ability to elicit change in their situation, may start "writing scripts"—and this is a dangerous turn of events. When an employee writes a script, they are already anticipating their manager or supervisor's response, before it has been given. Any negotiation or discussion that involves a compromise, etc. will have already been interpreted as something else, where the individual is being victimized. In such situations—although they may not always end in violence—there is little chance of changing the employee's opinion(s) about their situation.

Most mass shooters have a weapons fetish; this shouldn't be confused with someone who is a firearms enthusiast, or collector but rather someone with a fetish, is obsessed with what the weapons stand for/represent, and are able to achieve. Someone may enjoy recreational shooting, have a large number of weapons, and at the same time not fantasize about using them on others. However, for others, their firearms give them a sense of power, which they will take to help form their identity. Richard Farley owned a small arsenal, which he boasted to his coworkers at ESL about; he also talked, and made threats, about his ability "to take people with him," to a manager—when asked to clarify, he stated that he was prepared to kill both Laura Black and others. To commit a violent crime, you must have both the intent and the ability; Richard Farley clearly demonstrated he had both. Joseph T. Wesbecker, was no different, he would often tell fellow coworkers about his large gun collection, and how he would walk into Standard Gravure, and "show them" ("them," being the management). The threat was made so often—and never actioned—that it was soon discounted. When someone wants to demonstrate they have the ability and means to carry out a threat, it should be taken seriously.

This type of vocalization of violent intent, is one of the most obvious warning signals that we may have, yet it is often denied and discounted. Richard Farley told his manager that if he was terminated from his job, he'd have nothing to live for, and that he was prepared to punish and take revenge on those who were responsible for firing him; he was true to his word on this, it just took him two years and a restraining order to reach a point where he was sufficiently motivated to do so. Threats should not be taken lightly, especially when somebody has the means to fulfill them—everyone at ESL, knew of Farley's extensive gun collection. Farley didn't just make one threat, he made repeated threats. Wesbecker did the same. For Wesbecker, Pat Sherrill was a crusader, who had laid down a blueprint for taking control and revenge, on companies that had abused and mistreated their employees. Wesbecker expressed his admiration for Sherrill vocally—he didn't see Sherrill as a monster, he saw him as somebody who was demonstrating that there was a "new" way to respond to management abuse and victimization. This demonstrates a type of implicit intent, and should be taken as seriously as more explicit and direct threats.

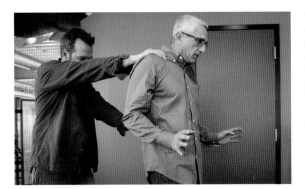

The same defense for dealing with a handgun to the rear, will work if you turn the other way. If the shooter's free hand is on your shoulder, you will know which hand is holding the gun. However, without this information, you will not know if they are holding it in their left or right hand—you can always try looking over your shoulder, to try to ascertain which is the free hand, and this is advisable because the shooter may be pushing you forward with his/her fingers into your back, and holding the gun close to their hip, etc.

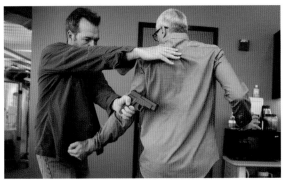
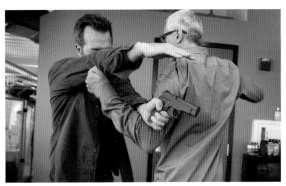

As you make your turn—this should be done tightly, and on the spot, so if your attacker is still moving, they will continue to walk past you; this will help get you further behind the gun, reducing the available distance that the shooter would have to pull it back in order to retain it—bring your arm down, and start to swing it/snake it up, under your assailant's weapon arm, both to move the gun away from you, and to start controlling the weapon arm. Continue to turn, stepping in close and deep to your attacker.

This will enable you to close enough distance to make an elbow strike to the attacker's face, while still having a secure control of their weapon arm. Your chest should be pressed against it, slightly hyper-extending the elbow. With this pressure on their elbow, and the complete control of their weapon arm, your elbow strike won't knock your attacker away from you. If you hadn't stepped so deep, or so close to your attacker, you would at this point only be controlling the weapon at the wrist, which would mean you probably wouldn't be close enough to make the strike, and may not have a secure enough control of the arm, to prevent the attacker pulling their weapon away, as they were moved back by the force of your elbow strike. Reach over towards the gun...

...and slide down the attacker's arm, to control it at the wrist; isolating their hand, so that it cannot turn/rotate at the wrist.

Bring your hand over to secure the gun, and then...

...turn it towards your attacker.

As it comes free, continue the rotation, and strike your assailant repeatedly with the barrel of the gun. In this situation, you should be looking to render them unconscious/unable to continue their rampage.

There has been an overwhelming focus on the mental health issues of active shooters; many of us want a simple and singular reason, as to why someone would turn into a killer, and if we can diagnose a shooter with a mental health condition, we won't have to ask ourselves difficult questions; e.g., how does a seemingly normal/balanced individual—perhaps someone who appears to be like ourselves—turn on their colleagues and peers and kill them? Joseph T. Wesbecker was suffering from depression, but depression alone does not make someone a killer. However, when depression is blended with anger and hatred, the futility and pain of existence, there can start to develop a desire for revenge. Killers like Pat Sherrill had already demonstrated a penchant and pleasure for killing; he was known in his neighborhood for torturing and killing cats. Although Sherrill—unlike Wesbecker - never sought out professional help for his mental health issues, it is likely he had an undiagnosed mental condition—killing animals is one of the three early warning signs that serial killers exhibit, normally as children (along with setting fires, and bedwetting past a certain age—it is believed these behaviors/actions reflect parental neglect and abuse, and it is this which is the cause of later predatory behaviors).

A threat made once, a spur of the moment remark condoning an act of violence, etc. shouldn't necessarily be a cause for concern. That said, if any of these five warning signs, are exhibited in conjunction with others, the threat should be taken seriously, and some form of respectful intervention should probably be made. If you are in management, dealing with a disgruntled and potentially violent employee at the earliest opportunity, is far better than burying your head in the sand, and hoping the problem will go away.

It may be that the shooter is armed with a long-barrel weapon, rather than a pistol or revolver. These weapons are relatively uncommon in workplace and active shooter incidents because they are not easily concealed. A disgruntled employee who has made threats, perhaps has just had a disciplinary hearing and turns up to work with a large duffel bag, is someone who requires our attention. Of course, there may be a million and one legitimate reasons why this individual is bringing a large bag into work, instead of leaving it in their car, etc. However, there is also one reason, for which the consequences are lethal.

With the weapon at your back, put pressure on the barrel of the gun, by leaning into it slightly—this will cause it to travel forward when you make your turn, helping you to get behind the muzzle. With a quick turn, the shooter will not be able to arrest their movement and will continue to lurch/walk forward. Depending on the amount of pressure they were pushing into your back with, they may find themselves jolting forward and experiencing a temporary loss of balance.

Reach under the barrel, with your left arm...

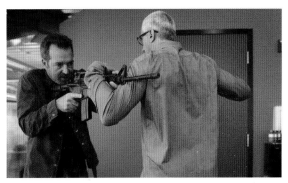

...and secure it by hooking, and pulling it to your upper arm/bicep—depending on where the shooter is holding the weapon, you may end up trapping their hand/arm, as well.

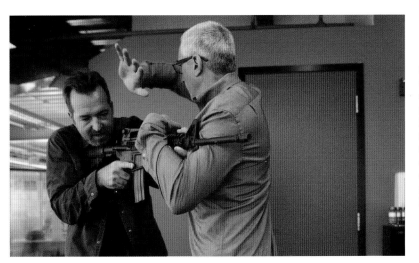

Continue your turn, raising your elbow up to clear the weapon, and deliver a slicing elbow to your attacker's face—depending on the length of your arm, and how far down the barrel you secured the weapon; e.g., the shooter may have already started to retain their weapon and pull it back, you may not be close enough to connect. Don't worry if this is the case.

One way to release the weapon would be to grab the stock, lift it over your assailant's left arm by pulling it up and over, and turn your body to the right; however, if your assailant is much stronger and/or taller than you, this can be problematic. For this reason, you may want to secure the weapon to your body first, and use your weight to help weaken your attacker's grip on the gun. Bring your arm over...

...and hug the weapon to your body so that it is locked against you. If your arms end up being folded over the ejection port, and the shooter fires their weapon, you will likely end up jamming the gun; the spent casing will have to be cleared, before the gun can be operated. If the attacker has the weapon's stock under his armpit, pull forward to release it, so that the weapon will be able to be turned/rotated.

Turn with your body, and lean your weight away from your assailant.

This will either weaken their grip, or cause them to release the weapon, entirely

Immediately turn in the opposite direction (to your right), bringing the stock of the rifle up and over your assailant's left arm. Pull away from your attacker, and transition the weapon to your hands, so that you can use it as a "cold" impact weapon. If you know how to operate a rifle, and clear a possible jam, you should do so, as the situation may necessitate the use of lethal force; e.g., the shooter may attempt to pull a second weapon, and/or attempt to get their weapon back—they may even do this to "force" you to shoot, having already planned to end their own life; either by committing suicide, or by having law enforcement shoot them.

Lethal Employee Interventions—For Supervisors & Management

If it is believed that there are warning signs that indicate an employee may be contemplating an act of workplace violence, or some other retribution against the company and its workforce, management should be committed to intervening beforehand—a company's employees are entitled to a safe working environment, and to not provide/compromise this, is a failing on the part of both management and the enterprise, especially if they have been alerted to, or recognize a significant threat or danger. The workplace environment should be one where employees feel that they can share their safety concerns—whatever they are—with supervisors and managers, and supervisors/managers feel that they are able to involve upper management and executives, without feeling that they are being judged for either creating a problem, and/or being unable to handle the situation themselves, etc.

One of Joseph T. Wesbecker's biggest complaints was that he was not being listened to, or taken seriously. A meeting with a troubled employee is not a disciplinary hearing—unless a particular work protocol or process has been broken—and shouldn't resemble one. Management should recognize that with a potentially lethal employee they only have power, as long as the employee "agrees" to recognize them as having it. Once they cease to—or are fired—the company will no longer have influence over them. "Coming on strong," only increased the sense of isolation that both Pat Sherrill and Joseph T. Wesbecker felt, and lead to them coming to the conclusion that they had no other alternative but to take revenge on those—and the company—that had disrespected them.

People who are frustrated and angry will talk, when given the chance—it is often the fact that they don't have the opportunity to express themselves, which causes them to fester, and their anger to grow—ignoring an angry person will not de-escalate any situation. People with a grievance don't like to be ignored, or have their concerns dismissed. If somebody at Standard Gravure had taken Joseph T. Wesbecker's complaints seriously, and shown him some respect in the process, then he may never have felt compelled to engage in his shooting spree. Ultimately, his contract may have needed to be terminated, if his future working demands had become more serious, and had effected production, but coming to a compromise over his time working on the folder, or taking him off it altogether, was something that had been granted to other employees. Unfortunately, management saw themselves in a position of power, from which they didn't have to engage with their employees and recognize their complaints—and the combative way in which they had beaten the Unions into submission, seemed one that would be effective against a single employee. And it may have been effective, had it not also been, for Wesbecker, the final straw.

An employee who is considering/compelled to engage in a rampage killing, will feel that they have nothing left to live for—whether they plan to end their life, expect to die in the process, or to be imprisoned, etc. Any meeting with such an employee needs to be positive and focus on their future, whether with the company, or if their contract is being terminated, on their future prospects, and employment opportunities/possibilities, etc. If in the meeting any threats are made, whether implicit or explicit, these should be noted, and taken seriously—rather than be met with incredulity and disbelief; as was the case at ESL, when Richard Farley, in such a meeting, instructed management that if they fired him, he would be back to take revenge. These types of threats should be anticipated in these types of meetings, and met with a calm response. A manager could respond, for example, by stating that everyone involved, has too much respect for themselves and the others in the meeting to be making such statements.

If you are the one terminating an employee's contract, do so at the end of the day when other employees have left—if you have a troubled relationship with the employee, have someone neutral and not involved conduct the exit interview. If the individual was planning a shooting spree, they may well have a weapon(s) in their car, and their termination/firing may act as the trigger which initiates it—in 2010 Omar Sheriff Thornton didn't leave the building after his disciplinary/firing but instead retrieved two pistols from his lunchbox, and went on a shooting rampage, killing 8 of his coworkers at Hartford Distributors, in Connecticut. If the building is vacant because everybody has gone home, then there will not be the high number of potential casualties needed for a would-be shooter to make their statement. This is also the reason you don't want to take breaks in the meeting, as the employee could use this opportunity to retrieve weapons, like Omar Sheriff Thornton did—keep the meeting short so there is no need for them to take a bathroom break, etc.

Many companies, as well as schools, mark out the parking spots for people who have positions of responsibility in the organization. Unfortunately, this can also allow disgruntled employees and ex-employees (as well as ex-students, etc.) an easy way of gaining access to somebody who they believe has had a negative impact on their life. Using a numbering system rather than displaying titles and roles, addresses this problem.

You should also have someone accompany them off the premises, and stay with them while they retrieve their belongings, etc. This may be a member of security or another member of the management team—if you can avoid having security escort them off the premises, or go to their desk/locker with them, then you will do much to preserve their dignity (if possible try not to have security visible, as this may make you look weak and afraid—have them ready and nearby to act, but don't have them in a position where it looks like you will require their assistance). Someone should stay with them at all times, as you won't want to give them any legitimate reason to return to the premises. Ask them if they are at the same address, or if there is another address that they would want you to mail any outstanding items to, such as paychecks, etc. along with a phone number you can give if anyone may want to contact them. Shut all the doors behind them that would give them a reason to have to contact or visit the company again.

It is also advisable not to park your car in your regular spot, where they will know where to find/wait for you. The longer you can give an individual before they have the chance for revenge, the longer they will have to rationally process what has happened rather than be overtaken by an emotional reaction; firing them at the end of the week will give them a longer time to cool off and not find themselves reacting emotionally to what has just happened. It is worth doing your homework to find out about the employee's background, and if they have "support" from friends or family members or whether they will be coming to terms with their job loss on their own; if this is the case, it may be worth offering, through a third-party, counseling and services that would help them get a new job and move on. This is not something that would need to be offered to everyone whose contract is terminated, just those that may pose a risk to the safety of the company and its employees.

A shooter may move you to where they have other executives and management held hostage. Your best chance for survival will most likely be to tackle the shooter, before you get there. If they are moving you, they are likely not looking to kill you in this moment, but perhaps looking to have all of management present before executing everyone. It may well be that they want everybody to hear and understand their grievances, and know why they have engaged in their shooting spree. Clay Duke spent nearly 6 minutes confronting a school board, in Panama City, Florida, about the termination of his wife's teaching contract, before attempting to assassinate them (2010).

As you turn (making a body defense), dip your right arm down, pushing the barrel of the gun away with your upper arm. This turning action should see you move out of the line of fire.

Step in deep, towards your assailant, aiming to get as close to them as possible. Due to the fact that they were moving forward, and the length of the barrel, they will find it difficult to pull the weapon back, and because your arm will now be under the gun, any attempt they might make to pull it down, in order to retain it, is not going to be possible—they could try to pull their weapon up, but this would only assist you in gaining control of it. Move your right arm as close to the stock as possible, and bring your left arm over the weapon.

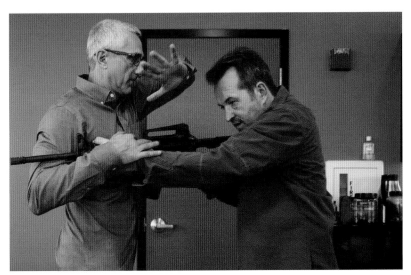

(Remaining photos in this sequence are shown from opposite side)

Initially trap the gun in the crook of your elbow, pulling it tightly to you. Your other arm should come over the weapon...

...to deliver an elbow strike to your attacker's face. Your turning motion should see your chest come to the weapon, so you can hug the gun to your body, giving you a greater control over it. If you were further away, and couldn't connect with the elbow, you could use a punch instead.

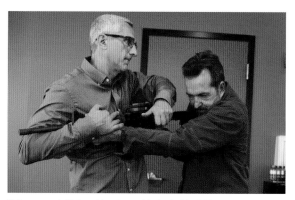

Bring your left hand back, and take hold of the weapon's stock. If your attacker has the weapon tucked under their armpit, pull it forward, so it will be free.

Lift/pull the weapon away from your attacker, keeping it close to your body, so that it is the turning motion of the torso, rather than the strength of the arm, that pulls the gun away.

The turning motion of the body, will compromise the shooter's grip on the weapon, and they will not be able to hold onto it.

Move away, and if you are familiar with the workings of the firearm, make it operable and prepare to use it against your assailant. It may be that they give up the fight, recognizing that the incident is over. If this is the case, instruct them to put their hands up, and prostrate themselves face down on the floor. If any movement they make indicates that they are going for a second weapon, or are putting themselves in a position to tackle you, you should use the weapon against them, without hesitation.

Conclusion

There are few things scarier than having to deal with an assailant who has both the intent—and the means—to kill you. No strategies and tactics can come with a guarantee, but even in extreme situations, there are always things you can do to improve your survival chances. In these situations, you do what you can—you may get shot as you and a group swarm a shooter, or as you try to get away, but that's not necessarily the end; people survive these injuries—it's sometimes possible to continue to fight, despite them. Jacob Ryker—who had been shot once already—took a bullet to the hand as he tackled the shooter to the ground, but he kept going. He knew what would happen, to both him and the others in the school cafeteria, if he gave up. It may be too much to expect to come through such incidents completely unharmed, and unhurt, when extreme and drastic measures are called for, such as tackling a shooter head-on, but we can hope to survive them—we can work to a plan for survival. In the end, we have no choice but to try.

The more people there are who understand how to effectively operate in an active shooter/killer incident, the more likely it is we will find allies who can assist us (and others) if we ever find ourselves in such a situation. Jacob Ryker was fortunate that others joined him in his tackle, as they had no training that told them to do this—if they had, it is likely that more people would have run along with him from the start, rather than joining him, later. It may be more comfortable and easier in our day-to-day lives not to think about these types of incidents and convince ourselves that we will never find ourselves in the midst of such events. However if we do, we will wish that we had trained for them—along with everyone else who is with us. Active shooter/killer incidents are rapidly increasing in frequency in the U.S. and we should train, drill, and prepare for dealing with them, whether that's in our schools, our places of work, or the places where we worship, (Dylan Roof, Charleston Church shooting 2015), etc.

There may be situations in which we have worked or studied alongside someone who is planning a mass killing. We may be privy to the warning signs—the threats they make, the admiration and fascination they have with previous shootings/killings, their constant blaming of others, their boasts about the firearms they own and the power that this gives them, etc. If this is the case, we shouldn't feel embarrassed about sharing our concerns with someone in a position of power, and neither should we discount or deny the evidence we have. If we are given pre-violence indicators, we should use them to our advantage and not dismiss them because we believe we are being paranoid or overly sensitive. There were many warning signs that Klebold and Harris were planning a mass killing, but they were not taken seriously because nobody could imagine that such a thing was possible. We must accept that these events do occur, that they can happen anywhere, and that we may have the relevant information that can prevent them.

PART II
Carjacking & Other Vehicular Crimes

There is a huge discrepancy between the presentation of carjackings by the media, and how they actually occur. Most carjackings, globally, involve unarmed rather than armed assailants (the U.S. is an exception to this with about 74% of all carjackings involving a weapon, 45% percent of those being with a firearm). Unfortunately, it can be difficult to gather accurate statistics on this crime, as not all countries have specific laws regarding what constitutes a carjacking and they are often recorded as both a property crime and a crime against the individual. For these reasons, it is often insurance claims (along with police records) that can give us a better idea of how these incidents occur and the types of scenarios/situations in which they take place. In the U.S., carjacking is a federally recognized crime that is defined as "the taking or attempted taking of a motor vehicle from the person or presence of another by force and violence or by intimidation." There are three major ways in which carjackings typically occur and these are as follows:

1. Targeting a moving vehicle, e.g., pulling alongside and forcing a driver to pull over using the display of a weapon, deliberately crashing into a moving vehicle (a rear-end collision), or tailing a moving vehicle and forcing it to stop, etc.
2. Targeting a car owner, who is not in the immediate vicinity of their vehicle, e.g., following a driver after they leave their vehicle in a parking lot, and then robbing them of their keys outside the lot, etc.
3. Targeting the vehicle when stationary, e.g., when it is parked in a parking lot with the driver still in, when stopped at a gas station, or when stationary at a junction, etc.

There are also less common and more specific scenarios in which such crimes may be committed, e.g., cars that are stolen during test-drives at a dealership, or as part of a home invasion, etc. There have even been bank robbers who have demanded the keys off bank staff, in order to use their car to drive to the getaway vehicle. Rather than focusing on such specific instances of carjacking, this section will look at the three most common methods—as described above—and how they apply in more general situations and settings, as well as preventative measures, and physical solutions to dealing with such assaults, both when in and around a vehicle.

This section will also look at other types of assaults that may occur within, or in the vicinity of, a vehicle, including sexual assaults, road rage incidents, and express kidnappings, etc., involving private-use vehicles, as well as taxis and ridesharing services.

Parking Lots

It would be unrealistic—and unhealthy—to stay in a state of conscious vigilance at all times; you'd quickly exhaust yourself and accomplish very little. We can learn a lot concerning Situational Awareness from observing how animals identify and respond to threats and dangers in nature. A gazelle's natural predator is the lion, yet it will graze peacefully and in a relaxed state within 30 feet of one that is sleeping; a sleeping lion is not a threat. What signals danger to the gazelle is the lion waking up—the lion's movement will attract their attention and they will quickly move away. Gazelles also have an innate understanding about the times of day that lions are most active and likely to be on the lookout for prey (it's good to know when you are most at risk); lions normally hunt around dusk unless there is a water source nearby that attracts prey during the day, which may cause them to change their hunting patterns, etc. A large part of a gazelle's awareness is based on their knowledge about the predators they face; this allows them to stay in a relaxed state for most of their lives while still remaining safe. Our own Situational Awareness needs to be founded on a similar type of knowledge and understanding concerning the ways in which human predators act and operate as it is these behaviors and actions that will alert us to the presence of danger. In human terms, we need to understand the differences between a sleeping lion and a hunting lion.

If you use a commuter rail or a transit stop at the end of a rail line (outside of a busy city), you may be surprised to learn that these stations often have some of the highest rates of crime out of any of the other stops in the network, including busy city center stations. If you look at the MBTA (Massachusetts Bay Transit Authority) "geography" of crime around the greater Boston area, you will find that there are two types of stations which account for most of the crimes committed on the transit network: end of the line stops and stops at the city center, that act as hubs, and interconnect with other railways and bus lines. The shared characteristic of both is that these stations are interchanges between other modes of transport which are fed by people changing from trains to the subway or from cars to the train, etc. At end of line stops, it is often in these parking lots, where most of the criminal activity is focused.

Parking lots in general—and specifically those that act as interchanges between different modes of transport—are the equivalent of watering holes to human predators; i.e., they attract a lot of potential victims. These are locations where we need to up our awareness, and be more vigilant: questioning the activities of those around us and our vehicle, looking out for places of concealment, and understanding the "blind spots" that would afford a criminal protection from natural surveillance, i.e., other individuals in the environment who would be able to see them committing a crime. We should also recognize how the time of day might be important in effecting criminal activity. Locations have a natural life-cycle of activity, e.g., a parking lot that serves a commuter line is going to be busy during certain hours, and less busy at others—a criminal may have observed that after 7 pm, there is a steady and regular supply of individuals who may have worked late, with the absence of large numbers of commuters—that may have existed in the previous hour—whose presence may have made committing a particular crime unobserved difficult/impossible. Understanding the ebb and flow of the environments you visit should be part of your overall Situational Awareness. The gazelle knows the time of day it is most at risk of being hunted (late afternoon/evening), and so should we.

Our fear system is operating all the time, and it is subconsciously taking in information, and storing it for future use. If you regularly use the same parking lot, at the same time of day, you may well over time, develop an awareness about the cars commonly parked there, and the people who are present—this can allow our fear system to identify new people and vehicles, as well as movements and behaviors that may be out of place. If the times when you are in the parking lot—such as early morning or late evening—are times when there are only a few cars and people present, strangers and their vehicles will stand out even more. The more you allow yourself to be "aware" in such surroundings, the more detailed the information your fear system will be able to store—this is not a conscious process of remembering, but a process of allowing yourself not to be distracted by other thoughts and contemplations, and being fully present in your environment.

In this state, you will both gather information, as well as allow your fear system, to have its attention drawn to things that are out of place, such as somebody pretending to go to a car, or open a car door, when it's not the owner you'd normally—or your fear system would—associate with that vehicle. This demonstrates a very high level of awareness, but it is one we are all capable of developing.

One of the things that criminals will try to do is claim legitimacy in an environment. They will try to make it appear as if they have a reason to be in a particular location. This is why it is important to stay observant as you move through an environment, so that you can notice "changes" in a person's behavior; e.g., does somebody who was doing nothing, suddenly make out as if they are going to their car, as you pass by? If your head is down, looking for your car keys or cell phone, etc., you will miss these types of signals.

Any time you move from one location to another, have what you need available to you, before you enter it; e.g., if you are moving from a train station to its parking lot, have your keys already out so you won't have to search for them, as you approach your car. This will allow you to keep your head up and recognize when someone is synchronizing their movement to yours by following you, approaching you, intercepting you, or waiting for you. In a 1984 study by Social Psychologists, Betty Grayson and Morris Stein, it was found that one of the physical cues that predatory individuals used to identify potential victims was walking with the head down—a signal of unawareness as well as depression and low self-esteem.

One of the first things an attacker will try to do is to put you in a disadvantaged position, such as compromising your posture, etc, so that you are less able to fight back. When we practice and train techniques/solutions we shouldn't assume that assailants won't use the environment to their advantage. In your compromised position, and particularly if there is a difference in reach, trying to use a simultaneous control and strike is going to be difficult/impossible; i.e., neither one of your hands will be able to reach your attacker's face or throat. As with all threats, you should raise your hands up in a submissive and placating fashion, as near to the weapon/weapon hand as you can. If the assailant simply wants your car keys— and the car—hand them over, however they may also want you to come with them, which you should never do.

With both hands, grab the attacker's wrist, pushing the knife away from your throat, and move your neck as far away from the weapon as you can—your body movement will be restricted due to your position, so most of your emphasis will be on moving the knife away from your throat—this is why you will want both hands on the wrist/arm. As you grab, start to rotate the arm, to move your attacker away, allowing you the space to start to gain your posture back.

Keep rotating your attacker's arm, so that they end up being pushed to the side. This will allow you the room to start to stand up. It will be hard for an attacker to resist this type of rotational force, as the muscles of the arm (biceps, triceps, deltoids), are designed to work in one plane. This means that you are working against the arm/shoulder muscles in a way which an attacker will find hard to fight against.

Keep turning the arm as you stand up...

...and bring your left arm, over your attacker's knife arm—all the time continuing to rotate their arm.

This same technique would work if the weapon involved was a gun pointed at your throat. Just as moving/turning the attacker's wrist moves the knife away from your neck, it would do the same with a firearm. The only thing that would need to change if it was a firearm would be the eventual "disarm."

Secure your attacker's arm under your armpit and clamp it to your body. As you do this, lean back slightly so that their weapon arm is being controlled by your bodyweight. With their weapon arm isolated, and their posture broken, they will be in no position to use their free hand/arm effectively. Their arm in this position, will mean that it will be well controlled by your bodyweight.

Keeping the arm securely isolated and locked with your left arm, release your right hand and start to put pressure on the back of your attacker's wrist/grip. If you were dealing with a short-barrel weapon, rather than a knife, you'd grab the barrel with your right hand and apply the same amount of pressure; using the barrel as a lever to open their grip.

Keep applying pressure to their hand, until the grip on the knife releases and the hand opens up. You can now scoop your own hand inside their grip and extract the knife.

Once you have the knife free, you should use it against your assailant to prevent them from making subsequent attacks—disarming someone of a weapon (even if you have had a chance to hit/punch them) doesn't mean that the encounter has ended. There may be occasions that you choose to use the handle of the knife as an impact weapon rather than cutting/slashing your attacker. Delivering concussive force is often a quicker way to disable an attacker than using the knife as an edged weapon. In saying this, situations determine solutions and if you believe it would be quicker and simpler to cut/stab your aggressor, this should be your course of action. If you will be hesitant for moral and legal reasons to cut your attacker, it is better to be decisive and hit them with it.

Even though you may believe that you have dealt with your attacker, don't waste time trying to get into your car. Under stress and duress, it is unlikely that the fine motor skills needed to press an unlock button on a key fob, or turn the key in the lock will be functioning. The other issue is that you won't know if your primary assailant is working with accomplices. It is better to assume that your environment has been compromised and your safest option is to exit it—you should only return to your car in the presence of law enforcement officers or professional security operatives.

Our fear system works a bit like a "spot the difference" game, where two nearly-identical photos are shown side-by-side but with one having certain objects/elements missing or added. Our fear system knows what a "safe" parking lot looks like—it knows how people act and behave, which cars and persons are present when there is no danger; it has taken a "safe" picture of the environment. When it witnesses a scene that isn't the same as the "safe" picture, it will alert you that something is different—it won't give you specifics, it just identifies the photographs as not being the same; just like when you look at two "spot the difference" photos, where it is obvious that they are not exactly the same, but it will take some investigation to be able to identify what the specific differences are.

If your fear system tells you that the pictures aren't the same, what you are seeing isn't the usual "safe" image, you should heighten your awareness and start investigating the reason and significance of the difference, rather than discounting it and switching off. There may be many reasons you could come up with as to why someone is trying to access a vehicle you don't associate with them; however, it is safer to be curious about their motives than to make an assumption which will cause you to ignore them. If you fear system has brought your attention to something, you should investigate.

Use of Keys and Other Improvised Weapons

One way to stay alert—and avoid switching off—when in a potentially dangerous or harmful location, is to hold onto your keys and use your grip on these as a "reminder" that you need to stay alert. You can also do this to prevent yourself from going into a state of denial, when your adrenal/fear system is triggered; e.g., if you are walking home late at night, and believe that somebody is following you, it is easy to go into a state of denial, and convince yourself that you are imagining things, etc. However, if when you first feel afraid, you take hold of your keys, you can remind yourself that while you are holding them you will need to stay alert and aware as you identify what caused you to become afraid. This will prevent you from denying or discounting the presence of a threat, which is a default human response/coping mechanism when experiencing danger. The other advantage that holding your keys will give you is that you will now have a weapon in your hand that you can use to defend yourself.

There is a common myth/misunderstanding that the correct way to use keys as an "improvised weapon" is to place one—or many—between your fingers as you make a fist. There are a number of issues with this. One is that it takes time to do so, requires both hands, and is hard to do surreptitiously. Another is that it is difficult to punch hard and retain a good grip on them in this position which may also increase the chances of injuring yourself when you strike. However, more importantly, it doesn't respect the nature of the weapon, which should dictate how it is used.

Holding it between your thumb and forefinger, and using it to slash and stab with like a knife, recognizes the properties of a key. Traditional Krav Maga teaches us to search for improvised weapons/objects that resemble things we can use to defend ourselves, such as shields, rocks, knives, etc. A key resembles a knife more than a rock, and so should be used like a knife, rather than as an improvised knuckle-duster, which is an impact tool used to deliver concussive force. When you slash and stab with it, aim for the eyes and throat—soft tissue which is vulnerable to such attacks. Holding it as you would when using it to open a car door also suggests that there is less premeditation than if you had it between your knuckles, which may help any legal case you're involved in following the assault.

Any object that you consistently carry on your person can be used to confirm and remind you of the presence of a threat. If you choose to use your mobile phone, you should categorize it as an object that resembles a "rock/stone" and use it in the same way to deliver concussive strikes.

Part of your Situational Awareness involves being able to identify objects within your environment that could be used as improvised weapons—as well as those items that form part of your everyday carry.

One object which is prevalent in parking lots is the car antenna/aerial. These long, flexible, stick-like objects can be easily broken off of a car and used as a defensive weapon.

Some types of car antennae are extremely long and share properties of both a stick and a chain. They can be used in a whip-like fashion to deliver stunning/paralyzing blows to areas such as the neck and face. Because they are extremely light, they can be moved at great speed and are difficult for an assailant to identify and block. Use of the weapon should also be coupled with constant movement to prevent an attacker from getting close to you. Remember that this weapon will be unable to deliver concussive force and should really be used as a distraction to cover your movement away or set up an entry for you to move in and deliver strikes, etc.

Understanding that parking lots are potentially dangerous places, we should look to limit the amount of time we spend in them. If we must wait for somebody, we are better off driving around the lot or arranging a better rendezvous point rather than sitting in our car waiting for them. However, we may have gotten into a bad habit of sitting and waiting in parking lots, and because nothing bad has happened as a result, we continue to do it. Unpunished complacency, is one of the main reasons that people don't engage in good personal-safety practices; e.g., the first time we decide to take a shortcut through a dodgy part of town, we may be nervous and fearful, the second and third times we do it we become less so, by the fifth and sixth time we're probably not even thinking about the risk to our safety, etc. The longer we engage in a bad practice, without a consequence, the more likely it is that we will conclude that we were being overly cautious and paranoid. This then effects other areas of our personal safety; e.g., if we were being overly cautious about the shortcut, it would probably be overly cautious to not sit/wait in a parking lot. The issue with this reasoning is, nothing bad ever happens until it does.

Carjackers and others involved in car crime, understand where the "blind spots" of a car's side and rear mirrors are, and will often use these areas of invisibility to disguise their approach. If you ever do have to wait in your car, whether it's in a parking lot or on the street, or at a red light or junction, don't just use your mirrors to check your environment, but look over your shoulder as well, so that you have a true 360-degree field of vision that will expose any blind spots.

By moving through a blind spot, an assailant will be able to get close to you without you realizing. With the gunman at this range, you will not be close enough to get control of the weapon. By opening the door and swinging it into the weapon you may be able to create a diversion but at this short distance, and having to get up from a seated position, it is unlikely that you would be able to either create enough distance, or get control of the shooter or the weapon before they recovered—that said, if you believe they are about to shoot, this option would at least give you a fighting chance (however it is more likely that they will want to make a demand of you, rather than assassinate you).

The gunman may order you out of the car and demand your wallet, or other possessions. At this point, the incident may seem like a straightforward robbery and carjacking. If the attacker wants your wallet, and car, then your best survival option is compliance. Any time an aggressor wants your resources, it is best to comply, as these can always be replaced. It is your ego that tells you not to acquiesce, your survival instinct knows that compliance is your best option; you should not battle against it.

Rather than simply taking your wallet and car and letting you go the attacker may start controlling and moving you towards the back of your car. This is the time to act, as the script has now changed and your assailant is no longer behaving like a carjacker/robber. It is obvious that they have further plans which involve you (these may not even have been evident to them at the beginning of the incident). It could be that this is an Express Kidnapping; i.e., you will be taken to a series of ATMs to withdraw money, etc. It could be that they will drive you to your house (they will have the address on your driver's license, or car's registration etc.) and force you to locate/identify any valuables you may own, etc.

The best time to act would have been before you were put in a compromising position; however, in reality we can often find ourselves overwhelmed by the assault, and miss these opportunities. We also must overcome our fear system's reticence to act when it isn't experiencing pain—even if we understand that not acting would lead to future pain. To expect that we'll always act in the moment is unrealistic and so we should train options for when our best opportunities are missed. Keep your hands up and your shoulders shrugged so that your attacker can see that you're scared. Try to move your hands back so that they are as near to the weapon as possible. Keep your fingers still so that your attacker isn't alerted by their movement as to how close they are to the weapon.

Quickly reach behind with your right hand to grab the top/barrel of the gun and start to pull it forward. At the same time, rapidly move your head to the left to get out of the line of fire and to make room so that you can pull the gun forward. The right-hand grip doesn't use the thumb to grip with, but instead wraps over the top of the weapon—when the weapon is behind your head, trying to judge where the barrel is, to get a grip involving the thumb is too difficult and requires too much accuracy.

Keep pulling forward and at the same time start to straighten up. Pulling forward on the arm and pushing your head back will allow you to quickly get your left hand onto your attacker's wrist. It is important to secure this as soon as possible as the grip on the gun with the right hand alone wouldn't be strong enough to hold onto the weapon if your assailant were to pull it back.

Straight away, start to turn out and away from your assailant, keeping their wrist locked in place with your left hand. Your grip on their wrist will be your pivot point and as you turn your body the attacker's gun should turn, bending their hand back and opening up their grip.

Keep turning and once you feel their grip loosen, violently punch the gun out of their hand. The sooner you can have it in your hand and out of theirs, the better your survival chances will be.

Without hesitation, use the firearm as a cold weapon to deliver concussive blows to your attacker; at this close range it is often more effective to shut the person down this way, than to try to shoot them, especially if you don't know whether the weapon is operable, or not. Now disengage from the environment as quickly as possible, as your assailant may recover quickly and/or be working with an accomplice. Once you have moved away from the location, phone law enforcement (you will want to return to your vehicle with some form of security, and alert the authorities that criminals are operating in that environment, so that they can up security and/or link this incident to others). If you were waiting for someone, you will want to alert them as well, so they don't come out to the parking lot.

Trunk Emergency Locks and Preparation and Planning

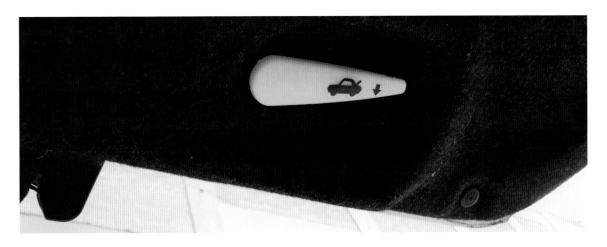

Since 2002, all cars manufactured in the U.S., are fitted with an emergency trunk release. This is usually a glow-in-the-dark handle located near the trunk latch. It is worth taking a minute the next time you have the trunk open to find out where it is; although the chances of you being bundled into the trunk of your car are remote, finding out where yours is ahead of time may prevent you from panicking and freezing in the moment, if you are. If you want to go further, you could keep a flashlight, a bottle of water, and a power/protein bar in your trunk along with a canister of pepper spray, etc.

A good part of upping your security and target-hardening yourself is planning and preparation. Knowing the potential threats you face and planning to mitigate your vulnerabilities in response to them should be a large part of your overall safety strategy. This Planning and Preparation Phase shouldn't be restricted to only looking at violent incidents, it should be extended to other areas of vehicle security. Part of your "car security" planning should involve learning how to change a flat tire (this is something you may want to practice in your driveway if you've never done it before) and/or keeping an emergency flat tire repair kit in your car—although you can drive slowly on a flat (if your tire bursts in a dangerous district/area) you will want to spend as little time changing a tire as possible, especially if you have to do this on a roadside where there is little traffic (natural surveillance), and it is late at night; don't rely on roadside assistance getting to you quickly. You may also want to extend this list of items that you have in your vehicle to an emergency car starter if you live in a cold area where there is a risk of your battery dying—getting stranded somewhere ultimately affects your personal safety. No matter your lifestyle/location, one of your most important and essential pieces of kit that you should have in your car is a first aid kit.

Part of your planning and preparation when driving involves making sure that you never have less than a half tank of gasoline/petrol, that your phone is fully charged—and you have a charger—and that you know where the hospitals and police stations are (and if they are manned or not—not all rural ones are). Rarely do we travel routes that we're not familiar with, e.g., we travel to work, we travel to places where we shop, go to the gym, etc. We should have a knowledge of where significant places are along the way, and how to change routes in order to get to them. If you get stabbed, it may be quicker for you to get someone to drive you to a hospital, rather than make an emergency call and wait for an ambulance, etc. Situational Awareness extends beyond your horizon and field of view and includes safe places that you can head towards in the event of an emergency.

Blind Spots

An often overlooked part of Situational Awareness is understanding the places of concealment that exist in an environment; this is something that criminals understand very well—they know where to stand and approach from, unnoticed. Every criminal will want to deny you the time and distance to respond and react so they will try to approach from an angle at which it will be difficult for you to notice them until it is too late to avoid or prevent the assault. One way to improve your Situational Awareness is to start having a curiosity about your surroundings, e.g., where could you stand unnoticed, how could you approach your car without drawing attention to yourself, how can you make yourself look like you fit in and belong in a location, etc? By recognizing your own actions and behaviors in these exercises, you will learn how predatory individuals act and behave when they are looking for prey.

Somebody looking to access you while you are in your car, whether this is at a junction where there are traffic lights, or in a parking lot, etc. will be aware that if they approach the driver's door by walking next to the car...

...they will appear in your wing mirror. Even if you are not directly looking at the mirror, there is a good chance that their movement will be picked up by your peripheral vision, and your attention will be drawn to them.

Criminals know that by approaching you at an angle, they will be in the mirror's blind spot...

...and their movement/approach will likely go unnoticed. We are acutely aware of these blind spots when we are driving, which is why we look over our shoulder before we pull out, in case there is a car overtaking us, etc. However, we tend to ignore/discount them when we aren't in motion. If we want to have true 360-degree awareness of our environment—and those who share it with us—we need to look over our shoulders even when our vehicle is stationary.

OC/Pepper Spray

In most U.S. states—and cities—it is legal to carry OC/Pepper Spray (in some states there are restrictions on the size of the canister and the percentage value of the OC, etc.). It is worth noting that not all "defensive" sprays are the same, and before selecting a spray, you should be aware of what it is that you're buying. There are basically three types, that are commonly classed as tactical/defensive sprays, but in fact have markedly different properties and effects:

1. CN Spray/Gas (2-Chloroacetophenone)
2. CS Spray/Gas (o-Chlorobenzylidene Malonitrile)
3. OC Spray/Gas (Oleoresin Capsicum)

CS and CN gases/sprays are irritants that cause the eyes to tear up, making it difficult for a person to see (CN gas also can cause vomiting in some people)—those sprayed/gassed may also experience a burning sensation on their skin. In contrast to these irritants, Oleoresin Capsicum is an inflammatory that causes the eyes to swell/close shut (not just tear up) and inflames the mucus membranes of the nose and throat, making breathing difficult and labored (if a person is sprayed, they will end up experiencing something akin to an extreme asthma attack). In choosing between an irritant and inflammatory, there really is only one choice; we want to inflame rather than simply irritate. Another advantage that OC Spray has over CS/CN is that its effects are almost instantaneous, whereas there may be a delay with the other two—with most attacks lasting only a few seconds, the quicker we can disable an assailant, the better.

When choosing a pepper spray, there are certain things you should consider. The first is the delivery mechanism. There are three basic delivery types, each with their own strengths and weaknesses:

1. Cones/Foggers
2. Streams
3. Foams & Gels

Cones/foggers deliver their spray in a cone-like mist, which means you won't have to be as accurate as you would, if you were using a stream or a gel—both of which would require you to aim and direct the spray into your assailant's face, where there is a chance that they could duck or you could miss, etc. If you are highly adrenalized and have a fast-moving attacker coming towards you, aiming a direct shot at your attacker's face may not be as easy as you'd think. One of the advantages of a stream or a foam/gel is that it is less likely to be affected by adverse weather conditions such as strong winds and less likely to be blown back towards you. There is also the risk with a cone/fogger of "contaminating" an area if you spray it in a room or enclosed space. I generally advocate cones/foggers to have in your car and for general carry (despite the seeming advantage of the stream. I have seen too many people—even in relatively low-stress training environments—miss their attacker with it; this doesn't mean that streams don't have their place, but for everyday use the cone/fogger offers a better hit rate). Foams/gels are good to have in your house for home-defense, and for use in other confined spaces, where cross-contamination might be a concern.

Although there is nothing technical about using pepper spray, one factor which greatly affects your ability to use it effectively is the finger you use to depress the button that releases the spray. Many people will automatically use their index finger to press down. The issue with this is that as they press down, they will tend to bend the wrist as well, which will direct the spray towards the ground, rather than at the attacker.

By using the thumb to depress the button, the wrist can remain locked so there is little danger of it bending. This may initially feel unnatural to some people as we are used to using our thumbs to grip. It is worth practicing so that this becomes the default way that you use the spray. You can either purchase an inert spray to practice with and/or simply train yourself to place the thumb on the button of your "live" tool without depressing it.

This sequence of photographs is demonstrated with the car window fully down, so that the correct way to spray someone—whether you are in or out of the car—may be understood.

When you select an OC/Pepper Spray, there are two values you should take note of; these are: the SHU value, and the percentage value. The most important of these is the SHU (Scoville Heat Unit), as this tells you the "heat"/pungency of the pepper spray, i.e., how potent the active ingredient is. A habanero pepper's heat rating is somewhere between the 100,000 and 350,000 mark—if you took this pepper and rubbed it in your eye, that would be the heat you'd be experiencing. At the time of writing, you can purchase a spray commercially that is anywhere between 3 and 5 million SHUs. The higher the SHU value of the spray, the greater the effect on your assailant. The percentage value simply refers to the percentage this active ingredient makes up when compared to the delivery agent that carries it, e.g., the water or oil it is contained in (if you have the choice—though it should not be a deciding factor—oil-based carriers, in civilian settings where stun guns, tasers, and the like are not being used, are preferred to water-based ones). I would suggest not going below 5% to make sure there is enough "active ingredient" to have an effect.

If you inadvertently cut somebody off in traffic, you may cause them to become angry and aggressive enough that they decide to follow you (this is an example of spontaneous violence where your actions and behaviors, whether real or perceived, have caused a person to become aggressive—if this was a face-to-face incident, you could attempt to de-escalate it, however because both of you would be in your cars this would not be possible). This is one reason why it is good to know the locations of hospitals, police stations and other areas where security and law enforcement are present, as you should head for these, rather than your home or workplace; you won't want this aggressive individual to know where they can find you in future. Unfortunately, if traffic is heavy and you are stationary, you may not be able to disengage and drive away easily, and your aggressor may decide to leave their car and approach yours.

As your aggressor approaches and attempts to open your door to gain access to you, one option you have is to roll down your window slightly (in the photos, the window is fully down, for illustrative purposes), and with your thumb on the pepper spray's button, prepare to spray your aggressor. Another option may be to sit tight with your central locking on and wait for traffic to start moving; however, your failure to engage your aggressor may in fact escalate the situation and if they have a firearm or heavy impact object, you may find yourself in an extremely compromised position.

Under stress and duress, you may find that your hands will start shaking, making it difficult for you to hold the can steady and aim straight. To compensate for this, you should spray a giant "S" in front of you so that you will be sure to cover your aggressor in spray. Start your "S" by drawing from right to left, over your assailant's head. You can see from the photo that although it's not going directly into their face, the spray mists and drops down under its own weight ensuring that your attacker's head/face will be fully drenched in it. The first thing that will happen to your assailant is their eyes will close, and moments later their breathing will start to be restricted.

Once you have drawn the top part of your "S," start to bring the can down so that you can draw the middle part. Your goal here is to spray a protective cloud of "mist" directly in front of you that an attacker would have to move through to get to you. The advantage of working this way is that if you are walking on a street or similar space, you can create this cloud even when your attacker is too far away for you to hit directly and then disengage by backing away knowing that they would have to come through the cloud to get to you. In reality, you would want to write several "S"s as you back away creating a tunnel of spray between yourself and the attacker.

At this lower level, start moving the can left to right. This will put more spray into your attacker's face, and will mean that if they try to duck their head/face to avoid being contaminated with the spray, they will still be hit with it. Finish off your "S" by drawing the bottom part, again from right to left. As soon as you can, roll the window back up tightly to limit the danger of the spray being blown back to you.

If you have the time and the clarity, it is advisable to turn off the fan in your car to reduce the risk of any spray being sucked into the ventilation system (better yet, hit the air recirculation button, to fully stop the intake of outside air). This is unlikely to happen as most air intakes are situated at the front of the vehicle, not to the sides and back, but it may be worth taking the precaution.

Unfortunately, OC/Pepper spray has come to be seen as a women's self-defense tool rather than as a general protection tool that can be used regardless of gender. There are several reasons why I believe it is an essential protection tool to carry and have in your car as well as your home:

1. It is recognized legally as a less than lethal weapon unlike a knife, firearm, or many other weapons.
2. There are no long-term injuries to your assailant associated with its use—the effects last 20–30 minutes.
3. It can be used at range, unlike a knife, Kubotan, baton or similar, and requires little training or the development of skills and attributes to support such training.

In any confrontation, one of the skills that will swing things in your favor is decisiveness: acting in the moment, without hesitation. Our decision-making process, however, can be slowed down by the presence of "peripheral doubts"—these are the questions we ask ourselves before acting; e.g., is our planned response to an assailant legal? Is it moral? Is it an appropriate use of force? What if it isn't effective? The more doubts we have, the more questions we must answer, and the less decisive we become. We know that pepper spray is recognized as a less-than-lethal weapon (in some states it is viewed more as a "distractant" than a weapon)—and that the police use it this way, so our intent when using it is clear; we don't want to use unnecessary force. The fact that there are no long-term injuries or conditions associated with being sprayed means that it is highly unlikely that our assailant will be able to bring a civil suit against us, claiming damages for physical, emotional, or psychological distress. Using OC Spray requires no athleticism or other physical skills and attributes, and it always has an effect; some people will fight through it, but these are few and while they may be combative, they will still be experiencing the effects and will have been debilitated to some degree. There are few, if any, adverse consequences to using it and therefore few peripheral doubts to affect your decision-making process: if you feel threatened and your aggressor is putting themselves in a position where they could harm you, spray them—you are legally entitled to do so.

Road Rage Incidents

There are many people who drive who believe that they're the "driver" and everyone else is traffic; i.e., they're entitled to be on the road while everyone else is only tolerated if they don't interfere, slow down and/or get in the way of their driving. In most instances, the expressions of rage at somebody else's driving—which conflicts with theirs—is restricted to signaling/gesturing and using the horn, however some drivers get so incensed at what they interpret as extreme disrespect, that they will follow the offender, tailgating them, flashing their lights, and/or making overtly threatening gestures, etc. They may at some point have a moment of realization, that to take the incident further, would involve them getting out of their car to physically confront the other driver when they stop (which may be something that they don't feel justified and/or able to do), and so eventually give up their chase. There are, however, individuals who are unable to control their anger and rage and are prepared to engage in a face-to-face confrontation, not caring about the consequences and ramifications (legal and physical) of their actions.

Not every country or state has legislation around "aggressive driving" (California has specific legislation that uses the term "Road Rage" and Australia has similar laws where they use the term "Predatory Driving") and so somebody who bullies you on the road may not in fact be breaking the law (unless they are in violation of other traffic laws, or driving to endanger), until they get out of their car to confront you; when their actions would be covered by "standard" assault laws.

Road Rage incidents may also occur over parking disputes such as blocking somebody in, parking in a space that belongs to them, or that they believe belongs to them, etc. In January 2016, a man in Boston was shot and killed after parking in a spot that another man had cleared of snow. People can be extremely territorial and it has been shown in studies that they will work twice as hard to get something back that they believe they've lost—or had taken away—than they would to acquire something new. This goes the same for "respect;" if somebody believes you have disrespected them they will work doubly hard to get back that lost respect, than they would in order to gain respect initially. Some people will go to great lengths to re-establish the respect that they feel has been lost.

Sticks, Baseball Bats, and Pipes

Unlike knives and guns, long objects such as bats and pipes are cumbersome to carry and difficult to conceal, which means they are rarely weapons that people come to a scene with; they are ones that are acquired from the environment, e.g., a tire iron that somebody retrieves from their car, a piece of piping that they find on the ground, etc. One of the skills you need to have when using improvised weapons is to be able to spot and select them before your assailant(s) does.

In a busy parking lot, finding an empty space can be extremely frustrating, and a driver may find themselves waiting for some time for a car to pull out of a spot. If you were to not realize that somebody was waiting and had "claimed" the space, and pull in before them, you may cause them to become spontaneously aggressive, and even violent. If it's a hot day and their air-conditioning isn't working, they may already be uncomfortable and angry and your action could be the trigger that moves them to violence (there are numerous studies that show sharp increases in violent crime during hot weather—if someone is physically uncomfortable they are more likely to react aggressively and violently to events that otherwise may not have bothered them). They may be so incensed that they look for some form of weapon to both increase their chances of coming out of the confrontation unscathed and to deliver as much punishment to you as they can. They may get a tire iron from their trunk, or look for something, such as a brick or a piece of piping in the environment. Although in most spontaneous situations, you will have the chance to attempt to de-escalate, and help an aggressor find non-violent solutions to the situation, once someone has pulled a weapon—whether improvised or carried—they will already be in an emotional state, that will make de-escalation extremely unlikely to be successful.

If you can position yourself between two cars, your attacker will be limited in the directions that they can generate force with the stick, and so will only really be able to make downwards, upwards and stabbing strikes with their stick/pipe.

Where possible, you should use the environment to your advantage. One way to do this is to use objects in it to restrict your attacker's movement—and the movement of their weapon. If you can limit and dictate the types of attack they can make, you will be better prepared to deal with them. If you can position yourself between two parked cars, you can limit your assailant's ability to make lateral swings with a pipe or other long weapon. This means that for them to use the pipe with any power, they will need to swing it downwards from overhead—there is a chance that they could try and stab out with it, to the front, but this is not a natural movement for most people and is an extremely uncommon type of attack. If you know how they will have to use their weapon, you will only need to focus on your response to this type of attack, and not have to spend time trying to recognize/identify the other possible directions that they may attack you from. As soon as they raise the pipe overhead, there is only one direction in which the bat is heading. Although the same defense can be used against a swinging bat, from all directions, knowing the one from which it is coming reduces a number of variables and allows you to focus on a single attack.

Your first reaction should be to disengage from your attacker, trying to get behind a parked car, so that you keep this obstacle/barrier between the two of you. However, it may be that you are not going to have the time and distance between you to do this, so you will need to turn and face them, in preparation for taking control of the weapon.

Immediately, bring your left hand up to your cheek—this is the hand which is opposite to your assailant's weapon hand; i.e., if they were holding the pipe in their left hand you would bring your right hand up. Your elbow should be down, rather than out, so that your arm doesn't stick out and become a potential target. At the same time, you should tuck your chin down and raise your shoulders up. Moving towards an oncoming weapon is not natural—our instincts will tell us to move away. The problem is that moving away, plays to the strengths of a weapon such as a stick or baton, which is a long-range weapon, and part of what we will want to do is take the advantage(s) of the weapon away. One way to ensure that you will move forward is to deliberately put yourself off-balance in that direction. If you raise yourself up on your toes as you bring your left hand up and lean forward slightly, you will direct your weight towards your attacker and almost "fall" towards them.

The majority of the power in any swinging bat, pipe, or stick, is contained in the last third. If you can move inside of this—then even if your arm or any other body part comes into contact with the pipe it is unlikely that you will sustain a serious injury. This doesn't mean that it won't hurt, just that you will still have a functioning arm to use after the strike. The most significant part of your defense is forward movement, to position yourself inside the swing of the pipe. As you step forward with your right leg to close distance, begin to extend your left arm forward, towards your attacker's right ear. Don't focus on the pipe itself, as its movement might trigger your flinch reflex and cause you to bring your arm up to defend yourself with—if the pipe hits your arm when it is in this overhead position, it will do serious damage to your forearm. It is useful to think of your left hand as being like a horse's blinker that will prevent you from seeing the pipe.

As you extend your arm, and move your body forward, bring your left knee up and slide forward on your right foot using a Glisha (sliding) step. Bringing your left leg up like this removes it as a potential target, if your assailant was aiming for your thigh/leg, rather than your head or body.

Your extended arm, will deflect the downward motion of your assailant's weapon arm. If you had to cover a greater distance, and couldn't close the distance between you fast enough, the pipe may well connect with your arm. Despite the pain of the initial impact, from this angle, the pipe will deflect and run down your arm. In this position, it is much less likely to be injured or broken than if you tried to block/stop the pipe with your forearm.

The raised knee, can be used to strike your assailant, further disrupting their attack.

Don't rush to disarm, instead control your assailant's head with both hands/arms and continue to deliver knee strikes. Most attackers will remain weapon-centric, and instead of dropping the pipe to free their arm to defend themselves, are likely to keep hold of their weapon—which unless they are trained in how to grapple at close quarters with a stick, will do them little good.

While keeping control of your assailant's head with your right hand/arm, start to slide your left arm down, along your assailant's weapon arm.

Continue to slide your arm down...

...until you can press the pipe to your side, with your left arm. At this point, grab your attacker's wrist with your left hand.

With your right hand, grab any part of the pipe that is exposed. You should now have hold/control of it with your body (the left arm hugging it to your side), and your right hand; By comparison, your attacker only has hold of it with one hand—if you extend their arm by stepping back, their grip will be loosened further.

By turning your body to your right, you will rip the pipe out of your attacker's hand/grip. You will now have hold of the pipe and can use it yourself as a weapon, against your attacker.

Take hold of the other end of the pipe with your left hand and drive it forward into your attacker—in this confined space, just like your attacker, you will not have room to swing it. As soon as you have an opportunity to disengage, do so, you are not there to punish your attacker, but to survive the situation, and the sooner you can get away to safety, the better.

Second, Third, and Fourth Phase Attacks

There is a big difference between a technique and a solution. Just because you have executed a technique successfully—such as disarming somebody of a length of piping—doesn't mean that the confrontation has automatically ended. An attacker can remain an active attacker even after you have disarmed them, and may continue to attack you, even though you now have their weapon. If every training scenario you practice ends when a disarm has been performed, you could be training yourself into a corner; e.g., if you finish every gun disarm with the attacker backing away and respecting your command to "Stay Back!" you are only training for one outcome and are not preparing yourself to deal with the assailant who will try to recover their weapon. A violent encounter may comprise of many different phases and dimensions, and these all need to be brought into our training; e.g., knives need to be pulled during clinch-work, multiple assailants need to be added during one-on-one encounters, etc.

One assumption you should always work to is that your assailant is armed, even if you can't see a weapon or you have disarmed them of one. Just because you have taken an attacker's initial/primary weapon away doesn't mean they don't have another weapon that they can use against you.

It may be that after you disarm your attacker of the pipe they were using to attack you—and even after you use it against them—they still wish to continue the fight. They may now pull a knife they were carrying (it may be that in their initial rage they forgot that they had this with them, or that they didn't want to initially use it because they wanted to try and maintain distance between you and them, and not get themselves in an up close and personal type of fight).

Due to the confined space, they will not easily be able to swing/slash the knife but will be limited to making forward stabbing actions. They may run towards you, preparing to shank you with the knife. Immediately, turn to face them, holding the pipe in your right hand, and placing your left hand, palm down, on the other end of the pipe—don't grab the pipe, as you want to leave the bottom of the pipe clear, in order to create an uninterrupted striking surface.

As your attacker brings their knife up towards you, viciously slam down the pipe into their arm—don't think so much about defending yourself with the pipe, but rather using it to cause as much damage and trauma to your attacker's arm as possible. As you make this action, you should pull your hips back, to create distance between the knife and your body.

The force of your strike, and the subsequent pain that your attacker will feel, will interrupt their timing and recoil of the knife. This will allow you to turn the pipe and use it to redirect their knife and weapon arm away from you.

If there is a solid surface available to you, you can ram/slam their weapon arm into it (in this case, the car door to your right). The force of this may cause them to drop the knife. If your attacker does release the knife, don't be distracted by trying to retrieve it yourself. Instead, take this opportunity to attack your assailant with the pipe.

With their weapon arm clear and unable to protect their head/body, bring the pipe back in towards you and...

...drive the end of the pipe into your attacker's face. You may need to make repeated strikes, in order to drive your attacker back and give yourself enough distance and time to escape safely.

Quickly disengage before your attacker manages to recover—don't concern yourself that your assailant still has their weapon, not every armed assault needs to end with a disarm. If you can get yourself clear of the environment, your attacker will no longer be a threat to you.

Weapons Training and Improvised Weapons

Although Krav Maga uses a categorization system to help us identify items in our environment that can be used as weapons, e.g., objects that resemble a stick, objects that resemble a knife, objects that resemble a shield, etc. (for a full list and explanation please refer to *Krav Maga: Real World Solutions to Real World Violence*, pp. 159–162), it is one thing to be able to spot an improvised weapon, and another to know how to use it effectively. This is why it is useful to do some form of offensive/defensive weapons training; if you don't know how to effectively use a stick or baton, identifying and picking up a length of piping or similar may not actually give you an advantage. In fact, if you have to hesitate, to think and work out how to effectively use it, you may be slowing yourself down in a fast-paced and dynamic encounter.

Your weapons training should aim to replicate your unarmed movements as closely as possible; i.e., you want to have a style/system of movement that is common to everything that you do. In the photographs below you will see how defenses against circular strikes with the baton resemble the 360 unarmed defenses we use (for a more detailed and comprehensive description and explanation of Krav Maga's 360 Defenses, please refer to *Krav Maga: Real World Solutions to Real World Violence* (pp. 41–50).

When blocking with a stick or baton (or similar), you should think of the weapon as being an extension of your arm, resembling a standard 360-Block. You should have one hand, holding the stick, with the other one supporting it; it is unlikely that you would have the hand/wrist/grip strength to keep the stick horizontal, when blocking, if you were simply to hold it with one hand.

When blocking circular strikes to the side, your stick/baton/pipe, etc. needs to be positioned vertically and pushed out to meet whatever attack is coming in. As with all baton work, you should support the baton with your left hand, rather than gripping it. If your top hand was wrapped round the long end of the stick gripping it, and somebody swung a baseball bat sideways that you needed to block, your knuckles and fingers would be exposed. If your hand is supporting rather than gripping, only the shaft of the baton will be exposed.

When blocking strikes, such as knife shanks, your objective is to stop the attack, rather than deflect it; this is the same whether you are blocking with a baton, or with the blade of your arm, and regardless of the direction the attack is coming from (above, below, from the side). Either one should be driven into your assailant's arm as hard and forcefully as you can. Because most knife attacks occur at close range, it is generally more efficient and effective to use your baton this way rather than trying to time a swing to intercept an attack; in such a case the attacker would only have to get inside the last third of the stick to negate the power of the swing.

Pipes, Sticks, and Baseball Bats When on the Ground

Moving towards an attacker wielding any weapon, whether that weapon be a bat or a knife, etc. goes against all of our instincts, and even if we consciously and rationally understand that this strategy offers us our best chance of survival, we will still have to overcome our emotional response, which will be to back away from danger.

Much has been written about the fight, flight, and freeze responses, however it is worth noting that the original study was conducted by observing the behaviors and actions of birds when attacked by predators (Walter Bradford Cannon, 1915). It should be understood that different species have different defense mechanisms and strategies that favor different responses; e.g., a flock of birds will scatter in a myriad of directions in order to confuse an attacking predator (a strategy a group can adopt/replicate when dealing with an active shooter), so flight is the preferred/natural solution for such a species. A rat will disengage and retreat unless cornered, in which case it will attack. These behaviors are common to prey animals. Human beings are not natural predators and are by default wired as "prey;" i.e., we would rather run or hide, than fight. This can cause us to naturally move away from a threat rather than engage with it—though with training we can learn to manage the response; this training may be formal, by attending realistic martial arts/self-defense classes, that adrenalize you, for example, or informal; e.g., you grew up in a neighborhood where aggression/violence was a common occurrence and so learned effective ways to deal with attacks through experience.

It is also worth remembering that the initial studies that coined the term "fight or flight" looked at responses when the threat or danger came from another species, e.g., birds being attacked by cats, etc. They did not look at intraspecies violence where the threat came from an animal of the same species, e.g., violence between birds, violence between cats, etc. In most intraspecies violence, conflicts are resolved through acts of posturing and submission, rather than through physical violence. There are times—even when confronted by an angry person swinging a bat—that we will fail to recognize the danger we are in, believing the act to be one of posturing/dominance rather than one intended to cause us harm. This potential confusion, coupled with our natural prey drive, can see us backing away when our best survival option would be to move forward and engage.

If somebody comes at you swinging a bat or stick and you are caught unprepared, there is a good chance that you will start to back away. If this sees you initially avoid getting hit, your fear system will tell you that this is a good strategy to adopt and you should continue with it. Our fear system works in the moment and has no foresight; if moving back means you don't experience pain it will tell you to keep doing it, even if logic tells you you'll eventually run out of room and get hit.

If you are caught by surprise (or have difficulty registering the nature of the threat, in the moment), you may find yourself moving away from your attacker, even if "consciously" you know this is not your most effective survival strategy. If you had a safe place to back away to (such as getting behind a parked car), disengagement would be a good strategy, however in an open environment, it will only be a matter of time before an attacker manages to close you down. One of the big differences between a training environment such as a studio/dojo, etc. and the real world, is the terrain. In real world situations it may well be uneven, increasing the likelihood that you could trip and fall.

One vital skill to have for surviving real-life assaults is the ability to break your fall (this is a good life skill to have as well, as most people when they fall—such as on ice—stick their hands out to protect themselves, which often leads to broken wrists and collar bones). When you fall, your first priority should be to land safely and in a position from which you will be able to continue the fight. Deal with your fall first and the stick/pipe second.

Make your breakfall, bringing your hands down to slap the ground, and tucking your chin to your chest, so that your head doesn't hit the ground. Continue the movement of the breakfall by rolling backward, and tucking your legs into you. Your feet should be positioned upwards. Your attacker will now have to change their attack from a side-to-side swing, to a downwards one, in order to continue their assault on you.

Explosively launch yourself upwards, propelling your feet towards the pipe, aiming to intercept your attacker's swing with the soles of your shoes. If you are wearing a sneaker with a thick and spongy sole, you will be able to absorb the impact of the pipe much better than the thin sole of a dress shoe, however your goal is to intercept the pipe before it gains much momentum and power.

You are aiming for inside the last third of the stick, towards your attacker's grip, where the pipe naturally has less power. You are not looking just to "stop" the stick; your goal is to kick it backward, interrupting your attacker's recoil of it.

Quickly bring your feet back in, before your attacker is able to swing the pipe back towards you, and then once again...

...propel yourself upwards, but this time launch yourself at your assailant's chest to kick/push them backward.

As your attacker falls backward, use the time and space this creates to get back to your feet. The most natural way to get back to your feet is to turn onto your hands and knees, and push upwards with your arms. The problem with getting up this way is that you will no longer be facing your attacker, and will be unable to defend yourself, should they recover and launch further attacks. This is why it is necessary to practice getting up from the ground while still facing your assailant.

The quickest and easiest way to get up while facing your attacker is to lift yourself up, with an opposite leg and arm (in this case left leg, right arm), and then pull the other leg through and behind you to get to standing. Keep your free arm out, so that you have something forward to defend yourself with, should your assailant attack you as you get up. It is probable that once standing you will still have to deal with your attacker, so you should prepare yourself now to move towards them, and get inside the range of their pipe, using the previous technique described.

Hard and Soft Breakfalls

Knowing how to break your fall is an essential self-defense skill—not because 95% of street-fights go to the ground (this myth comes from an incorrect interpretation/reading of an 1997 LAPD ASLET study that showed that 62% of arrests went to the ground; an arrest is very different from a fight)—but because if you do fall, or are knocked/pushed over, etc., not being able to break your fall may mean that you hit your head on the floor and are stunned or knocked out. This could result in you being unable to defend yourself from further attacks.

There are two basic types of breakfall: there are hard breakfalls, where your body absorbs the fall, and soft ones, where you try to roll out of the fall. In a hard breakfall, your aim will be to spread the absorption of the fall throughout your body so no one body part receives the full impact. Hard breakfalls are usually made when there is little room to move, and although they will save you on hard surfaces such as concrete (and are certainly preferential to just hitting these surfaces), they are less painful when performed on grass, floor boards, carpet, etc. Soft breakfalls require more room to perform but are useful in getting back to your feet quickly and can be performed on the hardest surface with little discomfort.

Hard Rear Breakfall

Starting from a neutral position (Unprepared Stance)...take a step backward and start to lower your weight. A common error, when people practice breakfalling, is to try and drop too quickly; if you can, you should attempt to lower yourself as close to the ground as possible before you actually drop/fall onto it.

Bring your hands up in front of your face to protect yourself from any frontal attack your assailant may make; e.g., they could push you to take your balance, and then follow this up with a punch to your face. Putting the palms up and out, will prevent/deny them this opportunity. Also, raising them in this fashion, will prevent you from putting them out behind you, which would be your instinctual method for breaking your fall.

Lower yourself further (think about walking backward into a low squat—when babies feel themselves losing balance, they simply lower themselves slowly and sit down, this is basically what you are trying to do here, while moving backwards, away from your attacker). As you do this, start to bring your arms in...

...before slapping them outwards, palms down, as you drop towards the ground, landing on your buttocks (this is how babies who are learning to walk "fall down;" they just sit down as they lose their balance). Make sure to forcefully exhale as you do this.

Roll backward from your buttocks through your back and onto your shoulders (hips lifted) so that no one body part stays in contact with the ground for too long; this way each body part absorbs and shares the extent of the fall without one single part taking all of the impact. As you fall, keep one foot on the ground and let the other one come up. If you keep your eyes on the foot as it rises, you will naturally tuck your chin in and prevent the back of your head from hitting the floor.

By keeping one of your feet on the floor as you roll backward, you can quickly get yourself into a good defensive position, bringing your hands up to protect your head (there may be multiple assailants when you end up on the ground and you will want to be able to protect yourself from all directions). Bring your foot back so you are ready to kick out at anyone advancing towards you such as an assailant who has pushed you to the ground and is following up with another attack. Turn the toes out so that when you kick out at your attacker's leg/knee your foot won't slide off (something it may do if the toes are pointing up.)

Soft Rear Breakfall

From a neutral position (Unprepared Stance)...

...start to take a step back, and begin to lower yourself towards the ground. If you are going to roll over your right shoulder, extend your right arm. As you do this, bring your left hand across, towards your right shoulder.

Lower yourself as you bring your left hand over your right shoulder. This will help you to turn your torso, so that you don't go directly backward (which would see your head hit the ground).

This photo is taken from the rear. It shows how you are not rolling directly backward but instead are rolling over your right shoulder, and somewhat to the side. At this point, your feet should be off the ground.

Your feet should now start to be kicked out behind you, with the aim of throwing them over your head. At the same time, you should start to bring your left hand towards the ground.

Kick your legs over your shoulder, and lift yourself up with your left arm, so that your head doesn't come into contact with the ground.

Start to push yourself up with your left arm, and kick violently backward with your left leg. The purpose of kicking back is to add backward momentum to help pull you upright.

With both feet on the ground, and your left arm at extension...

...pull yourself back to standing, and prepare to deal with whatever threat or attack may follow.

Real-World Ground Fighting/Survival

Most fights that do go to the ground will end up with one person standing and the other on the floor; there are few situations in which an attacker, given the choice, will give up their dominant position, and follow their target to the ground. If they do, it is generally because the nature of the assault dictates that they do, as with a rape or sexual assault—or because the environment forces them to do so, should they want to continue the fight—i.e. their victim falls into a confined space, such as between the seats of a bus/train, where the only way to really continue attacking them, is to go to "ground" with them, etc.

There are a variety of reasons you may end up on the ground: you may slip or fall, you may be pushed, thrown, or have your legs kicked out from beneath you, you may be knocked down with a strike, or be weighed down by numbers in a multiple-attacker incident, etc. Being able to defend yourself against a standing attacker when on the ground is the first "phase" of ground survival.

One attack that you might experience if you are pushed/knocked to the ground is some form/variation of a soccer kick, usually aimed at your head. One way to defend against such an attack is to use a similar defense that you would use to deal with the overhead pipe attack from the ground that we looked at previously.

It is worth noting that kicking somebody in the head when they are on the ground is usually looked on in most countries' legal systems as an excessive use of force, i.e., if you are standing and your aggressor is on the ground and there are no mitigating factors such as a gun, multiple assailants, etc., then the person you are dealing with does not constitute an immediate threat and so you should take the opportunity to disengage rather than "continue" the fight. Obviously, situations determine solutions and there may be times that such force is warranted; however it would be unwise to adopt a policy where by default you finish every technique/solution with a head kick against an assailant who is on the ground.

Whenever possible, you should look to create range and distance, between yourself and an aggressor; this will give you the time and space to react to an attack. Depending on the situation, you should either look to act preemptively, or step back into your interview/de-escalation stance (*Krav Maga: Real World Solutions to Real World Violence*, p. 14).

It may be that your aggressor makes a strong push towards you, before you have the time to do either.

While you may have normally been able to deflect the power of the push by blading your body and/or deflecting the push with an arm, it may be that, due to the uneven terrain, your attacker is able to knock you over. Your first priority is to make a successful breakfall, so that when you hit the ground, your head and body will be protected; and you'll be in a fit state and ready to continue to defend yourself.

As you raise your right foot up, ready to defend yourself, your attacker may recognize the potential danger of being kicked and move to the side. In all of our defenses, we should recognize our attacker's ability to respond to what we do, and change their tactics and attacks accordingly.

Recognizing that it would be unwise to attack, facing your feet, your assailant may move around to try to attack you from the side. Immediately, push off with your left foot, to turn yourself, so that you can keep your feet between you and your attacker...

...if they are moving too quickly, they will soon be in a position to launch a soccer-style kick at your head/body, before you'll be able to get into position to re-align them with your feet. To counteract this threat/danger, start to pull your knees back to your chest...

In preparation for turning and launching a two-footed kick at your attacker.

As you extend your legs, start to turn on your shoulders, so that you are better aligned with your attacker, and will be able to drive both feet with your hips.

Forcefully drive your feet into your attacker's chest. As they prepare to make the kick, your attacker will likely lean slightly forward, so that you will be able able to drive your feet upwards, into them.

Immediately, start to get back up to your feet (again without turning your back on your attacker, as you do so), and prepare yourself either to disengage to safety or to continue the fight.

Training in Confined Spaces—Defending Yourself in a Vehicle

In most violent encounters, you will quickly run out of space. There are few real world environments in which you will have unlimited room to move and maneuver; in most situations you will have walls, furniture, cars, and other objects which will restrict your movement. In a crowded bar or pub you may also have other people blocking and preventing your movements. When you are fighting/defending yourself in a car you don't run out of space, you start from a position of having none. Understanding how to move in a car is essential to understanding what can and can't be done in such a confined space and how to compensate for this.

One of the first things to recognize and understand is how to generate power in your striking from the seat of a car. When standing, most of the power in your punches will come from your legs, hips, and back. When confined to a seat (whether the driver's, passenger's or back seat), you will not be able to employ these body parts. Therefore, it is essential to know how to reposition yourself so that you can put yourself in a more advantageous position for striking, if you do ever find yourself being attacked in your car.

The sequence below looks at how to clear your seat belt in order to deal with an attacker who is coming across the passenger seat or through the center console.

If you are sitting with your seatbelt on when attacked, you will need to clear the belt, else you will find yourself trapped and pinned to the seat. You could try to release the seat belt at the buckle, however you may find that the fine motor skills to do this will let you down when put under stress and duress—also while you are doing this, you will be losing moments that could be spent getting yourself into a better position to deal with your assailant. To clear the belt, base your right hand on the center console—you will use this to push up from—and with your left hand catch the seat belt with your thumb.

With your left hand, push out in one fluid motion, and grab on to the steering wheel, keeping the seat belt hooked on to your thumb. Don't "jerk" the seat belt, as this will engage its safety mechanism, locking it in place. At the same time, start to push/lift yourself up with your right hand.

Keep lifting yourself up, using your left hand on the steering wheel to assist you. You will want to lift yourself up high enough that you will be able to move your right leg underneath you, so that you can position it on the seat.

Pull your right leg under you, so that you are kneeling on the seat. Once you can support your weight, thread your left hand through the belt, so it is no longer restricting you. You will now have both arms free to both attack and defend with.

Jam your left foot into the floor of the car and/or against the driver's foot well, so that you will have a solid base, from which to strike.

A large part of personal safety and self-protection is about planning and developing processes/ good habits. One good habit to get into is to always put the central locking on when you first get into your car, (after doing a quick scan from outside of the vehicle, to make sure it's empty before you get in), before putting on your seat belt and starting the car, etc. If you were to place a bag on the passenger seat and start to buckle up before you put the central locking on, for the time that you are engaged in this activity, a criminal would have an easy job of opening the passenger door and taking it—by locking the car as soon as you get in, this type of theft can be avoided.

Another reason you will want to secure the locks at the earliest opportunity is that an assailant may use the passenger door as a means of gaining access to you in the vehicle to control you and/or take control of the vehicle. Leaving your car, while there is an attacker still inside will go against all your "territorial" instincts. There is a sense of injustice—after all, it is your car and it's not right/fair that you would have to leave it; the other person should have had to leave.

In real-life situations, techniques as such often don't exist; e.g., there isn't a specific technique for dealing with someone climbing into your car and across the passenger seat. Instead, you will need to work according to established concepts and ideas, and follow some general principles concerning defending yourself in a confined space, etc. Whenever the passenger door opens unexpectedly, you should immediately start clearing your seatbelt. If your attacker has some skill/experience, they will have approached your car in your side mirror's blind spot so it would have been difficult for you to notice their approach.

Your primary goal will be to get your legs beneath you and the seatbelt clear, so that you are able to face your attacker squarely, and have a height advantage over them. It is worth remembering that your assailant will be working in the same confined space that you are, and facing all the same issues, so if you can start off in a more dominant/advantageous position, you will increase your odds against them.

The attacker may try to grab the steering wheel, in order to prevent you from trying to drive off as they climb into your car—or to assist them as they pull themselves into the vehicle. If this happens, firmly grab onto their wrist, to help prevent/inhibit their movement. In such a confined space, you will want to look to control the other person, in order to make your combatives more effective.

Rip their arm across your body, and pull them down. You will want to prevent them getting a dominant position over you, and having them sprawled out face-down, is a good way of doing this. With your other hand, grab their clothing around the shoulder area...

...and pull their head down, smashing it into the steering wheel and/or center console. In most cars, these areas are padded so it's unlikely you will be able to deliver much concussive force this way, however the sooner you can start disrupting their thought processes by delivering any type of pain, the better.

Keeping your assailant's head pinned down by pulling on their jacket/clothing, start to deliver hammer-fist and forearm strikes to the back of their neck with your left hand. Don't worry that your strikes will lack the potency and power that you're able to generate when standing, instead concentrate on delivering them in a continuous, uninterrupted fashion, that keeps your attacker's head pinned down. You should be looking to disrupt their attack, so that you can safely disengage from your vehicle.

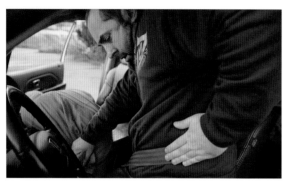

Keeping your assailant's head pinned down, find the seatbelt, which should be around your abdomen/stomach level, and place your hand along it. (Using clothing to control an attacker is extremely effective in restricting their movements, and it is often easier and more effective than trying to control an individual limb or body part, especially if there is sweat and/or blood involved. It is also much harder for an assailant to clear/remove a hand that is grabbing clothing, than one which is holding onto a limb, etc.)

Slide your hand down the seatbelt until you find the buckle to release it—this is your quickest and most effective way to find the buckle, rather than trying to search for it with your hand. The advantage of doing everything by feel, is that you can keep your eyes focused on your attacker and scan your surroundings to see if there are any other threats present.

Once you have unbuckled yourself, start to extricate yourself from the vehicle. Many people make the mistake of trying to force/fight an attacker out of their car, instead of fighting their own way out. If you think of the amount of time, and what you would have to do, to force your attacker back out through the passenger side door, it is clear that getting yourself out safely is a much simpler proposition. The sooner you can end a situation, the better, as you never know if there are third parties in the environment who can come to your attacker's assistance. You can always return to your car with law enforcement, later on.

Get out of the car and get clear of the environment. Your safety has been compromised, and it is not worth staying to find out if there are any other dangers present. Keep your attacker's head pulled/pinned down as you exit. If you can safely remove the keys from the ignition, do so, but don't have this as a priority.

From a personal safety perspective, however, it will be much easier and quicker for you to disengage than it would be to force the other person out. This would be the same if someone attacked you in your house when you were alone; leaving your house is much easier than trying to fight your attacker out of it, especially if there is a huge weight/strength discrepancy between you and them and/or multiple assailants are involved, etc. Any location where you are attacked, whether it is a public space, your car, or your home, is a place where your safety has been compromised and one which you should leave/evacuate, at the earliest opportunity.

Disengaging and evacuating your home or car can get complicated when you have dependents present, e.g., if there are other family members in your house, young children in your car, etc. In these instances, you will need to take into consideration the safety of these other individuals—if you have an infant in a child seat in the back of your car, you would want to extricate them from the seat as part of your evacuation process. If you are attacked in your home when family members are present, evacuation may not be an option and disengaging to a safe room—along with family members—that you can secure and barricade may be a better strategy in that case. You still should not be looking to try to force your assailant(s) out of your home but rather to get your family to a safe place from which you can call law enforcement. These are strategies that you will want to talk about with all family members, in an age-appropriate manner, before such a situation occurs.

It may be that the attacker makes an armed, rather than an unarmed, assault. Dealing with weapons in a confined space is extremely difficult as you won't be able to make a significant body defense as part of your solution. Neither will you be able to generate enough power with your combatives to seriously disrupt your attacker. This means that most of your attention should go to controlling the weapon and taking away an attacker's ability to move it.

Sometimes certain pieces of legislation/safety precautions that are designed to keep us safe from one type of danger may force us to change our actions/behaviors in ways that can put us at other risk in other ways. Due to laws around texting and using mobile phones when driving, you may decide to pull to the side of the road, to make a call or respond to a text, etc. In doing this, you will make yourself vulnerable to a mugging/robbery and/or carjacking. While using hand-held devices when driving is certainly a huge safety risk, we should be careful not to exchange these risks for others.

In any threat situation, if the attacker simply wants your resources (such as the car), give them over. If their demands involve moving you to another location, on the other hand, your best survival option, in almost every situation, is to resist and fight back. With a threat, there is likely to be some form of dialogue, where your assailant will instruct you what to do and/or give their demands. Use this as an opportunity to get your hands as close to the weapon as you can without alerting them; e.g., shrug your shoulders and bring your hands up in a submissive manner.

Once you determine that it will be necessary to deal with the situation physically (they have demonstrated an interest in you, not just your possessions), grab your assailant's weapon arm at the wrist, and push the gun away from yourself (you are going to start pulling the gun across your body as you do this). At the same time, try to pull your body back, as much as is possible, pressing it into the seatback. As you pull your body back, also do the same with your left hand, so that it doesn't end up in the line of fire.

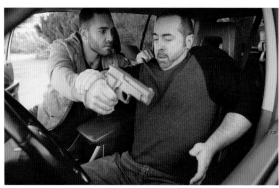

As you push the gun forward, start to pull your attacker's arm across your body, and rotate your left hand, in preparation for grabbing the barrel of the gun with an underhand grip—if you use an overhand grip to grab the barrel, there is a danger that you will muzzle yourself, wrapping your hand around the end of the barrel; this is especially true if you are dealing with a small-frame revolver or pistol, where the barrel is extremely short. Coming at the gun underhand is also more surreptitious, and less likely to be spotted than attempting an overhand grip from this position.

In a confined space where your movement is restricted, you will not be able to move with the weapon if your assailant tries to pull it back. This means that you will have to restrict and secure the movement of your attacker's weapon arm so they aren't able to try to retain it. To help facilitate this, start to bring your arm over your assailant's weapon arm, as you go to grab the gun. By pulling them forward, you will affect their balance and compromise their base; this will restrict and limit their ability to respond to what you are doing.

Stretch and extend your attacker's arm, securing it so there is no way they can pull their weapon back. If they try to pull their weapon back, they will also have to pull you, and due to your relative body positioning, they will not have the strength/leverage to do this. Keeping your attacker's arm secured, start to rotate the gun, using the barrel as a lever to open up your attacker's grip.

Once you have the weapon clear...

...transition it to your hand that is nearest your assailant...

...and use it to deliver concussive force (making sure that you don't muzzle yourself with it).

At the first opportunity you have, disengage and evacuate from your vehicle, keeping the weapon close to your body, and pointed away from you.

There is a common misconception that driving while talking on the phone is no more distracting than talking to a front-seat passenger. The difference is that the passenger will also be observing what is going on in your environment, and their intonation and speech will change if they suddenly see a car pull out, or someone slam on the brakes, in front of you, alerting you to, or confirming, the danger. However, because they aren't in the environment with you, the person on the phone will keep talking in exactly the same way as they were before, creating a distraction from what is happening around you.

Attacks from the Back/Rear Seats

Many people will use their key fob to locate their vehicle in a parking lot. The danger of this is that it both identifies the car you are heading to, and in many cases unlocks it, allowing a predatory individual to gain access to your vehicle—even if the remote fob only unlocks the driver's door. With this open it is possible for a criminal to turn the central locking off and climb into the back seat to hide. If your car has tinted windows, it may be difficult to spot someone hiding there. Even if you don't unlock your car remotely, it is a good habit to check the backseats before entering your vehicle.

A group who have identified your house as a target for a potential home invasion may determine that their best method of gaining entry to your property is to abduct you at another location—where you are more vulnerable, and more easily accessible—and then drive you (or force you to drive) to your house. It may be that they need you to turn off the alarm system, direct them to valuables, etc. and this is your worth to them. Afterwards, they may even use your car to transport the goods they steal from you, while leaving you and your family members tied or locked up.

Most people's routines are fairly predictable and in most cases it isn't difficult for someone (or a group) to carry out some basic surveillance on you to work out where you will be at a particular time, e.g., a gym class you attend regularly, or your regular arrival/departure time from work, etc.

In many cases, an attacker will not present you with an opportunity to control their weapon—they will keep the weapon back, out of your reach. Where this is the case, you may want to think about ducking down, and exiting the vehicle rather than attempting a disarm. Depending on the position of the gun, the driver's seat and headrest will make it difficult for the attacker to keep it trained on you, as you move to your left, towards the door. It should also be understood that in almost all abduction attempts, you have the most value to your assailant in the early stages, and the least value in the later stages. This means that your assailant is less likely to use their weapon in the first moments of such an assault, as you will have no use to them dead.

Before you move to control the weapon, try to get your hands as close to it as possible. Your attacker will be expecting you to put your hands up, so you should take advantage of this assumption, by doing so. At the same time, use this movement to mask the fact that you are moving your body back so that it is as far behind the muzzle of the gun as you can get it.

Quickly turn your nearest hand towards the weapon, and wrap your fingers over the barrel, putting your thumb behind the hammer (or where the hammer would be, if it is enclosed).

Don't just pull the gun forward; instead turn it by rotating your wrist and then pull forward. Rotating your wrist—and therefore the barrel—will get you out of the line of fire much faster than if you simply pull the gun forward. At the same time, bring your left arm/hand across to take control of your attacker's wrist.

With both hands (the one that is holding the weapon, and the one on the wrist) start to pull your attacker forward explosively, straightening their arm.

The seat will eventually prevent their body from moving any further forward, and their arm will be at full extension. At this point, as you keep straightening your own arm, they will be unable to hold onto their weapon.

If you were simply to disarm your assailant at this point, it is likely that they would be able to continue the fight—it may be that they have a second weapon that they could bring to bear. Keeping hold of their extended arm with your left hand, bring your right arm (the one holding the weapon) forcefully down onto their extended arm.

This action will hyperextend their elbow, and likely cause a dislocation, however in many instances the dislocated joint will simply reset itself, and while it will be painful, it may not actually render the arm inoperable; this is something that should be remembered whenever you perform any type of armbar—an adrenalized/drunk/drugged up attacker may fight through the pain.

Once you have hyperextended the arm, throw your attacker backward—your assailant should want to pull their arm back, so their movement will assist you in doing this. Then...

...pull it forward again, driving your attacker's head into the seat/ headrest. Make sure not to muzzle yourself, keeping the gun turned away from you at all times. All of these movements, are to distract, and disorient your attacker, rather than deliver concussive force.

Once again, throw them backward, as you start to make your disengagement.

Don't rely on the weapon being operable and useful to intimidate/force your attacker to comply with any demand that you make. It may well be an imitation or unloaded firearm, and your assailant will be aware of this. Instead, exit your vehicle as soon as you can and make for a safe location.

It may be that rather than using a firearm to force compliance with a demand, your attacker chooses to use a knife or other bladed weapon.

If you identify that someone is getting into your car, your best survival option in almost all cases is to exit it—far better to have room in which to work than fight in a confined space, especially where weapons are involved. Violence, however, tends to happen extremely fast, and sometimes you will miss the opportunity to disengage.

If your assailant is using a knife to try to control you or get you to acquiesce to a demand they will likely hold it close to you. This will allow you an opportunity to "cry" your hands into position, and get them close to your attacker's weapon arm/hand. In this moment, you can talk to your attacker, asking them what they want, telling them that you have money, etc. Don't introduce "new" ideas into their script, by asking them not to kill you, stab you, etc. They may not have considered these things (the offer of money is one that can buy you time, or offer a less dangerous alternative, i.e. you can hand over money, but the introduction of an idea that would do you harm, should be avoided). Stay "on script," and give them no reason to think about using their weapon against you.

Quickly make a "hook" with both hands, and explosively pull your attacker's weapon arm down. It is important that you start your pull from the space over their arm, rather than hooking it and then pulling. The first thing your attacker should feel is their arm moving suddenly downwards, rather than your hands being placed on their arm, and then feeling it being pulled down. If you don't attack the arm with movement, you will be giving your assailant a chance to respond and with a knife at your throat, even an unintended flinch response could be deadly. As you make the hook and pull down, pull your head/neck back, away from the knife—as part of your body defense.

Keep your attacker's arm pinned to your chest. One of the first things you should look to do when dealing with a knife, is to take away its movement—if it can't move, it can't cut you. Once the knife is clear of your neck, you should pull it into your chest, rather than continue pulling down.

Slide the thumb of your left hand around your attacker's wrist, keeping it pressed into your chest. Start to move your right hand around, so that it can also get a good grip on your assailant's wrist/arm.

Once you have a solid grip on their wrist, transition your left hand so that your thumb can be pushed into the back of your attacker's weapon hand. Ideally, you will want to apply pressure between the bones of the middle and ring finger, as this will start to open up your attacker's hand, loosening their grip on the knife.

Drive their hand down towards the center console.

You can pin it here with your right hand...

...and use your left hand to open the door and evacuate the vehicle. Once outside, head for a safe place (in any environment you are in, you should have a safe location that you head towards in the event of danger—this is part of your self-protection planning and preparedness).

Getting into Cars with Strangers

All of us have social networks; at the center are our close friends and family members who we have strong ties to and at the edges and peripheries are individuals we have weak ties to, e.g., former coworkers who we don't see anymore, old school friends we have lost touch with, etc. Bordering these peripheries are individuals who we may see regularly but don't actually know, such as parents who drop off and pick up their children from school at the same time as us, or fellow commuters. Outside of these loosest connections are those we think of as strangers. The truth is, most people are strangers to us outside of the contexts in which we experience them; e.g., we know how a coworker behaves and interacts with us in a workplace setting but we don't necessarily know how they would act and behave with us in a social setting where alcohol is involved, etc. If we've never experienced them in this setting before then they are, in this context, a stranger to us. This may seem a touch paranoid; however, predatory individuals are extremely good at shifting roles, so that we don't see or treat them as strangers.

One of the first personal safety rules that we are taught as children is not to get into a car with a stranger. Our parents probably gave us this rule when we asked if we could play in the front yard unsupervised. We were warned that if anybody pulled up and asked if we wanted to go with them to see some puppies or similar, we should refuse and then find a parent to tell them what had happened, etc. The problem with this personal safety rule of not getting into a car with a stranger is that even as adults we associate this rule with the same context, i.e., a stranger pulling up and asking us to get into their car, and while predators may target small children this way (though it's not the most common way children are targeted, either), they are going to use different methods and approaches to get their adult victims into their vehicles; they are going to shift their role so that they aren't seen as a stranger and thus, the rule of not getting into a car with a stranger won't seem to apply to them.

Predatory individuals know how to get us to recategorize and redefine them as something other than a stranger—they know we have safety "rules" around strangers and one of the quickest ways to disarm us, is to get us think about them as being something else. One situation in which we often tend to redefine strangers, is when on a date with them; even if we've never met them before, we start using the term "date" to refer to them, rather than stranger—and even if we do know them but haven't ever spent time with them in this context, we should still look on them, and treat them—from a personal safety perspective—as a stranger. If we meet somebody online and agree to go out with them, we can follow every good piece of safety advice we've been given, such as telling a friend where we will be meeting them, choosing a busy location etc. and still be at a huge disadvantage if the person we are going on a "date" with is a sexual predator.

Most sexual predators are extremely skilled social players who find ways of making themselves attractive to their victims. They may even give their victims the "illusion" of control—and thus get them to lower their guard—by letting them choose the time and location of where they meet. If you start to use the term "date" to describe your relationship with someone you have met online, you will have made the first step in not thinking of them as a stranger. Experienced predators possess great social skills and are extremely adept at putting their targets at ease. They know that in an initial meeting that you will be careful and guarded, and they will do everything they can to put you at ease, and allay any fears you may have about them. There is a good chance they will be good-looking, and charming—not fitting the stereotypical profile, of sexual predators being socially awkward and desperate characters.

The hope for any date is that it is successful; and the ultimate judge of whether it is successful or not is both parties wanting to see each other again. A sexual predator understands this. Towards the end of the meal, they may say something along the lines of, "This has been great, I haven't had such a great evening in a long time. It would be a shame to end the evening now. I know a great bar across town. Why don't we go and finish the evening up there? One drink, we don't have to stay out late as I know we both have work tomorrow. What do you say?" They've complemented their date, flattered them, and just given them a "second date" ahead of schedule—not only do they want to see them again, they're unable to wait to do so. Predators are extremely skilled at identifying what their victims want and then offering it to them. As the two walk to their cars, the predator may say, "Tell you what, let's take my car. It's stupid to take two, and it's not the easiest place to find. Come on, I'll be designated driver. I can drop you back here afterwards." They've just created a very socially awkward situation; something predatory individuals will do, knowing that most victims won't want to embarrass themselves by bringing up their safety concerns, or won't want to offend them by implying that there may be something nefarious about their behaviors/actions. With a bit more pressure and pushing, possibly questioning their dates concerns by stating that nothing untoward is going to happen, etc., there is a good chance that they'll convince them to get into their car. Despite believing that they'd never get into a car with a stranger, if their date wants to go for that drink with them (the "second date"), in many cases, they will.

This personal safety exception may have been made several times in the past with no bad outcomes, reinforcing to the person that it's unlikely any thing dangerous will happen on this occasion, either. There are no exceptions to personal safety—and to make them plays into the hands of the predators.

You may have read this thinking that the gender roles assigned involved a male predator and a female victim and that the motive was rape/sexual assault. While this could be the case, it doesn't necessarily have to be. There are dangerous and predatory women out there, and when we add weapons and accomplices there are no low-threat situations. It could be that the predator is a woman looking for male victims to involve in an express kidnapping—she drives you to a location where she meets an armed accomplice who then drives you to a series of ATMs, forcing you to make withdrawals; they may even keep you as a hostage overnight (or for a few days) locked in the trunk of the car so that they aren't limited by the daily withdrawal limit on your card—they may keep you hostage until your account is run dry. Men will often believe that their personal safety won't be compromised by a woman they feel they can physically overpower; however, criminals have used women to lure men since the beginning of time. Not getting into a car with a stranger is a piece of advice that applies to everyone.

Taxis and Ridesharing Services

One of the types of strangers we may interact with are "Known Strangers," these are individuals who we don't personally know, but who provide services that we may use, or that cause us to interact with. These can include police officers, delivery persons as well as taxi drivers and those working for ride sharing companies.

When considering which type of taxi/ridesharing service you should use, there are certain things from a personal safety perspective that you should consider. Personal safety isn't just about protecting yourself from violent individuals, it is far more extensive than this. One thing to consider is the risk of being injured in a road traffic accident and the possible consequences of that. It is worth checking which services limit the hours that a driver can work—in Boston, taxi-drivers sometimes work "Iron Shifts," driving for 24 hours straight; obviously getting into a car with a driver who hasn't slept for 23 hours poses a risk to your safety. It is also worth understanding the insurance that different providers are obligated to carry. You don't want to be involved in an accident where the provider's insurance is unable to cover your medical expenses. Different cities, states, and countries have different requirements and it is worth being up to date on these. If you travel to another location, this should be something you consider as part of your travel security preparations.

Regardless of which type of service you use, where you sit in a hired car effects your safety. The safest place for you to sit in a car is in the front passenger seat. Here, you can keep a closer eye on your driver, and you also have easier evacuation options than if you are in the backseat; e.g., the driver may have put the child locks on, preventing you from exiting through the rear doors.

One of the reasons a fight might go the "ground," and see both combatants on the floor, is if the environment dictates that this is how the fight must be fought. If you are attacked in a confined/enclosed space, such as a car, you will effectively be fighting and defending yourself as if you were on the ground. This is one of the reasons why you should practice ground-fighting in enclosed spaces, where there is little room to move and maneuver. You will need to check that your ground survival techniques and solutions are effective in these spaces, and possibly amend them accordingly if you find that they need space, and an even platform/surface to work, etc. If you think about the real-life situations in which you might end up on the ground, in many of them there will be objects such as furniture and/or crowds, that will restrict your movement and ability to perform certain techniques.

You may find yourself in a dangerous situation if your taxi/ridesharing driver pulls over into a deserted lot, in the course of your journey. If they have engaged the child locks on the back passenger doors, you won't be able to open them from the inside. This means that you will effectively be trapped in the back of the car, with the front passenger and driver's doors offering your only escape route. If the goal is to sexually assault you, the driver will likely climb over the center console in order to access you. For personal defense in confined spaces—such as cars, subway carriages etc.—a foam or gel pepper spray would be more suitable than a stream or cone, as there is less risk of cross-contamination, which might effect your ability to defend yourself.

As the driver starts to climb through, forcefully kick and stomp their chest. Brace yourself in the back seat so you can drive your kick into them with force. If you are able to, roll down/lower the window. If it only goes down part-way, take your mobile phone or other available object and start smashing the glass out. Start at the edges of the window (these are the weakest points) and use the corner of your phone—you want a small focused striking surface, rather than a large one. Car side windows are made of tempered glass and are extremely strong and resistant to large impacts, and so to break them, you need to concentrate your force. It is worth having in your own car a glass-breaking tool and seatbelt cutter, in case you ever get trapped inside; e.g., as part of a traffic accident.

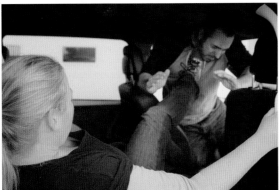

Use your kicks to buy you the time to get the window open or smashed so that you can reach through and open the door from the outside. Make noise if you can—there is always a chance that somebody may hear you and call the police —but at the same time don't rely on this happening. Shouting at your attacker will also help you regulate your breathing as it is common for people under stress and duress to hold their breath, exhausting themselves. Shouting also puts pressure on your attacker; they may grow concerned that someone could hear you—getting them to doubt a part of their plan (that they chose a deserted spot) may cause them to doubt other parts of it, as well.

If you are unable to get the door unlocked and exit the car, your attacker will eventually find a way to get control of your legs or get past your kicks—it is highly unlikely that you will be able to hold them back indefinitely or cause enough damage to stop their attack. Still, they should now be tired from the struggle/fight and be hesitant when dealing with you for fear of getting hurt. Sometimes in fighting for survival you move toward this goal by incremental steps, rather than in one single go. This truth of real-life violence rarely gets conveyed in self-defense classes, where students are often taught that a particular technique, will solve and instantly end a situation.

As the driver clambers through and tries to get control of your legs, bring your hands up, ready to control their head, and pull them between your legs. If you can control both their hips and their head, you will have complete control of them.

Grab their head and pull it forward into your chest. As they fall forward, wrap your legs around them, and pull them down towards you—you want to take away any support and base that they have, so that they're unable to either kneel or stand.

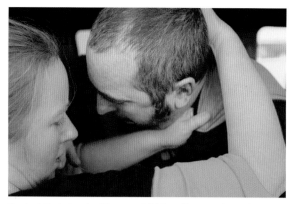

Control their head with your right hand/arm, and reach across their throat to the inside collar of their shirt or jacket, with your left hand. Hold the material firmly between your thumb and top two fingers.

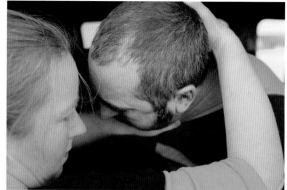

Don't pull the material around, but run it between your fingers, taking all the slack out of it, so that it is wrapped tightly around your attacker's neck. Keep your right hand/arm over the back of their head to keep them pulled close to you. If you have taken away their base/support, they will not be able to push themselves upright, onto their knees/legs.

You will now be left with all the loose material from the clothing in your left hand—pass this around the back of their neck, to your right hand.

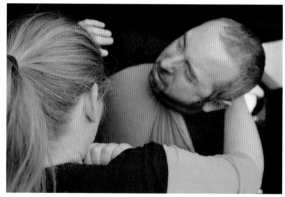

Pull down on the material, wrapping it tightly around your attacker's neck. It will be extremely difficult for them to resist this movement. You will also be restricting blood flow to the Carotid Processes, which will start to cause blood to be flushed from the brain—this clothing choke will eventually render them unconscious. This is not the primary goal/aim of the clothing wrap, which is to use the t-shirt to roll/pull your assailant of you; however, anything which debilitates your assailant will help to increase your survival chances.

Keep pulling down with your right arm, turning your attacker's head and body. You can assist your pulling motion, by pushing your attacker's nose, to help turn their head. Make your palm rigid, and angle it in along the side of your assailant's nose, at a 45-degree angle—think of the nose and the eye as forming a 90-degree angle and driving the ridge of your palm in at 45-degrees.

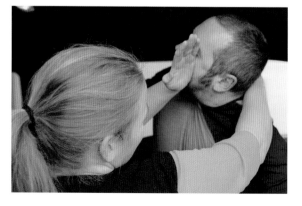

Once you have your aggressor's head and body turning, start to release the control you have on them with your legs. This leg control was intended initially to restrict your assailant's movement; however, you will now want them to be able to move, so that you can roll them off of you.

Keep pulling and pushing until you have completely rolled your attacker off you.

You should now be over the attacker, with them pushed into the floor/foot well. If necessary, slam palm-heel strikes into your attacker to stun them further. Don't get overly focused on these, and if you can escape without using them do so, as the longer you remain entangled with your assailant, the more likely it is that they'll find a way to get back in the fight.

As soon as you are able, clamber over the attacker and through the center console, so that you can bypass the child-locked rear doors, and exit through the front.

Use your attacker as part of the floor, pinning them down with your foot/feet as you escape. Make your way to what you can identify as the nearest populated area. If you are unable to do this by sight, because you are in a built-up area, listen for noises, such as the sound of traffic, that can help guide you.

Some of the photographs in this sequence have been taken with the rear passenger door open; this is for demonstration purposes to help capture what is happening—in reality, the scenario assumes that the rear doors have been child-locked and cannot be opened from the inside.

It is worth letting any driver you use know that you are familiar with your environment and the route(s) they may take. At the very least, this will prevent them from overcharging for your fare and at the other extreme, it will make them realize that if they change the route to take you to somewhere remote you will be aware of this at an earlier stage. Asking the driver which way they will go, and offering them two alternatives; e.g., "will you be taking Mystic Avenue to 93 to avoid the construction?" will give your driver an idea that you are familiar with the best way to get to your destination. If you are traveling in a foreign city, it is a good idea to study the different routes a driver might take from the airport to your hotel, etc. Let people know you are aware of your environment.

It is a good idea with any taxi or ridesharing service not to have them pick you up or drop you off at your house or work, but rather have them meet you one street over. This may be slightly inconvenient, however, it prevents the driver from knowing where you live and gives you the freedom to report them for any inappropriate behaviors or misconduct, etc., without the fear of any reprisals; e.g., if because of your complaint they are fired from their job, they will not be able to find/locate you.

A good personal safety habit to get into is not to discuss or reveal too much information about yourself to strangers including "known strangers." Criminals and predators are always on the lookout for information that might be of value and use to them. Often, people in taxis and ridesharing services are uncomfortable with being driven in silence and will strike up/take part in conversations with their driver and end up over-sharing information with them. There is also a sense that because this driver is someone we are unlikely to see again that we may give away private details that we'd be more guarded about if it was someone that knew us—this is why people will often unburden themselves to complete strangers, such as a fellow passenger on a train or airplane (the close proximity of being next to each other can create a sense of false intimacy). Predatory individuals are also skilled at getting people to open up about things they'd otherwise keep private. One way they do this is to use our natural urge to reciprocate; i.e., if someone tells us something intimate, we will feel the need to reciprocate by sharing something private about ourselves. We do this to keep the relationship with the other person "balanced," and so as not to create an uncomfortable atmosphere; it is less socially awkward if we are both talking about private things than if only one of us is.

It would be incorrect to say that all or even many taxi and ridesharing drivers are criminals/predators; however, it is a job where a lot of information that can be useful to a criminal can be gathered; e.g., if you have a taxi driver pick you up to take you and your family to the airport, they can easily find out where you are going, and for how long, and make a judgment based on this and your luggage, whether there will be items of value in your house, etc. It may be that they themselves aren't an "active" criminal, but will pass this information on to those who are.

Ridesharing services are often used by those avoiding having to drink after driving, looking to get away from a potentially unsafe location etc. In the realm of personal safety, these services can be useful and have their place. As with all safety measures, we need to be aware that we could be trading one risk for another. Proper planning/awareness of our routes, knowing where to sit in the car, and knowing how to defend ourselves in confined spaces, can drastically improve our survival chances should our driver harbor harmful intent towards us.

External Dangers When Driving

We are creatures of habit, and spend a lot of our lives following pre-written scripts. Predatory individuals understand this and will use these scripts against us. If we are involved in a road traffic accident with another vehicle, our default behavior will be to get out of our car, to inspect the damage and exchange insurance details. It is likely that we will do this without thinking—and this may be the reaction that a predator relies upon. If the accident occurs in a remote area, and it looks as though it may be deliberate/set up, e.g., you are rear-ended on an open road where there are no other vehicles—you may want to consider whether getting out of your car is a safe option, especially if you are on your own, and the other car has multiple adult occupants. By having photocopies of your license and insurance details in your car, you can cut down on the interaction you have with the other party and remain in your vehicle simply handing these through a gap in your window. You can ask the other driver to hold their documents against your window so that you can photograph them with your mobile phone.

Be aware of what information about yourself is available to others who may have access to your car, such as valet services. If you keep your registration documents in your glove compartment, then they will know where you live, and if you haven't separated your car keys from your house keys, this will enable them and/or others to burgle your house while you are out to dinner. Make it easy for yourself to separate your car keys from your others when using valet services. There are key rings specifically designed to detach just one key for this purpose.

If when driving, another car pulls up alongside you and a passenger points a gun at you, motioning for you to pull over, don't try to speed up in an attempt to out-run them. You will not be able to drive faster than a bullet. Instead, slam on your brakes, and let the other car go past you. Make a quick U-turn, and drive to a safe location; e.g., a police station, hospital, or populated area, etc. If the car also turns to follow you, empty your can of OC spray out of the window (you should have a can in the door of your car when driving, just don't leave it there as extremes in temperature can interfere with it), to create a cloud of spray behind you. There's a good chance this will be sucked up by the other car's ventilation system, affecting everyone in the car, including the driver who won't be able to see. (Note that this is an extreme response to an extreme threat, and should only be used as a last resort, as pepper spraying someone as they drive can endanger others on the road.)

If you believe that you are being followed, you may want to check that the car behind you has actually synchronized their car's movement to yours. You can do this covertly or overtly, i.e., not letting the other driver know that you have picked up on the fact that they are following you or making it clear to them that you have. A clear way to test, and also demonstrate that you know you are being followed, is to keep driving around a traffic circle, or make only left or right turns, so that you are driving in circles—if the car behind you copies your movements, it is a good bet that they are following you, for whatever reason; and you will have demonstrated to them that you know this. A more covert way to check if someone is following you, is to take a right turn, followed by two lefts, and another right, which will put you back on to the original road that you turned off from—there is no legitimate reason that another car would have replicated your movements, when they could have simply driven straight on. If you do pick up on the fact that someone is following you, make for a safe location, such as a police station—part of your self-protection planning should be to know where these, and other safe places are located within the environments you frequent.

If your way is blocked by protesters or a crowd when driving, and none of the members of the group are threatening you or putting you at risk, you will be on extremely dodgy legal territory if you attempt to drive through them; even if you try and do this slowly and in a controlled manner. It is always good to keep up to date through the news, and social media, as to where there might be areas of civil unrest, demonstrations, etc. This will allow you to choose alternative routes and avoid these locations.

If your way is blocked by an angry mob, who is clearly threatening you (and has the ability to cause you harm—such as having bricks, and similar that they can launch at your vehicle), and you have no room to turn your car around and disengage, you may consider abandoning your vehicle, or driving through the group in front of you. If you don't believe you can evacuate your vehicle and get to safety, you may be forced to drive through the group—this will only be successful if you can get beyond them, otherwise the crowd will swarm over you and your vehicle. Drive at a consistent speed, where you can force people out of the way, without knocking them down, where they may get trapped under your car; your goal should be to give everybody a chance to move away from your car while recognizing that if your survival is threatened, you will need to do whatever is necessary to defend yourself, and those in your car.

How you hold the steering wheel when driving is also important as you don't want to break your fingers/thumbs if involved in an accident. The air bag may deploy to prevent a serious concussion in the event of a collision; however, in the moment before this happens, or in the case that the airbag doesn't deploy, your hands may come off the steering wheel, breaking your thumbs.

If you drive holding the steering wheel with your thumbs wrapped around it, it is likely that if you are involved in a collision, or you have to brake with extreme force, that your thumbs will be broken, as your arms/body are flung forward—the air bag should deploy before your head hits the steering wheel, and your seat belt should limit some of your body's forward momentum; however, as soon as your hands slip off the wheel during impact, your thumbs will likely break.

By resting your thumbs on top of the wheel when you drive, you will prevent this from happening. If your hands come off the wheel during a collision, your thumbs won't get caught on the wheel and be broken. In tactical driving, the airbag may be disabled to prevent deployment in a collision that could impede the driver. If the airbag is operational, a hand position at nine and three o'clock will prevent some of the common injuries from airbag deployment.

Side-of-the-Road Carjackings

In certain countries, geographies, and regions it is not uncommon for drivers to be held up at junctions and traffic lights. In some instances, it is possible to time your approach to traffic lights so that you won't have to stop your vehicle, however, this isn't always possible, and there may be times when you find yourself in a stationary vehicle having to deal with an armed assailant(s). One of the reasons a carjacker or carjacking gang may use a junction is that if the road approaching the junction is long, it gives them time to identify a car that they may be stealing to order, e.g., there is a prearranged buyer for a particular make/model. A group may position themselves along a road and either observe the car from a distance or have an accomplice positioned further up the road who can call/text/signal those at the junction when a suitable vehicle has been spotted—when it approaches, they can have a decoy walk across the road, forcing the car to slow down or stop.

One of the major reasons why a criminal may choose to "jack" your vehicle while you are in it, rather than break-in and steal it at a time when you are not there, is the improved alarms and security systems that are fitted in modern cars. An expensive car is likely to have an expensive alarm and/or immobilizer which will prevent the car from being started without the presence of a key fob, etc. Rather than try to bypass and overcome these systems, it is often easier and less time consuming (and requires no technical knowledge) to take the car when the driver has already started it and switched off the alarm system. This also means that if the car has a steering lock, it doesn't have to be broken and then repaired before selling it on—this might not be so important if the car is stolen so as to be used in another crime such as a get-away car or in a "ram-raiding" incident—in which an SUV or estate/station wagon is reversed through a shop-front/window in order to burgle the place.

The greater the technical improvements in security become, the more likely it is that criminals will involve the owners of the assets they are trying to steal in order to bypass these systems. This is the same for home security as it is for vehicular security; e.g., home invasions will start to replace burglaries in certain instances, just as carjackings replace car theft. This is referred to as "functional displacement."

When you approach an intersection, widen your field of vision, so you are not just looking straight ahead at the car in front of you. This will allow you to observe the actions and behaviors of people near the junction. Don't tailgate the car in front of you. You will want to have enough space to maneuver around it if necessary. If you can see the bottom of the tires, and some road behind the car, you will have sufficient room to move around it in the event of a threat/danger (even if this means mounting a curb, etc.). If you lose sight of the tires, you will have to reverse first, in order to get past it and if there are other vehicles lined up behind you, this may not be possible.

A common tactic in carjackings is for an attacker to make out that they're crossing the road, forcing traffic to stop. There are other ways to do this, such as having a person lie in the road, pretending to have been hit by a car, and in need of medical assistance—or even staging a road traffic accident. (Predatory individuals and groups will often look to take advantage of people's good nature, setting up scenarios that create an opportunity for someone to be a "good samaritan".) Two people may work together; one stopping the traffic, while the other approaches the car, using the blind-spot in the side mirror so that their approach goes unseen.

Look to your side, as well as to the front, when you are stationary, and use your mirrors to assist you in getting a 360-degree view of your environment. If you see a threat or potential danger, consider whether you can exit the scene safely...

...and if you can, do so. Whether you were the original target or not, if you are no longer in the environment, they won't be able to target you.

If you are targeted for a carjacking, you may be told to lower the window, so that you can listen to and follow your assailant's commands and instructions. If these involve you getting out of your vehicle, so that it can be stolen, you should comply. There is no reason to risk getting shot trying to protect a resource asset, such as your car. Alternatively, you may be instructed to stay in your vehicle, and release the central locking, so that the second assailant can get into the car with you—possibly to search you while you are physically trapped, with a gun pointed at you, and can't respond. This is where you must decide whether it is safer to comply or enact a physical solution.

If you believe that the incident doesn't seem like a situation where your attackers just want to take your car, you may decide that your best survival option, is to try and disarm your attacker of their weapon. To do this, you will need to make the assumption that if the second assailant had a weapon, they would have shown it by this point—sometimes we have to reach decisions, without having all the information, because we don't have the time or the means to gather everything we may want in order to be fully informed of our situation. Have as an automatic response, that whenever somebody threatens you with a weapon, you shrug your shoulders up to indicate that you are scared, and bring your hands close to the weapon— this should look natural and non-threatening.

Your initial defense should see you grab the wrist and push the gun away from you, while bringing your other hand towards the barrel. Try to push yourself back in the seat, using your feet to drive you back, so that you have some form of body defense, to accompany this.

While you are seated—without the ability to stand up—and your attacker is upright and mobile, your priority has to be to prevent your attacker from retraining their weapon onto you. To do this, once you have both hands controlling your attacker's weapon, and weapon arm, pull them across your body, and at the same time bring your elbow over their arm, in order to lock it to your body.

Once your assailant's arm is trapped, slam them into the side of the car. This disruption should interrupt any thoughts they had in the moment about trying to retain their weapon.

Keeping your attacker's arm trapped—even if they try to pull back, your elbow will be pulled into the car door, preventing you (and the weapon) from being pulled any further—start to turn the gun, using the barrel as a lever to break your attacker's grip on it, and open up their hand.

Keep turning the gun until you have released it...

...and then throw your attacker's arm away from you and quickly drive off.

Targeting of Vehicles and Individuals

Much of our non-anecdotal research and understanding around carjackings comes out of South Africa where this is an extremely common crime. It should be noted that a crime in one geography doesn't necessarily define the crime in another; however, in many types/areas of violence there is a degree of universality and so there are many lessons that can be learnt and translated from events in a particular locale.

In many cases, gangs/individuals will target specific vehicles (either because they are high-priced, highly-valued—because of their reliability—or are otherwise desirable or in demand, whether for parts or as an entire vehicle), but they will also occasionally target the individual(s) in the car. It is worth noting that there are primary and secondary motives that are involved in all violent crimes. It may be that the primary motive is to obtain a specific vehicle, however those that engage in such illegal activities are also motivated by anger, and the need for power and control. It would be naïve to think that such motivations aren't present in violent crimes. This may mean that they target the individual, rather than the vehicle. Many South African carjackers have stated that they enjoyed the power and control that they had over their victims, and at times found themselves targeting those who dressed in expensive suits, or who were seen to put on the central locking when in their presence, etc. just to teach them a lesson. In security terms, it is always best to be the "Grey Man," the person who doesn't stand out in any way, but simply blends with the crowd.

In many instances, there are different roles that individuals play in a carjacking, and it is worth understanding what these are so that you don't fall into the trap of thinking that you are only dealing with one individual. In carjackings committed by groups, there are usually three distinct roles, sometimes performed by the same individuals, but sometimes not. These are (Davis, 1999):

1. The Pointer—The individual pointing the weapon.
2. The Driver—The person who will drive the vehicle.
3. The Searcher—The person responsible for searching the victim and the vehicle for items of value.

It may not always be apparent that these roles are performed by separate individuals; however, it would be risky to assume that someone who seems to be an individual attacker is actually alone. Rather, it is better to scan and look around you to see if other individuals are involved before acting/responding to the threat/danger.

Although carjackings seem to be the preserve of young men, women can also be involved, often given the role of slowing vehicles down, causing them to stop, or engaging with drivers in parked vehicles, etc.

Driving/Travelling In Foreign Countries—Kidnapping and Hostage Taking

We tend to think of kidnapping as a relatively simple crime whereby a person gets taken by an individual/gang and held until a ransom is paid; however, there are many different types of kidnapping—some physical and some virtual—and it is worth understanding them so that we can understand the different types of kidnapping threats we may face and our vulnerabilities to them. This will enable us to make effective risk-assessments and put appropriate security/counter-measures in place to prevent and deal with them. The main types of kidnapping are as follows:

1. **Basic Kidnapping**—These are where individuals who are deemed to have sufficient resources to pay for a ransom (but not for security personnel, etc.) are taken and held until a specified amount is paid. The ransom amounts are normally small enough that they can be paid relatively easily and in a short period of time. A tourist or business traveler in a foreign country may have more value to a kidnapper in this geography than when at home; e.g., $3,000 or $4,000 in the U.S. may be too small an amount for a criminal to risk kidnapping someone for, but in a South American country this may be considered a large enough amount of money to make the risk of kidnapping someone worthwhile.

2. **High Net Worth Kidnapping**—These are the kidnappings that are featured in Hollywood movies, ones that involve experienced gangs targeting multi-millionaires who enjoy a high level of security and demanding extremely large ransoms. The Planning and Preparation Phases in these types of kidnappings are long and involved and the ransoms reflect the time, personnel, resources and energy that go into them.

3. **Tiger Kidnappings**—These involve a gang or individual taking someone hostage in order to force another person to comply with a demand/engage in another criminal activity; e.g., the family of a bank manager may be taken hostage while he is forced to provide a gang entry to the bank where he works along with his security pass/entry codes, etc.

4. **Express Kidnappings**—An individual or group abducts an individual and takes them to a series of ATMs to withdraw money. The victim may be held overnight to get around daily withdrawal limits—in fact, they may be held until the account has been run dry. In some cases, this will be a feature of a Basic Kidnapping where a person will be held for ransom, and during that time also have money withdrawn from their account. Those paying the ransom may be loathe to freeze the account during this time in case it puts the hostage at risk.

5. **Virtual Kidnappings**—The perpetrators wait until they are sure their victim is unreachable, such as travelling in a foreign country with poor communications, and then "pretend" that they have taken them hostage, demanding that a ransom be paid for their safe return. These types of "kidnappings" have to be conducted quickly and before the person who was supposedly kidnapped is able to be reached. This makes the ransom relatively small. Criminals will often use social media to search for these types of victims, looking for individuals who post that they will not be able to be contacted for a certain period of time due to travel, etc.

6. **Political Kidnappings**—These are where individuals are taken hostage in order to affect political change. The main issue in most of these incidents is that there is little room for negotiation, unlike in kidnappings in which money is involved.

7. **Child & Spousal Kidnappings**—In the U.S., these are the most common types of kidnappings and usually involve an ex-partner or estranged wife/husband, taking their children and/or the ex-partner hostage; usually without any predefined ransom terms in place; e.g., when hostage

negotiators track them down and ask what their demands are, they usually haven't yet thought about this.

8. **Bridal Kidnappings**—These are common in certain cultures and communities and represent a form of "forced marriage," where a groom kidnaps his bride—often raping her to convince her to stay and settle down with him. In many of these cultures once she has lost her virginity, she will be viewed as worthless by her family and community so she may feel that she has no choice but to stay with her "new husband."

Crime and violent crime are often geographically specific; e.g., bridal kidnappings are more common in central Asia and Africa than they are in North America; this is not to say they don't take place within certain communities in the U.S. and Canada, etc. just that they occur less frequently than Child & Spousal Kidnappings—which make up the most common type of kidnapping in the U.S.—and although Express Kidnappings are committed every day in the U.S.; they do not take place with the same frequency, or complexity/organization as they do in South America, etc. Express Kidnappings in the U.S. tend to be single-transaction events, involving one ATM and one withdrawal, as opposed to those in South America, where a person might be held for several days, to get around daily withdrawal limits.

A crime that may be profitable in one location, region or country may not be worthwhile in another. The limited resources that a targeted person has may not be enough to pay a ransom in one locale but will be sufficient in another; for example, the costs and risks of kidnapping an individual in the U.S. may make the ransom too large for most "easy" targets to pay; however, in Mexico this may not be the case. This means that your risk for kidnapping goes up and down as you move from region to region. Being aware of this will allow you to take precautions and reduce your vulnerabilities when you travel.

It is generally easier to provide security for physical assets than it is for people; e.g., a house or building can be fitted with secure locks, restricted entry systems, alarm systems, etc. All of these things are designed to prevent unwanted access, by putting physical and technological barriers in place that make it extremely difficult for criminals to gain entry. People are much more difficult to protect—it is much harder to prevent access to a person than it is to a building or other physical space. One of the times when a person is most at risk is when they are traveling, whether they are walking, driving, taking public transport, or taxis/ridesharing services. In these types of situations, it is hard to prevent criminals from gaining access to them—unless there is an extensive team of CPOs (Close Protection Officers), protecting them at all times; and even then, it is often possible for a criminal(s) to get close enough to an individual to cause them harm. When in a foreign country, and/or unfamiliar city, it is worth recognizing this risk and employing some basic safety habits/procedures in order to restrict and limit your vulnerabilities.

If you are visiting a foreign country and will be driving, there are certain security precautions that are always worth taking. You should procure for yourself an IDP (International Driving Permit), this allows you—along with your own driver's license—to legally drive in a foreign country (if you are hiring a car, this may well be a requirement of certain letting agencies). One of the benefits of having an IDP, is that you can use it as a form of ID in place of your passport when driving—in some countries, where the police are susceptible to corruption, they may take/confiscate your passport if you are involved in a minor traffic infraction, making it difficult for you to get it back, without paying a bribe or granting a favor. If you will be driving in such regions, or if you don't want to carry your passport on you at all times, this is a good alternative form of ID. As with all documents that you take with you when traveling, make sure that you have both a photocopy of them (a physical backup), as well as an electronic copy available to you—don't just have one stored on your phone as this could be stolen, but instead email copies to yourself so that whatever happens to your belongings, you will always have access to them.

We often have a tendency to trust hotel staff—they can appear to act as a bridge between us and the local community, e.g., they speak the language, know the customs, what the appropriate cost/prices of things are, and can direct us to local attractions. But we should understand that those who work in the hospitality industry are usually poorly paid and may be involved with the criminal fraternity so we should not be overly trusting of them. You should not to use hotel staff to book transport, such as taxis and the like, and instead take responsibility for this yourself, e.g., they may well set you up with a driver who has criminal/harmful intent towards you.

You may find yourself taken by your driver to a quiet part of town, where a gunman steps in front of the car waving a gun, forcing it to stop. They may open the door and pull you out—looking to transfer you to another vehicle. It may well be that hotel staff are involved, and have been through your room, ascertaining whether you are someone who has resources/access to money, and whose family and/or business will be able to pay a significant ransom.

If you had checked the route beforehand and kept an eye on the road, you should have realized that the route the driver was taking was moving you away from, rather than nearer to, your destination. At this point, you could have threatened to call the police/security forces if he didn't amend the route. If you had taken a photograph of the car's license plate before you got into the vehicle, you could text/email it to a friend or associate with instructions to contact the police, etc. upon realizing you might be in trouble. You could also take a surreptitious photo of your driver, when you get in the car, and send this as well.

Your assailant may now grab you in a side headlock, and put a gun to your head. Immediately, bring your near hand up as close to the gun as you can, and tell them that they can have your wallet, phone, anything that they want, etc. This will appear as a totally natural response when being manhandled and controlled in this way. Bend your legs, so that your body is upright, rather than allowing your attacker to bend you at the waist, which is what they will be trying to do; i.e., they will try to break your frame and posture so that you are bent forward and in too awkward a position to do anything.

In this position, it will be impossible for you to move your head—the reason your assailant is holding/controlling you in this way—and so all of your defense will rely on you clearing the gun, so that you are not in the line of fire. Rapidly bring your hand up, catching the barrel of the gun between your thumb and index finger. You will need to grab and secure it as you move it—don't grab and then try to move it, as this will give your attacker a moment in which to act, while the gun is still pointed at you. At this point, you have value to your abductor—they may need your pin number if it is a express kidnapping, or may need you alive for another purpose—and so they will be less likely to be thinking about using the gun at this stage. At this moment, it is a tool to force you to comply with their demands.

As you move/grab the gun, spear your right hand through the gap between your assailant's weapon arm and their body, in order to be able to control their weapon arm, to prevent them from pulling the firearm away from your grip. You will need to secure both the weapon and their weapon arm to prevent them from retaining the gun.

Rather than "grab" the weapon arm in a conventional grip using the thumb—which may see you get your thumb caught on clothing—when you spear it through, keep the thumb and the fingers together and form a hook, and use it to pull their arm into their body. At the same time, keep rotating the barrel away from you. Wherever possible when disarming weapons, try to turn them towards your assailant, to give them a problem they must deal with; i.e., put them in the line of fire, rather than simply directing the barrel away.

As you rotate the barrel, start to stand up/straighten. Use a combination of your shoulders pushing up, under your attacker's armpit/arm, and pulling in on their weapon arm, to start to compromise their balance. Continue to rotate the barrel of the weapon, away from you.

Once your hand is over your attacker's, push down forcefully to release the weapon—rather than continue rotating it.

Once you have the weapon in your hand, slam the barrel into your attacker's face. Repeat as many times as necessary to force their grip around your head/neck to loosen enough to pull away. In close-quarter situations it is often better to use the weapon "cold" rather than "hot", to deliver concussive force against your assailant, to render them unconscious. Despite the impression that movies may give about the effectiveness of firearms, shooting someone may not immediately stop them, depending on where they are hit and the caliber of the bullet, etc. and so it may be quicker and more effective to strike them with the weapon, until they are disabled and no longer a threat.

As soon as you can get away, do so—keeping the gun close to you and as unnoticeable as possible, so that you don't get mistaken for your attacker by any law enforcement or security personnel who may have received a call that an armed assailant is in the area. This is where it is good to understand the areas and routes that a driver may pass through and use in getting you to your destination, so that if you are stopped along the way, or involved in a road traffic accident, you will be able to make your way to safety. In this situation, you won't know where you are, and should head for populated areas, with the weapon concealed.

Although it is rarely experienced, other than when being controlled by trained individuals, it is worth understanding and knowing how to escape from holds such as the "Full Nelson." This attack is an effective way to immobilize an individual and isolate/restrict their arms. If somebody knows how to apply this hold effectively, they will raise one arm higher than the other, taking your spine out of alignment and tilting you to one side. Unfortunately, this manner of applying it will nullify many "standard" and conventional escapes.

As you are pulled/bundled out of the car, your assailant may move behind you, in preparation for controlling you using a Full Nelson. Obviously, if you can prevent them from moving behind you, and deal with them combatively—or run and make an effective escape—this would be preferential; however, if you have been taken by surprise and your movement compromised, this may not have been possible.

Once your attacker elevates your arms, and pushes on the back of your neck/head, you will find it difficult to move. Many conventional/standard escapes from this hold will see you end up on the ground or in another disadvantaged position. This may be acceptable if you are engaged in a one-on-one fight, where there are no time constraints; however, in an abduction scenario where there may be multiple individuals involved, surviving a situation using incremental steps (improving your situation bit-by-bit) may not be an effective option.

As soon as you feel that your arms are being lifted up, raise them both and reach behind your head...

...to grab your assailant's hand/fingers. You may have to feel for which is their top hand. If their left hand is on top, use your left hand to work the fingers, if it is their right, use your right hand.

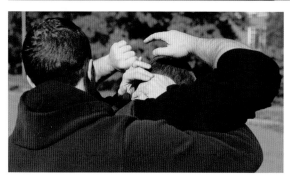

Peel one off—the little finger/pinky finger, will offer the least resistance, and be easier to bend away from the hand.

Start to bend the finger back to pull your attacker's arm away, releasing their control of you, and the pressure on the back of your neck/head.

As you pull down on their finger, bring your other arm (your right) explosively down to break your assailant's control of it—you will end up pinning your attacker's arm to your side.

As soon as your right arm is free, grab your attacker's wrist so that they are unable to turn/twist out to relieve the pressure on their finger. This way, you can control your attacker's movement/direction.

Apply pressure to your attacker's finger to force them to the ground. Any pain that you inflict upon an assailant is not for its own sake, or to punish them, it is to create opportunities for you; either by putting them in a disadvantaged position, or by taking the fight out of them. Any person who attacks you—regardless of your relationship with them—should be seen as a problem that needs to be solved. At the moment they attack you, you should not think of them as anything else. Do not care for their well-being or the pain that they have to endure, simply deal with them as a problem that must be nullified, so that you can get away.

Once you are free from your attacker's control, start moving—don't stay to examine their condition, or whether you need to apply further force, etc. If you have an opportunity to make distance and disengage, take it. The only important factor in this equation is your safety and survival.

Conclusion

Reality-based self-defense means looking at what our realities are. If we are people who spend time in a car, whether driving or as a passenger, we need to know how to defend ourselves in and around vehicles—this is our reality. Fighting when in a car means knowing how to fight within confined environments and when on our backs/on the ground, with restricted space, etc. Our training must reflect this reality and prepare us for it. More importantly, we should look at the preventative measures that we can take in order to avoid having to physically defend ourselves in these situations.

It is estimated by the American Automobile Association (AAA) that Americans on average spend seven 40-hour weeks in their car every year. That is a significant part of anyone's life. Understanding the risks and dangers associated with being in a vehicle and looking at ways in which these can be mitigated and dealt with deserve our attention. Even if we don't drive, we likely use cars in some form—either as a passenger in a friend's car, or as a client/user of a taxi/rideshare service—and so we should know how we can successfully prevent and deal with physical assaults in this environment.

PART III

Home Invasions

Risk is not universal. The level of risk one person has regarding certain crimes, may differ to others based on a variety of factors, including geography; e.g., you are more likely to be the victim of a crime involving a firearm if you live in the U.S. as opposed to the UK, and you are statistically more likely to experience gun violence in Chicago than in Boston; there are also areas in Boston where you are more likely to face an armed assailant than in Chicago. Therefore, a one-size-fits-all approach to determining risk just isn't effective. It is impossible to draw up a definitive list of the most likely or common attacks that people may face. There is no way for such a list to be appropriate for every demographic and group—the types of attacks that women will face, for example, are often very different to those faced by men. It is not just geography and gender which affect risk, age also comes into play. When it comes to social violence, you are much more likely to be involved in a violent confrontation if you are in your twenties than if in your forties. There are obviously exceptions to this, as your lifestyle choices—such as who your friends are, and the places you socialize in—can see you exposed to more violence, than a younger person. When you go to assess risk, all of these things need to be considered. While anyone can be targeted for a home invasion, there are demographics and locales, which will be more at risk than others; if you are a middle-class homeowner in South Africa, your risk is statistically higher—all other things being equal—than if you are a middle-class homeowner in a quiet suburban town in the U.S. When we try to ascertain the level of risk we face, we must look at the types of threats that are appropriate to our situations/lifestyle.

Although we tend to think of home invasions as being financially motivated, there are in fact a myriad of reasons why someone may target you, while you are in your home; e.g., an ex-partner may force their way into your home, to kidnap you and your children, because they've been declined visitation rights. In the U.S., most of the hostage situations that the FBI has to deal with, involve ex-partners and family members; rather than terrorist or criminal groups. Kidnapping is actually a much more "ordinary" affair than the typical Hollywood depiction. The fact that there can be many motives and reasons behind a home invasion has meant that many countries, regions, and states don't have a distinct legal definition of what a home invasion is; e.g., is a home invasion in which a homeowner is tied up and forced to reveal where they keep their valuables the same as one in which an ex-partner forces their way in to their old house and kidnaps their own children? In such cases, the individuals committing these crimes would be tried on several offenses, such as breaking and entering, assault, kidnapping, hostage taking, etc., rather on a singular crime of "home invasion." For the purposes of this section, we will define home invasion as the forced entry of a private home with the intent to commit a violent crime such as robbery, assault, kidnapping, etc.

Home Invasions vs. Burglaries

Burglars, when they select a property, are looking for unoccupied houses and apartments—this is why most residential burglaries happen during the day when people are at work—whereas those individuals and groups looking to procure valuables by way of a home invasion want the homeowners to be present. They may want them present for several reasons:

1. They don't know how to bypass the alarm system so they will target the property when the system is switched off—when somebody is in the house.
2. They need the occupants to open a safe or disable a security code.
3. They need the homeowner to direct them to where valuables/cash are hidden.
4. They want to rob the homeowner as well as the house; e.g., take their cash and credit cards as well as items in the house or commit an "express kidnapping" in addition to the home invasion; i.e., drive the owner to a series of ATMs (they may even keep them hostage overnight to get around daily withdrawal limits).
5. They want to steal the homeowner's car as well as rob them.

There may even be secondary motives at play; e.g., as part of the robbery, they may plan to rape/sexually assault the homeowner, etc. Unfortunately, many of the things which will deter a burglar—such as signs of occupancy—will act as a "green light" to somebody looking to commit a home invasion. Burglars are largely non-confrontational characters who don't plan on interacting with anyone. Most burglars, if disturbed in the midst of their crime, will take the chance to disengage if given one, whereas the exact opposite is true of those conducting home invasions; they are looking to use violence or the threat of violence to force the occupants to comply with their demands.

It isn't only the wealthy who are targeted for theft-motivated home invasions. One group that is at high risk of such criminal acts are those who are socioeconomically disadvantaged, who may not have bank accounts, and therefore store all of their wealth in cash. There are many groups and individuals who will specifically target such individuals, especially immigrant families who may have several members of the household working cash-in-hand jobs or who have to cash in their paycheck each week because they don't have a bank account. In such cases, the group will generally target the home when there is just one family member present and the others are out at work; this may be an elderly parent/grandparent who will be less able to defend themselves. After forcing entry, the individual will be forced to reveal where the cash in the house is hidden, either through the use of violence, or the threat of it.

One common characteristic of many home invasions—especially when information is required from the homeowner such as the location of valuable items, the combination to a safe, etc.—is the extreme force and violence that is used, greater than is needed to force compliance and/or subjugation. Often, the initial beating that is dealt upon entry, or when first coming into contact with the homeowner(s), is severe and brutal and acts as a warning against any future thoughts of resistance or escape. The goal of this is to terrify the victim to the point where they will be a passive and "willing" accomplice in the crime. Overwhelming violence is a potent tool in forcing compliance and preventing resistance. This is why it is important to either quickly engage and/or disengage, as you will be dealing with individuals who are committed, aggressive, and looking to physically, emotionally, and psychologically incapacitate you. The only way to deal with extreme violence is with greater violence, or by not being there; i.e., quick and immediate disengagement.

Methods of Entry—Forcing a Door

Most people, when they open their front door, aren't expecting somebody to charge in, and aren't prepared to deal with the surprise of somebody forcing their entry. It may be that the person forcing their way in, was at the bank where you made a substantial withdrawal; and although you may have taken precautions against being mugged, such as distributing the cash about your person, and taking well populated routes home, etc. you may not have picked up on the fact that you were being followed. Your attacker may have waited a few moments, for you to drop your guard, before ringing the doorbell, or knocking on your door.

If someone has targeted you for a home invasion, opening the door to them, may see them charge into you, knocking you backward. Staying on your feet is almost always preferable to going to ground, but it isn't always possible. Terrain can be a big determining factor for stability, and although you may train on a flat and level surface, you should not expect your terrain/environment to reflect that.

If your foot gets caught on a rug or similar, you could lose your balance. If you feel that your balance has been compromised, start to lower your weight. If you are going to have to drop to the ground and perform a breakfall, the shorter the height from which you have to fall, the better. Many people make the mistake of trying to "drop" from the height at which they realize they have lost balance, rather than first lowering themselves. As you fall, bring your hands up to protect your face, in case your attacker tries to strike you.

As you lower yourself down—think of it as simply sitting down (this is the way that babies learning to walk break their fall)—raise one foot into the air, making sure that you keep looking at it, as you drop. This will force you to tuck your chin into your chest, and prevent your head from snapping back and hitting the floor. Your breakfall will have failed you if you are unconscious due to a concussion. As you land, start to bring your arms out and down (palms down), and slap the floor.

Keeping one foot on the floor, roll back, and lift your hips off the floor, elevating your leg, and aiming it squarely at your assailant's chest. Don't direct it at their groin. If you kick your attacker in the groin, it is likely that they will double over, and possibly fall on top of you. There are very few occasions in which you will want to deliberately bring an attacker to ground with you. Kicking the chest gives you a large target to aim at, and will allow you to move your assailant backward, rather than double them over.

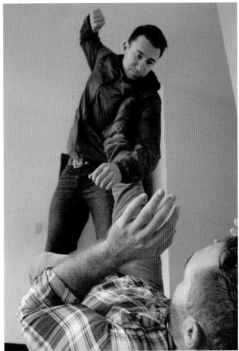

If your attacker bends over in order to try and punch you they will provide you with a "flat" target to kick, which will allow your kick to be fully absorbed. Keep your hands up by your head—there is always the chance in any situation—including ground—for multiple assailants to get involved, and it is good to be able to protect your head, in case a second assailant suddenly appears and starts aiming kicks towards it. You should not need your hands to stabilize yourself, so they may as well be in position to defend yourself.

Forcefully kick your assailant back, driving through with your hips; extend them as part of the kick.

As soon as you have the room and time to get up, do so. In reality, you may have to keep delivering kicks repeatedly to create the necessary space. To get up, place the same side arm/hand (in this case the right) as your kicking leg close to your hip, and lift yourself up. Your left supporting leg and your right arm, form two diagonally opposite corners that you can use as a base, from which to lift yourself up.

Keep your left arm up in front of you as you stand up, and back away from your attacker. Try to create the range and distance to give yourself time to react/respond, should your attacker attempt to continue their assault. It may be that they decide to back away, because what they thought would be a simple smash and grab has become more complicated, or it could be that, now they have gained entry to your house, they will not want to give up this opportunity.

We never want to assume that every action we take will have the desired effect, so we will look at ways to deal with an assailant who reacts/responds to your kick by stepping back—or slowing their advance—so that it doesn't connect with them. If an attacker can avoid being pushed/knocked back, they will be able to continue their assault while you are still on the ground.

As you go to make the kick, your attacker may anticipate what you are planning to do, and instead of continuing to move forward on to the kick, arrest their movement, and instead grab your leg.

Here, they could throw it to the side, so that it is no longer an obstacle to them...

...and step over it, to deliver a stomp kick to your head. Immediately, bring your arm up, to make an Inner-Forearm Block, and start to turn/roll your body, so you don't offer them a static and flat target. Normally, the hands are open when blocking, however because there is a danger that your fingers may be kicked and bent, it is worth making a fist in in this case, to protect them.

As the foot comes down, turn your body, and start to push outwards with your forearm, you will want to not only deflect the kick, but also push the leg out to load your attacker's weight on it, when it hits the ground.

Keep turning your body, and pushing the leg out. The wider you can get your attacker's feet to be, the less mobile they will be, and the longer it will take for them to shift/readjust their weight and initiate another attack.

As soon as their foot hits their ground, and weight is loaded onto it, start to turn onto your front, and wrap your forearm around the front of their ankle.

You can hold their foot in place with your other hand as you bring your forearm around and in front of their ankle. Although your assailant's weight should already be loaded, so that they will be unable to easily lift their leg again to stomp you, by pinning the foot/ankle with your hand, you will make it even more difficult for them.

Once your forearm is in place, drive forward with your shoulder into the back of their lower leg. At the same time, pull back with your forearm. This will cause them to lose balance, as you drive forward into their leg.

Keep pushing forward and downward with your shoulder, while at the same time pulling back with your forearm. As they lose balance, most of your attacker's focus will be on breaking their fall.

This will give you the time to get up—hold their leg down as you do this, so they are unable to get up, themselves—and then stomp on their ankle/Achilles tendon, before disengaging. Even if your stomp kick doesn't cause serious damage and trauma, your attacker is likely to hesitate and check it, and see if it can bear weight before fully standing up. This delay will create extra time for you to exit safely.

There is a tendency when disengaging from an assailant to panic and "run from danger", rather than to "run to safety". As you exit, you should still be aware of your environment, and the potential dangers in it, so that you don't run into a second assailant, or into traffic, etc. It is good to set up safe places in the environments you commonly spend time in, such as a friend's house you could head to in the event you are attacked in your own.

There are many things that can distract us from our own security and play to a predator's advantage. If we are facing a natural disaster such as a hurricane, extreme flooding, etc., almost all of our attention will be directed toward surviving and managing this situation—and our assumption is likely to be that this is where everybody else's attention will be directed as well. Unfortunately, there are those individuals who will look to exploit such situations and prey on those who are unaware of their presence and unprepared to deal with them. One thing that anyone living in an area susceptible to natural disasters knows to do when one is predicted is to make sure that they have a good quantity of cash available in case the banking system/cash machines/ATMs go down and are unavailable in the aftermath. This means that there are likely to be a number of individuals holding significant sums of cash in their houses. With everyone's attention focused on the impending disaster, a knock on the door can easily be thought to be a neighbor in need or someone bringing an update/information concerning the situation. Even when our focus is on our immediate situation, we shouldn't forget our personal safety policies and procedures, and this includes how we open our front door.

If when you open thedoor, an attacker pushes from too far out, they may not disrupt your balance so significantly that they force you to go to ground. If you can, take advantage of their push, to move yourself backward to create some space. An attacker will try to deny you time and distance, and if you are able to gain these back, you will have significantly improved your survival chances—as you will have the room to recognize and identify threats and dangers.

As your attacker follows you into the room, they may start to raise their leg in order to make a stomp kick. As they do, bring a hand down, and line it up with their ankle. As their foot comes up higher, your hand should track and stay level with their ankle, so it is well positioned to make the block. It doesn't matter, which hand you use to make the block, but you should also employ a body defense, leaning/turning away from the attack, so you aren't reliant on a successful block.

When the kick is aimed at your midsection, you will want to make a "scooping" block to defend yourself with—simply "cup" your hand and scoop the leg past you, as you move to the side. You are not trying to actually catch the leg—so the thumb should be positioned next to the fingers (so it is protected)—but deflect/pull/guide it passed you. Your goal is to help your attacker "extend" their leg, so that their weight will be transferred forward. You are working with the movement of the kicking leg; i.e., their leg/weight is already moving in this direction. You should never try to work against a person's movement and force, only with it. As your attacker's leg falls/moves towards the ground, catch it with your foot and sweep it.

There is a difference between a "sweep" and a "reap." When you reap a leg, you load the majority of the attacker's weight onto the limb, and then take the support away. With a sweep, you take the leg/foot where the individual is intending to place their weight. In this situation, your attacker is trying to put their foot on the ground, after they have made the kick, and you are taking away the limb, before it is in place. To get a better appreciation of how reaps work see *Krav Maga: Tactical Survival*, pp. 202-204.

If you time your sweep well, you may compromise your assailant's balance to the extent that they end up on the ground, however they may have the ability to remain standing. Even if this is the case, they will need to recover from the loss of balance that they experienced when you swept them. Coupled with this, their stability will be compromised, and their weight will be loaded in such a way, that they will need to shift it, in order to become mobile again. Both of these things will allow you the time to commit to a significant attack. Obviously, the position of the attacker in the photo offers a good opportunity for a groin kick from the rear, which could be used here.

High kicks, and especially those to the head, are tools that should be used carefully and sparingly. It would be wrong to say that they don't work in real-life situations, because they can be useful to deliver extreme concussive force against an assailant, which in all likelihood will end the confrontation. However, they do carry risks, which need to be mitigated; e.g., they are relatively slow when compared to punches, they put you in a potentially compromised position, and they require a high degree of skill. The best/easiest way to mitigate these—and other—risks is to only attempt such kicks when your assailant's position is so severely compromised that they stand little chance of countering or responding to your attack.

Although a certain degree of flexibility is required to throw high kicks, it is not the key factor; leg speed is. The faster you raise the knee up, the easier it will be to kick high. The weight of your shoe will also help swing the leg higher. You should aim to connect with the shin, rather than the instep, as it is a much stronger part of the leg—kicking with the instep of the foot, may also put a lot of stress on the ankle.

Once your environment has been compromised, you should look to exit it. It is much easier for you to disengage than to try to force your assailant out of your house. Although you may have stunned them, your attacker could recover quickly, and if they have a weapon on them, they will now likely choose to draw it. If you have family members in your house, such as children, or elderly relatives, who may be unable to quickly exit with you, you should try to get everyone to a safe room, that you can secure, and from which you can call law enforcement.

Roundhouse Kicks

One of the most versatile kicks in Krav Maga is the roundhouse kick. Most stomp-style kicks, such as the back kick and front kick, are best used in response to an assailant's movement; e.g., when they move in towards you, as they are usually too slow to use against an attacker who is in a "neutral," and uncommitted position from which they will be able to easily see them coming and move out of the way. The roundhouse kick, especially when delivered to low targets such as the legs, is quick enough to deliver that an assailant who hasn't committed their weight forward/is moving forward will still find it difficult to avoid and counter.

Many people believe that the power in a kick is generated by the leg, however to kick effectively the whole body needs to be involved. In this sequence, the roundhouse kick will be delivered using the right/rear leg. To employ full body power, both arms should be active, assisting the torso in moving/turning, so that the muscles of the back can be used to turn and pull the right hip forward, and add torque to the turning/swinging action of the leg. The right arm should be up guarding the head/face, as the right foot pushes off from the ground. As the kick starts, the toes of the supporting foot will be pointing forward—if we were to use a clock face to describe the orientation, they would be pointing at 12 o'clock.

Much of the power of the kick, comes from turning/pivoting on the ball of the supporting foot, which will allow the hips to open up—the result of this is that the kicking leg can swing freely in a wide arc. As you do this, your right hand should start to travel down, to help turn your back, and provide torque/rotational force in your torso. As the right arm/hand starts to pull behind you twisting your torso, your left hand should start to come up to guard your face. As the knee raises, start to pull your foot back towards your right buttock.

Continue pivoting on the ball of your foot, turning your body, and your leg, into the kick. You should commit enough movement and force to the kick, that if there wasn't a target/person to absorb its power, the sheer momentum of the leg would spin you right around in a 360-degree loop. As you turn, you should start to extend the kicking leg, towards the target.

As you strike the target, extend the leg. You should be looking to drive it into the target. If you are throwing the kick against the upper leg/quadriceps, you would be trying to press/drive the muscle as hard as you could against the bone, causing as much trauma as possible. If the kick is to be delivered against the ribs, you should be driving fully through to ensure that you crack them. Your striking surface is the shin, rather than the foot. Your supporting foot, should now be positioned around the 7 o'clock mark/position, and your left arm pulled up in readiness to guard your head/face.

From the reverse angle, you can see how far the right arm must be pulled back in order for the rotational power of the torso to be added to the kick.

The roundhouse is a versatile kick, with a high success rate, of both landing and causing significant trauma. The striking surface of the shin is large and if aimed at large targets such as the legs, the chance of connecting is high.

Dealing with Pushes When Prepared

You are not going to be taken completely by surprise in every situation. It may be that you are able to create enough time and distance so that you will be able to see your assailant's attack coming and be in a position to respond to it, or that your attacker doesn't follow up their initial attack immediately, giving you the time to prepare before their next assault. It would be incorrect to think that every physical altercation we may be involved in happens from a position of complete surprise; in fact, we should do

People will often leave the storm doors to their basements unlocked because they trust the locked basement door at the bottom to keep intruders out. An intruder could get in through the storm doors, pull them shut, and then spend as much time as they want, unobserved, breaking down the interior door. When we consider our home security, we don't want to provide criminals with any concealment points around our property.

everything we can to try to predict and identify violent incidents before they happen so that we can hopefully avoid them or at the very least be prepared and ready to deal with them and not caught off-guard.

Both burglars and those who commit home invasions are likely to have carried out some form of surveillance on your property; you and your house may have come to their attention as they trawled your neighborhood looking for opportunities—they may have noted the times of day when your car was in the driveway and when it was not, and even tested methods of entry to your house such as whether window air-conditioning units were loose and could be pushed in and whether garage and basement doors looked to be substantial or could be easily kicked open. It could be that they were also provided information about your property from those who have access to it such as cleaners, gardeners, handymen, and the like, or they may even have fulfilled one of these roles themselves in the past and know the layout of your property and what valuable items you have.

One of the weak points on a door is the "strike plate"—this is the part, which the latch-bolt (and possibly dead-bolt) slide into when the door is locked. It is the part of the lock which secures the door to the frame. In many cases, these plates are only secured by short screws which may barely attach and hold it to the frame. If the door was forced/kicked in, it is very likely that these short screws would be ripped out, and the door would fly open. If the wood of the frame is starting to rot or dry out, so that the screws have little purchase, this will reduce the structural integrity of the lock even more. To make your door more secure, look to get a longer striking plate, with multiple screw holds, and use the longest screws that the frame will allow—the more points at which the plate is attached to the frame, and the deeper the screws are driven, the less likely a burglar or other criminal will be able to kick/force the door.

When you open the door, a discreet way to prevent a push-in, is to position a door wedge, under the door and support it with your foot. If an assailant tries to charge the door, they will now be met with solid resistance. You shouldn't look on this as a preventative measure, to stop them getting into your home, but to buy you the time to unload a canister of pepper spray at them–having a can by your front door, and building in a process that sees you, put the door wedge in place, and have the spray in your hand, when you open the door, will help improve your safety from these types of attack.

Simple precautions such as parking your car in your garage, rather than in the driveway, will deny both burglars and home invaders information as to when your property is, and isn't, occupied. Like all security measures, this is intended as a means of "target displacement;" e.g., you don't have to be the hardest target, you just have to be harder than those around you so that others are chosen as easier targets.

One common method criminals will use to get you to open your door is to pose as some form of delivery person, either standing with a package at your door that you may have to sign for or placing a package/parcel at a distance from your front door so that you have to come some way out of

A package left at a distance from your house may cause you to come outside to retrieve it, allowing a criminal to access your property if you leave the door open, as you do so.

your house to pick it up. Both methods provide opportunities for them to gain access to you and your property. They may be in uniform to look the part but in the current "gig economy", where many people are working ad-hoc, part-time jobs delivering for various companies, this is no longer a necessity to be convincing. It may be that you are targeted in this way and as you open the door, the "delivery man," pushes you in.

As you open the door, you could be pushed backward. You may be caught by surprise, but you should try to stay on your feet, if you can...

...and begin to bring your hands up (so that you are now in a semi-prepared stance). Sometimes, all you have time to do is create space and get your hands up, ready to protect yourself. As you do this, your assailant may look to repeat their attack, and push you again. This type of repetition, where an attacker repeats the same attack over and over again, is fairly common (especially in incidents of social violence), as most assailants don't "plan" beyond their initial assault, and lack the skills and abilities to be creative in their attacks.

As your attacker goes to make their push, turn/blade the body to deny them a flat surface to push against—even if you are late in doing this, and they have their hands on your chest, turning in this way should cause their hands to slide off your body. As you turn, make an Inner-Forearm Block, to deflect their hands/arms past you. Your solution should include both a hand-defense (the block) as well as the body-defense (the turn).

Keep rotating your torso, with your arm fixed in place; your body moves your arm, not the other way around. As your body turns, rotate the arm inward, so that the palm is now facing you. This rotation acts to "drag" your attacker's arm past you.

Once you have successfully defended the push, use your blocking hand to throw a Horizontal Hammer-Fist at your attacker's head. To deliver this strike with power, "unwind" your body from its rotation, so that it is the body moving the arm.

For a complete description of the Inner-Forearm Block, see Krav Maga: Real World Solutions to Real World Violence, *pp. 56–58, and to learn more about Horizontal Hammer-Fists, please reference* Krav Maga: Tactical Survival, *pp. 23–27.*

After throwing the Hammer-Fist, keep striking, by throwing a straight punch/strike to your attacker's head. Use the unwinding movement of your torso to add power to your straight strike. Be aware that your attacker will likely try to cover up, to avoid getting hit with these strikes/punches and so it will be necessary to change targets in order for your combatives to be effective.

If your assailant moves to protect their head, start to use lower body combatives, such as knees, to attack unprotected targets. By striking multiple, different targets, your assailant's attention will have to shift from protecting one area—such as the head—to protecting many. This will be a much more overwhelming experience for them, and one that is much more likely to cause them to emotionally crumble, than if they believe they can simply cover up one target, and limit the effects of your striking. Try to overwhelm them with multiple, continuous strikes that will cause them to feel vulnerable.

If they start to move away from your barrage, and you have an opportunity to take their balance and sweep their leg, do so. While their balance is compromised, they will not be thinking about defending themselves or attacking you; all of their thoughts will be directed towards trying to remain on their feet. As they step away from you, grab their clothing to pull them backward, and then kick/sweep their foot away before it has been placed on the ground or the weight has been fully loaded onto it.

As your assailant falls backward, use this opportunity to disengage and get away to a safe place.

Being Pushed in Through Your Door as You Enter

Any time you enter or exit your house, you are vulnerable to being pushed in. Once somebody has you inside with the door closed, they won't need to worry about being seen. If they have carried out sufficient surveillance on your property, they will know how much time they have to commit whatever criminal activities they've been planning whether that's a robbery or sexual assault, etc.

Two sets of doors, where the outer ones are unlocked, present a security hazard. A criminal can close the first set of doors behind them, and either wait for the homeowner unobserved, or force the second set of doors open, without anyone on the street being able to see them do this.

It is important to make sure that any entranceway/door to your house that you use enjoys good natural surveillance; i.e., that it is visible to neighbors and/or pedestrians who pass by your property. If these access points, and the areas surrounding them, are visible to passers-by and others in your neighborhood, it will be difficult for criminals and predatory individuals to hang around outside them without being conspicuous. This is why you should cut back trees, hedges, and any shrubbery that may obscure people's views of your doors and entranceways. Good lighting, ideally motion-activated, is also important. There is a tendency when people are selecting "security" lights to choose the brightest ones with the most glare. Unfortunately, these can create strong contrasting shadows that can allow criminals a place to hide—they can also end up "blinding" the homeowner when they approach their own door. It is better to use several softer lights that extend over the environment, lighting up all areas and spaces that a person could use to conceal themselves. Using several lights will also allow you to cover a greater area and make it harder for a criminal to find an approach to your property that isn't covered by a motion sensor.

Shrubbery and bushes can offer privacy to occupants...

...but they can also conceal and hide those who are trying to break into your property.

Often when there are "common" areas in a building, such as shared hallways, lobbies, and the like, an assailant can gain access to wait for you. They may follow one of your neighbors in and call a neighbor on the intercom saying they are a repair person and that the intercom to your apartment isn't working, etc. They may even take advantage of somebody who lives in the building propping the front door open or pretend to be opening it as they exit. There are many ways that a criminal can gain access to the shared and common areas in an apartment building or similar. If they have targeted you, they may wait concealed in one of these areas until you return and then follow you to your apartment. As you unlock and open the door, they could push and quickly follow you in.

If you are pushed into your home from behind...

...Take a large step forward, to maintain your balance and arrest your movement. Many people will try to stop too quickly, rather than slowing themselves down gradually; this is often the reason that they fall over when pushed, and end up on the ground. Instead, you should move away from your attacker, gradually reducing the momentum. This will enable you to stay on your feet, and give you more time and distance to react/respond to your attacker, once you have regained your balance, and are stable again.

If you can, take a further step with your left leg, and try to stop your movement, by loading your weight onto it. This will put you in a good position to perform a back kick against your aggressor if they follow you into your apartment. Before you make the kick, you should look over your shoulder, so that you have a good visual on your aggressor. Make sure that you keep your chin tucked in, so that if your assailant was close enough to punch you, they wouldn't have a clear target to aim for. Any time you have to turn during a confrontation, you should protect your chin/face.

To add power to your kick, use a Glisha/sliding step to propel your body towards your assailant. Slide backward on the supporting leg, so that your bodyweight is added to the power of the kick.

As you lift your leg, pull your knee away from your attacker, to "chamber" it. This will allow you to engage your Glutes/buttocks into the kick, rather than rely solely on the power of the quadriceps/upper leg to extend the leg. Your knee should be pulled back, so that it is at least level with your Glute/Buttock. While you are in this position, your hands should be brought up to guard your face. These can be pulled down, as you extend the leg to add torque to the kick—whenever you strike; whether it is a kick or a punch you should look to engage every body part.

Extend the leg towards your attacker, driving your heel into their body. Although you will have brought the arms down as you turned your body, keep your chin and face tucked. Aim to connect with your assailant's chest, rather than their stomach. Although this means kicking somewhat higher, the result will be that they are moved backward, instead of "folding" over your leg, which would likely be the result if they were kicked in the stomach/groin.

Don't ever rely on one single strike to finish a fight. After throwing the kick, turn outwards, and step with the kicking leg, while delivering an outwards Hammer-Fist with your right hand; i.e., step towards your assailant with the kicking leg—your kick should have moved your attacker back and created the space to make the strike.

Using the momentum of your turn, follow up your Hammer-Fist with a straight strike, using your left hand, and shortly after it, a Roundhouse-Kick with your left leg. Your strikes should blend seamlessly together, without any interruption.

Step down with your kicking leg, and use this weight shift to add power to a straight strike with your right hand...

...closely following up with a right Roundhouse-Kick (See the section on Combining Upper & Lower Body Strikes with an Overlapping Rhythm, for a complete description on how to execute this combination). Although what is detailed and illustrated in this sequence looks like it is a set of prescribed movements/attacks, the different attacks should be chosen and flow together, based on the space you have, your attacker's movements, and the positions you find yourself in, after each attack. The general idea, is to overwhelm your attacker by hitting them high and low, from opposite sides, with continuous strikes, so that they are unable to effectively cover, or predict where the next attack is coming from.

Although this style of continuous striking is very effective at providing a machine-gun-like flurry of attacks, which will be difficult to defend and counter, each individual attack will lack the power that could have been generated, were it thrown as a single, concentrated strike. Because of this, it is often necessary to break up the rhythm of such an attacking sequence by delivering individual, powerful attacks. Once your assailant has been overwhelmed by your continuous assault, deliver a powerful front kick...

...with the intent of driving them out of your apartment...

...and immediately close the door, so that they can no longer gain access to you. Although it is often easier for you to exit your apartment/home, rather than force your assailant out of it, there are times when an assailant may be blocking your access/disengagement route, or there may be others you can't leave behind in the environment, leaving you little choice but to drive the attacker out. You may want to use a continuous striking pattern, to create space and time, to get to a safe room, or find a weapon—improvised or otherwise—that you can use against them.

A good safety habit to use when you enter your house, is to close the door as soon as you're inside. Many people will leave the door open as they organize bags and any other objects they may have in their hands. This can give individuals who may have missed their original opportunity to push you inside a second chance to gain access to your house and anyone in it.

Continuous Striking and Striking Rhythms

Few real-life fights involving committed assailants who are prepared to get hit end with one strike. While there may be those aggressors who don't recover from being hit (more often due to shock/surprise, rather than the concussive force of the strike), if a determined, adrenalized assailant decides to attack you—regardless of reason—it is unlikely that a single strike will be sufficient. In an unarmed conflict, striking/punching is a zero-sum game; if you're not striking your assailant, they're striking you. This is why in such conflicts it is necessary to fill the space/time of an encounter with strikes and other assaults against your attacker.

Sometimes all that is required when dealing with an assailant is to attack them repeatedly with the same strike, e.g., moving into them throwing the same punch, Hammer-Fist, or similar. However, if you are always attacking the same target with the same weapon, there is a good chance that your attacker will react/cover and render your assaults impotent and irrelevant. If this happens, you must be prepared to change to different targets that may require you to use different weapons—it could be that you start delivering punches/strikes to the head and your aggressor covers up, protecting this target, requiring you to switch to another such as throwing knees to their body or legs. Alternatively, you could keep changing targets from the start so that you don't find yourself in this predicament/situation.

Your striking patterns can be as simple or as complex as the situation merits, and may need to contain different rhythms in order to bypass your assailant's defenses. As soon as your striking patterns become predictable, your attacker—if they haven't emotionally crumbled under your onslaught—will be able to find a way back into the fight. By altering and interrupting your rhythm, you will take away the predictability of your striking sequence. At first, this will be a conscious skill, but as you become more adept in your striking, your ability to mix up and change your rhythm will be in response to your assailant's movement and the environment you are in.

There are three basic striking rhythms that your continuous striking sequences should be able to employ. These are:

1. Metronomic
2. Overlapping
3. Broken

If you want to deliver the most powerful strikes, a Metronomic/Regular rhythm needs to be employed. This will allow you to dedicate and focus all of your body's movement into each single strike. The issue with Metronomic Striking is that there is a gap/interval between each strike; as one strike/punch is recoiled, and the other begins its movement. Although the recoil/pulling motion assists the pushing/punching motion to add power, there is a time where both striking arms are in transit and this is an interval in which an aggressor can recover and find their way back into the fight. When you think of a Metronomic Rhythm you should think of it in terms of 1-space-2-space-1-space-2, with the numbers representing strikes/punches and the space representing the transition between them.

With Metronomic Striking, the body is fully committed to each strike/punch; the body is fully bladed/turned into the strike, weight is transferred and committed forward, the knees and the hips are sunk, the striking arm fully extended, etc. This is how maximum power is delivered into the punch. However, if the same degree of commitment and power is to be delivered into the next strike, using the other hand...

...the punching arm must be recoiled, the left hip must pull back while the right is pushed/driven forward, and the right arm pushed forward, as weight is transferred back and then forward. In this moment, there is a gap/interval between the left punch and the right—this is necessary in order for there to be a complete transfer of power between both strikes/punches, however in this transition an opportunity may be presented to an assailant to either recover from the first punch, and/or interrupt the striking action of the second.

At some point in a confrontation, you will want to deliver full/maximum power with your strikes, as these will allow you the best chance of seriously concussing your aggressor, however you should be aware that when you introduce Metronomic Striking—where there is a gap between your strikes—you may be vulnerable to a counter-attack. This is why you may want to combine Metronomic Punches with other rhythms so that your assailant is not in a position to take advantage of these gaps.

Although striking/punching metronomically delivers the most power to your strikes, as the body and weight is fully committed to each punch, there are times when you will want to deliver many strikes in as short a time as possible. This is where you will want to employ an Overlapping Rhythm to your attacking sequence.

Overlapping Rhythm

When you employ an Overlapping Rhythm to your striking pattern, you will initiate your second strike, before the first is pulled back and/or as you deliver the first strike. This will cause both strikes to land extremely close together, with little space between them. You will sacrifice some power in hitting this way because you won't be fully committing weight and power to each strike; however, you will be able

In this photo, a left punch has been thrown, with a right punch following closely after, before the first punch/strike has been recoiled. It can be seen from the body position that bodyweight has not been fully committed to either punch.

to land a greater number of strikes in a shorter period of time, clustering them closely together. It may help to think of Metronomic Striking as being like an artillery bombardment, where shells have a greater effect than bullets, but time needs to be taken to reload, with an Overlapping Rhythm being like automatic fire, where there isn't a need to reload, and so it is possible to have consistent and continuous firepower, even if each individual round lacks the impact of a shell.

It is possible to combine upper and lower body strikes to overlap, so that an assailant gets the feeling of being attacked at all angles, and completely overwhelmed. It should be remembered that any attacker will react and respond to your strikes, and are unlikely to stand still for you; this is one reason why you may want to attack with an overlapping rhythm, so that you will be able to land multiple strikes before they have the chance to move.

Combining Upper and Lower Body Strikes with an Overlapping Rhythm

The following sequence shows a straight left punch, followed by a straight right punch, followed by a low roundhouse kick, executed with the right leg. Each strike sets up the next, and is thrown in a seamless, continuous combination, using an Overlapping Rhythm. This allows for the strikes to be clustered closely together.

When clustering strikes together using an Overlapping Rhythm, forward momentum can be used to add bodyweight and power to the strikes. Because each strike will not have the benefit of a full body movement, moving forward with each punch is one way to add power to them. With Metronomic Striking, the body would be fully bladed with each punch, however if the right punch is to be thrown before the left is retracted, this setup won't be possible.

Before the left punch is pulled back, the right punch is launched.

As the right punch is delivered and the arm extended, the right leg begins to follow the forward movement of the right punch...

...in order to land a Right Low Roundhouse-Kick.

The kick should follow just behind the punch, and not be delivered at the same time. You will want your attacker to focus on dealing with the punch, only to realize a fraction of a second later, that they also have to deal with the kick. In this moment of indecision, where they will have to work out whether they should defend against the punch or the kick, it is likely that both attacks will connect. This is one of the advantages of using an Overlapping Rhythm over a Metronomic one; when each attack is easy to identify, and recognize, and there is time, space, and distance between them, an aggressor will have a better chance of defending against each one. When there are several distinct attacks clustered together and overlapping, each one will have to be dealt with, and the brain is not usually fast enough to deal with them all.

Both the punch and the kick should benefit from the turning motion of the torso and the fact that the right hip is moving forward. After the punch has been delivered, keep turning and extend the leg to complete the roundhouse kick.

You should be fully committed to the kick, pivoting on the foot of your supporting leg, and extending your kicking leg, so that it cuts/chops through your attacker's thigh/leg. You should aim to connect with your shin bone, rather than the instep of your foot. If your attacker was to step back, the momentum of the kick should spin you all the way around.

Breaking the Rhythm (Being Unpredictable When Striking)

Sometimes it is necessary to interrupt and break the rhythm of your striking sequence if/when it becomes predictable and easy for your assailant to anticipate your strikes and respond to them (by blocking, covering, or countering, etc.) Inserting broken rhythms into your continuous striking sequences is a good way to ensure that you don't fall into a predictable pattern. The method/rhythm can also be used to interrupt the blocking pattern of an attacker who may have started to mirror your intentional metronomic striking pattern.

This sequence begins with a left-hand punch...that is followed by a right. When delivered metronomically, both of the strikes will likely be blocked relatively easily, as they are thrown as individual punches with space/time between them.

If the combination is repeated; i.e., a left punch is delivered...followed by another right, both are likely to be easily dealt with. It is likely your assailant will have fallen into their own rhythm, which mirrors yours. This is the time to break your rhythm.

Instead of striking again with your left punch, which is what would be expected from the pattern you created, you should now pull back the right hand to throw it again. Your aggressor, predicting a left strike, will likely have already started to commit to blocking it, even though there is no punch to block. This will allow your actual punch—delivered with your right hand—a clear route to travel down. Breaking your rhythm, once an attacker has fallen into time with it, is a great way to get past a person's defenses.

It is important to remember that however hard you are able to hit, you should never rely on a single strike to end a fight. Scoring knock-out blows in a dynamic confrontation is extremely difficult to do. You may of course get "lucky" or pull off the perfect strike; however, this isn't very common. In most incidents, you should try to overwhelm your assailant with continuous strikes in order to cause them to emotionally crumble and/or increase the likelihood of a concussion through the cumulative effects of your striking. Your continuous striking patterns can be extremely simple, such as delivering a succession of hammer-fists or they can be more sophisticated/complex whereby you strike from a variety of angles and levels in an unpredictable fashion.

To be a well-rounded fighter, you will want to be able to control the rhythm of your striking and be able to change targets as necessary—this relies on you being able to respond to your attacker's movement and defenses rather than working to pre-set combinations. Your striking should flow and be continuous in nature, whether to create a disengagement opportunity or to concuss your assailant. The sequence below illustrates how you might change targets, working from left to right, from low to high and back again to overwhelm an assailant from multiple levels and directions.

There should be no pre-set striking pattern that you adopt in training and plan to use against any aggressor. Their movements, the positions they end up in, and how they respond to what you do, should determine how you follow up your initial strikes; e.g., they may move back, they may move off to the side, they may cover, etc. You can never predict how an assailant will respond to your attacks, and so you must be flexible; e.g., if they cover up their face/head when you throw punches at it...

...choose another target and attack with lower body combatives, such as knees—with your rear foot back as you make the punch with your left arm/hand, it will be in a good position to deliver a powerful driving knee strike. If your attacker reacts to this by dropping their hands to protect the body...

Punch/strike the face again, with your other hand, and follow it up...

...with a rear roundhouse kick, having the leg follow the motion/movement of the punch. You can use an overlapping rhythm to confuse, and overwhelm your assailant

Before they have time to react, bring the right leg back and swing in another Roundhouse-Kick using the left leg. To deliver the second kick with power, you can turn it into a metronomic strike—having used the right punch—and kick in an overlapping fashion to buy you the time to do this. In these five strikes, you will have attacked on different levels/heights, at different targets, from different angles, and different sides. Such a continuous striking sequence is extremely difficult to successfully defend against. If you change your striking rhythms within it, as described, you will greatly reduce the predictability of your sequence.

Break-Ins

Another method that those planning a home invasion can use is to break in to your property and wait for you to return home. If this happens then you should assume that it is you that is being directly targeted; i.e., they didn't need you to turn-off/disable an alarm system in order for them to gain entry, etc. It could be that they need you to locate items of value, provide them with the combination for a safe, etc. or it could be that the reason they are invading your home is not a financial one; e.g., they could be looking to sexually assault you, force you to comply with another demand (such as giving them the keys and access codes to your place of work, where they are planning to commit a secondary crime), or punish you for some wrong-doing you have committed against them or a family member. Such break-ins are not opportunistic crimes and shouldn't be equated with surprising a burglar who has broken into your home—as has been stated burglars aren't looking to engage with you and most, given an exit opportunity, will take it.

A simple safety precaution that you can adopt when in your home is to check all of the rooms when you first enter your house–starting with the rooms on the ground floor. This way, you will know that all of your rooms are still secure, and that nobody is in your house before you relax. It will also give you the opportunity to see if you've been burgled, or whether somebody has attempted to break in. In the process of this optical sweep, you may encounter someone looking to attack you, as you make your way up the stairs.

Although dealing with high kicks in real-life situations may not be a common occurrence, there are times when the environment the confrontation takes place in, means that you won't be engaging with your attacker on the same level. This may mean that an assailant ends up making an attack at a target they wouldn't normally select with that particular weapon; e.g., a kick to the head. High Kicks–those above the waist–do have self-defense applications for real-life, and you should be adept at dealing with them.

As the kick travels towards you, turn with the body to blade it. Using this motion, bring your forearm across to make an Inner-Forearm Block, knocking the leg out of your way. You should aim to strike it hard enough that it compromises your attacker's balance as you don't want to leave them in a position where they could follow their kick up with another attack.

It may be appropriate in some situations to follow up your block with some form of attack (such as if there were family members on the second floor), however, if you know that the house is empty and don't know whether your attacker came with any accomplices, it may be better to use the turning motion of your body to get into a position from which you are able to exit/disengage safely. It is worth noting that in a confined space, on uneven levels, you will not be able to use skilled footwork and control of range to the same degree that you would on a flat, even, stable surface. To a certain degree, the uneven terrain takes away some of the advantages over your assailant that your training might give you.

Keeping your arm up to cover your head in case they try to swing their leg back and catch you with the heel of their shoe/boot, quickly make your escape.

Home Invasions and Mistaken Identities

You may not be the intended target of a home invasion but still find yourself the victim of one. In the U.S., a good number of home invasions involve criminals who mistakenly identify individuals and properties; e.g., they force entry into your home in the belief that it's another property and/or that you are somebody else, such as a drug user who owes them money, etc. It could be that somebody who they are targeting used to live in your house and they're not aware that this is no longer the case. It may be that they have just come out of jail and are looking for a former associate who has now moved or incorrectly remember the house number where they lived. Even if they recognize that you aren't the person they were looking for, they may still cause you harm, believing that you are a family member, or somebody who is part of a criminal fraternity/gang, that their intended target belongs to.

Once a criminal has created an opportunity, such as breaking into your house, they are likely to try to exploit it for everything that it's worth, even if it wasn't part of their original plan. Just because you may not be the person they came looking for, it doesn't mean that they won't try to gain something from you. In the summertime, window air conditioner (AC) units can offer easy access to your home, as they can be pushed in through the window, unless they have been screwed into the frame or secured in some way. This can enable someone to break into your house and wait for you, and could see you entering your house and being confronted by an armed intruder.

As soon as the weapon is pulled, you should raise your hands up in a submissive manner, getting them as close to the gun as you can without drawing your attacker's attention to their proximity to it—you can talk to them as you raise your hands so that they are focusing on what you are saying, and not on your hand position. You should raise your hands by shrugging your shoulders rather than by simply lifting them up. Shrugging your shoulders and bringing them close to your ears is body language that communicates a sense of fear to your assailant - and you want them to believe you are afraid as they are less likely to believe that you are intending to, or capable, of physically dealing with them.

If you have been mistaken for someone else and the person is demanding information you don't have you may decide that your best chance of survival is to try and disarm them of their weapon. The body should move the hands, not the other way around. Make a body defense by turning and blading your body, pulling your head out of the line of fire. This turning movement will move the left hand into a position from which it can grab the barrel of the gun—close to the trigger guard - and redirect it. Your second hand should come to the back of the gun (where the hammer is located). You will now have two hands on the gun, against your attacker's one.

Keep turning, and pulling the weapon - it should be your body's turning movement that pulls the arms. Every strike, every pull, should be powered by the body turning and shifting weight, rather than relying on the strength of the limb. Your pulling motion should be rapid, and begin to take your assailant's balance. Attacking balance is one of the best ways to disrupt an attacker, and take their attention away from whatever they are doing. If you are dealing with a semi-automatic pistol and the gun goes off while you are holding the barrel (with a strong enough grip to prevent the slide from moving) the weapon will jam. By preventing movement of the slide, the weapon will not be able to eject the spent casing, and reload another bullet.

Quickly start to turn the weapon towards the attacker using the barrel as a lever. This will compromise their wrist and prevent you from being in the line of fire, in case they are able to regain their balance and pull the weapon back. It will also loosen their grip on the weapon, so you can make a disarm. As you continue the disarm process, your attacker may try to retain their weapon by pulling it back towards themselves (and away from you)...

...Which could see you becoming engaged in a wrestling match over the gun; i.e., your attacker tries to pull it back towards them, you counter by pulling away, etc. Although you will have two hands on the weapon, versus your assailant's one, they will also have a free hand, with which they could potentially attack you (punch, grab, push, etc.), and so you don't want to stay engaged in this wrestling match for long. They may initially be very weapon-centric, but at some point they will realize that they have a free hand, that they can use against you, and you will need to change what you are doing before this becomes apparent to them.

Your biggest concern, and greatest danger, is that they could manage to get their weapon free, and then shoot you (they may not have initially been intending to use the weapon, but now that there is a "fight" over it, where their safety has been compromised, it is more than likely they will). To prevent them being able to recover their weapon, you must keep them from being able to pull it back. To do this, turn the barrel of the gun away from you, and let your left arm follow the movement, so that your elbow is brought over your attacker's weapon arm.

With your elbow over your attacker's weapon arm, they will only be able to pull the gun back a short distance, as your elbow will jam up against their body. Now that you have their weapon arm fully controlled—you should be squeezing it against your body, at the same time—don't resist the pull but instead move in with it, stepping behind your attacker's lead leg; aim to get your knee behind theirs. You can use this leg to block their movement if they try to pull away by stepping back. This movement should see you knock into them, taking their balance somewhat. Keeping an assailant moving and off-balance, is one thing that can help take their focus away from the weapon.

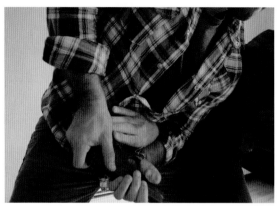

To disarm from this position, simply pull your right hand up, in a tight motion, working against your attacker's grip...

...and rip it out of their hand. Transfer it so that you have it secured in your right hand, and immediately use it as a "cold" weapon...

...to strike your assailant with the barrel.

At this close range, where there is little room or time to get away, you will need to disrupt and damage your assailant to the point where you will have the time to safely disengage (if there are other people in the house with you, you may need to further incapacitate the attacker, so that you can facilitate a complete evacuation of your property). Using the weapon to deliver concussive force is a much more predictable and effective means of ending the conflict, as opposed to shooting your attacker.

There are many issues when it comes to using a disarmed firearm as a hot/ballistic weapon. There is the assumption that the weapon is loaded and operable (if it is a semi-automatic that was fired when you had control of the slide, it will now be jammed, and require clearing—something that will take time), and unless your shots can "mechanically" shut down your attacker, they may well be able to continue fighting you even after being shot and draw another weapon to assist them in doing so. Even if you are dealing with a loaded and operable weapon, you may find yourself unable to deliver lethal force to another person and so will fail to use the weapon—or you may hesitate as you consider all of the moral and legal ramifications of potentially taking a life. Using it as an impact weapon takes little thought or consideration, as there are fewer potential consequences to doing so.

Home Invasion—When Your Assailant Is Already in the House

One of the elephants in the room when it comes to self-defense and personal safety is that statistically most violent incidents will involve someone who you know rather than a stranger—we might like to think/convince ourselves that these statistics don't apply to us but unfortunately they do, and it is important that we acknowledge them. One of the biggest obstacles that we have to overcome when we are attacked is being unable to accept our situation for what it is—even when we are experiencing the pain and ferocity of an assault, we may still respond with denial and disbelief, telling ourselves that this can't be happening to us. Most people—unless they have a history of trauma—tend to believe that bad things happen to other people, not to them, and so when attacked they find themselves caught in a state of denial. When our attacker is someone we know—and perhaps trust—we may have even more trouble/difficulty accepting the reality of the assault and determining the best way to respond; e.g., are we even allowed to fight back? And if so, with how much force? Is it right to hurt someone we know even if they are hurting us? We may be baffled and confused as to why our assailant won't stop when we ask them to and have trouble squaring their now violent disposition with the seemingly friendly, caring and considerate one they may have demonstrated before.

In this section, we will take a brief look at partner abuse, and stalkers/stalking—situations where your aggressor and/or assailant is someone you know. Even if you are not in an abusive relationship or being stalked, this is a section worth reading, as situations—however unlikely—can always change, and being prepared to respond is always better than being caught having to react.

Abusive Relationships

When we think about abusive partners, we tend to think about physical abuse where there is a male antagonist and a female victim—possibly with the abused explaining away her injuries as having walked into a door, etc. Studies by the U.S. Centers for Disease Control and Prevention estimate that one in four women and one in seven men will experience severe physical abuse from a partner in their lifetime—this type of violence is much more common than we may think and effects both genders. Relationship abuse is much broader than just physical abuse, covering many other elements and types of interaction, some of which lead to psychological and emotional injuries.

There are five basic types of abuse, and for them to be considered abusive they must form a pattern of incidents and events that are carried out consistently over time.; i.e., if something just happens once, it may be a reaction, that is regretted and never repeated, rather than being used as a tool/tactic of abuse. The five types of abuse are:

1. Psychological
2. Emotional
3. Physical
4. Sexual
5. Financial

Psychological abuse involves the use of threats and intimidating actions and behaviors that are designed to invoke fear, panic, and anxiety. These threats can be targeted at both you and your partner, and can even be hidden in seemingly flattering language; e.g., "if you ever leave me I'll kill myself"—however you look at it this is a threat, and with all threats there is a consequence if you act/don't act in a certain way. Threats, whether explicit or implicit, are designed to get you to change the way you act and behave and are therefore a means of control. Often, an abuser will get their victim to take responsibility for their abusive actions and behaviors; e.g., "if you go out with your friends tonight instead of staying home with me, I won't be responsible for my actions." Not taking personal responsibility, and projecting that responsibility onto the target/victim, making them to "blame" for the abuser's actions and behaviors, is a classic form of Psychological Abuse. A survey conducted by Women's Aid (a UK-based charity that provides support for victims of abuse) found that 88% of victims said the criminal justice system did not take psychological harm into account as being a form of abuse, with 94% stating that this type of mental cruelty/abuse could be more hurtful/painful than physical violence.

When a partner uses Emotional Abuse, they are in some way, shape, or form attacking the self-esteem, and confidence of their partner—someone who is caused to doubt their worth and is unsure of themselves is less likely to break away and leave the relationship than someone who is confident and self-assured. Often, emotional abuse will be couched in such a way that it could be misconstrued as some form of compliment; e.g., "You're lucky that someone like me, loves someone as unattractive/fat/ugly as you." Sometimes, emotional abuse is much more targeted and directed—"You're not going out dressed like that are you? You look like a whore." Abusers will often subtly chip away at their partner's self-esteem over time, sometimes using humor to disguise what they are doing. They may remark, with laughter and a patronizing smile, that their partner is so stupid, when they make contributions to a conversation—and do this over and over again. It is hard for someone not to question their intelligence when this happens repeatedly, and this is in fact the abuser's goal. If their partner complains about this type of abuse, or asks them to stop, it is likely that they will be told that they are being too sensitive, that they can't take a joke, etc. This is in itself emotional abuse, as the feelings/emotions of the other person are being discounted and denied.

Not all physical abuse results in injuries, and/or leaves bruises. An abuser can throw a glass against a wall, near where you're standing, leaving you unharmed—scared, terrified, and in fear for your safety maybe, but physically unharmed. Blocking your way and preventing you from leaving/entering a room won't leave a mark, yet it is still a form of physical abuse and if repeated demonstrates a pattern of abuse. Snatching a TV-remote (or similar) from you in an aggressive fashion probably shouldn't be classified as abuse on its own; however, if your partner repeatedly grabs and snatches things from you, this is a behavior that may indicate more serious/consequential physical abuse in the future such as locking you in a room, and/or physically attacking you; these types of abuse rarely happen in the early stages of a relationship and are things which are built up to gradually, over time.

Sexual abuse can take many forms. It can involve forcing sexual acts that a partner has expressed discomfort with and doesn't want to engage in, or not respecting their reproductive rights; e.g., refusing to use a condom when you have sex or deliberately not taking birth control precautions that were agreed upon. Disrespecting and ignoring the sexual choices and preferences of a partner is a form of abuse and not something to be taken lightly or disregarded. One group who experiences sexual abuse from an intimate partner an alarmingly high rate are teenage girls of high school age. A CDC study reported that 21% of young women in this group experienced physical and sexual abuse at the hands of a partner they were dating. For many, the belief was that this type of violence and abuse was acceptable and something they should expect as part of the relationship. In another study (Teen Research Unlimited, May 2009) 82% of parents believed, and were confident, that they would be able to spot the signs of this type of dating abuse; however, when tested on what these signs were/looked like only 42% were able to. Nobody is born with the appropriate skills to identify when someone in their care is in an abusive relationship—this is something we need to educate ourselves about. Their lack of dating/relationship experience creates the conditions in which young women are at risk for intimate partner violence, and especially sexual abuse, with many lacking the skills and the confidence to set the necessary boundaries that would prevent them from becoming victims, and in many cases, repeat victims (as they become used to operating and functioning in these types of abusive relationships). It is part of our role as parents, guardians, teachers, and leaders of community groups that interact with this population, to help educate them as to what is acceptable behavior within a relationship and how to set boundaries so they don't become victims of sexual abuse.

One of the major reasons that women—especially those with children—in physically abusive relationships don't leave their abuser is due to a lack of financial resources; e.g., the abuser controls the money and the bank accounts. When this is the case, the victim is not only being subjected to physical abuse, they are suffering financial abuse as well. An abuser who is looking to have full and total control over the relationship won't have it until they can also control the finances. However committed someone is to a relationship, and however "nice" their partner seems, it is never a good idea to hand over complete financial control to them, giving up financial resources that they may need at a future date —this can include the abuser forcing/coercing their partner into quitting their job. Financial abusers often start their campaign for control of their partner's resources by criticizing their spending habits, such as accusing them of spending too much money on certain things; e.g., name brands rather than shop ones or spending too much of their income on clothes, etc.

One form of financial abuse that is often over looked is "coerced debt." This is where an abuser uses their partner's credit cards to buy themselves things and then leaves their partner with the responsibility of paying the debt. They may well make promises to pay it, with the partner knowing that their only chance of recovering the money relies on them staying in the relationship. The abuser also knows that when their partner is unable to pay off the credit card(s), their credit score will be so negatively affected that it will be extremely difficult for them to acquire new credit or rent an apartment in their own name. If the abuser is also controlling all the finances coming into the home, their partner will be financially stranded. Coerced debt is a form of financial control and economic exploitation. A study by Michigan State University found that 59% of women who had been involved in abusive relationships had seen their partners run up debts under their name.

The Cycle of Abuse

In the cycle of abuse (a social theory developed by Lenore E. Walker in 1979 from a study of 1,500 female victims of domestic violence), there is a tension-building phase which precedes the actual violent outburst/incident—there are obviously relationships wherein the physical abuse is constant or even a part of daily life for the victim; however, in most cases physical abuse manifests itself in outbursts that are built up to, followed by a period of reconciliation in which the abuser demonstrates regret and remorse for their actions, and a time of calm, before the next tension-building phase begins. This "tension-building" phase is characterized by a breakdown in communications and a general sense of unease within the relationship. In most incidents, there is a "trigger" event that brings on the physical assault, such as an argument about how money has been spent or a sexual act that has been refused, etc.

Covering Versus Blocking

Even if it has never turned physical in the past, a heated argument may create the igniting spark for an abusive partner to attack you physically. In an attempt to control you, your partner may grab you by the throat and slam you against the wall.

At this close range and proximity, with your movement restricted by the wall, it will be very difficult for you to make a block that would intercept your assailant's strike, and so instead of trying to make a block, it would likely be more effective to try to cover, bringing your arm up around your head, to protect your face. Although covering would be ineffective against a weapon, if you know that the person is unarmed, it can be a good option.

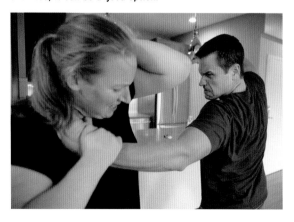

If an abuser has been unsuccessful in the argument, they may feel justified to use physical force against you, and may even feel that you have made it so this is the only option left open to them. They may feel backed into a corner by the argument, and that they have no choice, but to control you physically. Our instinctive response to having our throat grabbed/airway restricted is to start to bring our hands up to clear the choke.

It is worth noting that when defending the head against punches, it is really only the face that is vulnerable, the rest of the skull is fairly thick, and while punches to the ear are painful, under adrenaline they are unlikely to incapacitate you. This is why our natural reaction to being hit is to turn our face away, and turn the thicker parts of our skull towards our attacker. By bringing your arm up tightly against your head (protecting your ear) and turning away, you are working with your instincts. This movement will also weaken your attacker's grip on your throat.

While protecting your face from your attacker's repeated blows, pluck down on their wrist...

...ripping their hand from your throat. This action should also pull them somewhat forward, compromising their balance. Once you have dealt with their attack, and are no longer pinned against the wall, you can look to make your own attack. Start to release the arm that was pressed up against your head, in order to use it to strike with.

Because your attacker will probably still be striking/punching you, your attack will also need to be able to protect your face. When you bring your arm across your face to wind up for your strike, make sure that it is still covering most of it. It is okay to look over your arm, but you won't want to expose the complete eye-socket, as if a punch lands here, the pain may be debilitating.

Unwind and unleash a powerful forearm strike into your attacker's neck. Make sure that you drive through with it, so that your assailant not only receives the impact of the blow, but their balance is taken, as well.

As you make your forearm strike, pull your other arm up, ready to deliver a downwards hammer-fist. Make sure to raise your weight, and pull your hip back as you bring your arm up. This will allow you to sink your weight and bring your hip into play when you make the strike.

Bring the bottom of your fist/forearm into your attacker's neck...

...and then repeat. Never assume that one strike will be enough, but at the same time you should deliver every blow with the idea that it should finish the fight. Continuous—"Retzev" in Hebrew—striking doesn't have to be complicated. Your goal will be to simply deliver as much firepower as you can in the shortest possible time, like a machine gun. The goal of your striking will be to cause your attacker to emotionally crumble and create time for you to escape.

Deliver enough strikes to create an opportunity ...

...for you to push your attacker away and disengage. It doesn't matter if this is your house/apartment or not, if your environment contains a danger, you will need to evacuate. Your ego may tell you that your aggressor should leave, rather than you, however staying to try to make this happen, either verbally or physically, would compromise your safety. Once out of the house, you should either call law enforcement and/or make your way to a friend or family member's house.

Be aware that law enforcement may not be able to evict your partner from your property—even if they don't live there—unless they determine that they are a threat to your safety which may involve you bringing charges against them. This is because the police may not be able to determine whether they are a tenant who has a legal right to be in the property—if they deem them a threat to your safety that is another matter but as a general rule, the police are reluctant to involve themselves in these types of civil disputes as it can be hard for them to determine who has a legal right to remain in the home.

Recognizing Abuse

Most people who are in an abusive relationship, don't want to admit that this is their situation; that they are being victimized, whether it is psychological, emotional, or physical, etc. Many victims feel sorry and are apologetic for their partner's behavior, even seeing themselves as the cause/reason for it. Trauma occurs when someone is subjected to a highly emotional and stressful incident that they were unable to influence or control. When this happens, they will often try to avoid feeling ashamed about their inability to prevent and deal with the abuse that they received—as social creatures, we will try to avoid shame at almost any cost. One way we do this is to transfer our shame, which is public, into guilt, which is private. Unfortunately, guilt involves us taking the blame for what has happened (even though it wasn't our fault). However, dealing with this guilt is preferable to the shame that we feel, about not being able to stop what is happening to us. Because of this, we often end up blaming ourselves, rather than our abusers, for the abuse that we receive.

When trying to understand and recognize if we are in an abusive relationship, we will first need to accept that we are neither responsible or to blame for the abuse, whether it is psychological, emotional, sexual, or physical. Nobody deserves to be treated with threats or derogatory remarks, nor should anyone have to fear for their physical safety. However much we may try to rationalize our situation by normalizing it and convincing ourselves that all relationships resemble ours, this is simply not the case.

Controlling Your Assailant While Striking

Sometimes much of the power of a strike is translated into movement, rather than being absorbed by the assailant—this can be a good thing if it causes the brain to "shake" in the skull, resulting in a concussion. However, it can also mean that an attacker may be able to "ride" the strike, and limit the effects of the impact. One way to avoid this happening, is to control their head, and restrict its movement when you strike. You can use your striking to set up this type of control; e.g., after delivering a forearm strike to your assailant's neck...

...start to reach your arm around their neck. Your strike should have moved their head downwards, so that even if there is a height discrepancy, you will still be able to reach.

Don't trap your assailant's head under your armpit, as this will prevent you from turning it, and taking their back/spine out of alignment—and it is by doing this that you'll be able to control someone much larger and heavier than yourself.

You shouldn't pull your assailant's head down, but rather circle your arm around it, in order to turn it.

Keep turning your attacker's head, so that it comes past your armpit. You will want to catch the back of your attacker's head under your armpit, but still be able to see their right ear. From this position, you could apply a Guillotine Choke —explained/described in *Krav Maga: Real World Solutions to Real World Violence*, pp. 176-177—but here, we'll look at using strikes against your assailant's face from this position; before disengaging.

Keeping control of their head, raise your right arm high, and make a fist...

...and then smash it down into your attacker's neck, making impact with the bottom of your fist.

Immediately bring your hand to your attacker's face...

...and pull upwards, raking your assailant's eyes...

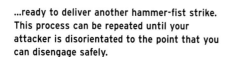

...ready to deliver another hammer-fist strike. This process can be repeated until your attacker is disorientated to the point that you can disengage safely.

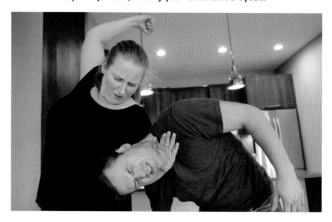

Who Abuses and Why

We tend to think that other people are like ourselves, and think like us; even possibly holding to the same or similar beliefs to us, etc. This isn't always the case, and in some instances, the person we are communicating and interacting with is operating with a totally different belief system and is in fact working with an alternative reality to ours. Alternative views/realities are common in individuals with personality disorders. Two particular disorders which feature heavily in abusive relationships are:

1. Paranoid Personality Disorder
2. Narcissistic Personality Disorder

While the *Diagnostic and Statistical Manual of Mental Disorders* (DSM) defines paranoia by its symptoms and manifestations, because it is a diagnostic tool, the root of the disorder is that those who suffer from paranoia see the world as being a black and white place with no gray areas; they need to be able to distinctly label and categorize every behavior, action, and event in such a way that it can be neatly compartmentalized. Paranoid individuals have a blueprint of how they feel the world should operate and try to fit/match reality to it. In relationship terms, when you are with this type of person, there will also be a blueprint for how you should act and behave and if/when you don't adhere to it, the response will be one of confusion and suspicion; i.e., they won't understand why you aren't acting and behaving in the way that you should.

The other thing to understand about dealing with paranoid personality types is that they also believe that every incident, everything you say and everything you do, is related. They have a very ordered view of the world and everything needs to be put into a particular box, and related to every other box, as it's mapped out on the blueprint.

A person with Paranoid Personality Disorder will find it difficult to accept more than one reason for an outcome. A partner arriving late for dinner may be asked why they weren't able to make it on time; after all if they "valued" the relationship to the same extent as their partner, they would have taken into account all of the things that may have caused them to be late. Initially, they may cite the reason that they weren't on time, as being down to traffic, but later in the conversation mention that a work meeting overr an. Although both, to differing degrees, may have been responsible, the fact that only one was mentioned in their initial explanation, will cause their partner to become suspicious; i.e., why was one reason mentioned later than the other? In their black and white world, the initial reason given isn't the same as the second, and so they will have trouble working out which one is correct. This can cause them to believe that their partner is hiding something from them, and result in them manifesting many of the symptoms that the disorder is defined by, e.g., distrust, suspicion, and the belief that others have malevolent intent towards them.

Hair pulls are an effective way of controlling a person's movement, as pulling away from it will cause extreme pain. They are also the types of attack, which people make when extremely emotional, and can be a signal that extreme violence is likely to be used.

Rather than try to enact a physical solution from your disadvantaged position, raise your hands up in a placating manner, agreeing to move/go with your attacker. This will allow you to get closer to them. This is referred to as "Crying Yourself into Position." Sometimes you will need to get into a better position before you engage with your attacker.

Keep moving closer. This will both take a lot of the pressure and pain away from the hair-pull, and allow you to get your hands closer to your attacker's face—without them realizing that this is your intention, and that you are actually planning a physical response. As you move towards them, talk to them, agreeing that you will go with them, etc. Let them focus on your words so that they don't question your movement or intent.

Once you are close enough, bring your right hand to the back of your assailant's head—to support it—and at the same time drive your fingers into their face, ripping and gouging their eyes. There is no prescribed method to this, other than raking and clawing at your assailant's face with your fingers

You can push upwards, directing your attacker's posture and movement—this will move their focus away from the grab, and give them a problem to deal with, lessening the control they have on you.

Rake downwards, dragging your fingers and nails across the flesh of the face and eyes. Your goal is to viciously attack their face, ripping and gouging, giving them the incentive to move away from you (which will mean they will need to let go of your hair).

You can turn your attacker's head to change their direction and movement. In all of your attacks, try to emulate the frenzied nature of a wild animal, which will commit 100% to its attack/defense.

As soon as you feel their grip release, and that they no longer have hold of you, push both yourself and them away, and make for the nearest exit. Make your way to a safe place, such as a neighbor's or friend's apartment—this should be somewhere your partner doesn't know about, or where they are unlikely to come looking for you.

Narcissists, believe that they are the most important people on the planet and that they can do no wrong. They are always looking for someone to blame. It doesn't matter whether it's their personal, social, or work-life, if things aren't going as well as they should be, it's always someone else's fault. Many narcissists are underachievers; they believe that the world owes them something and that they shouldn't be expected to make any effort to better themselves; they are simply entitled to everything. They may believe that they should have gotten better grades at school/university, that they should have been hired for every job they applied for, and/or that all of your friends should show them more respect, etc. Often, those in abusive relationships with narcissists will find themselves making excuses to friends and family members about why their partner isn't achieving the things that they keep proclaiming they have, or should have.

Narcissists believe they are perfect, and that there is nothing about their personality which requires work or development—they don't need to grow; it is those around them who need to. Suggesting that there may be areas of their life that they need to work on and improve is likely to upset them, and cause them to become emotional/angry.

If you attempt to criticize somebody with a narcistic personality type, or disagree with them in any way, they are likely to become angry, aggressive and possibly physically violent towards you. To them, all criticism is unwarranted, and they will react/respond badly to it, however well-meant it was on your part. Rather than just controlling your movement by grabbing your hair, your partner may is throw you around by it, in a rage, with the intent of causing you as much pain as possible.

One of the problems when you are being thrown around in this manner, is that it will be very difficult to do anything in terms of escaping until you have dealt with the movement and stabilized yourself.

In order to stabilize yourself, you should first bring your hands up...

...and over your head. If you are being thrown around by your assailant, it is likely that your arms/hands will be up and out already, as you try to maintain your balance. A fight is a dynamic thing that involves movement, and if someone has grabbed your head, they are doing it in order to try to control you and prevent you from countering their attack. This is why your primary goal in this situation should be to try and stabilize yourself - and reduce the pain, which may be prevent you from being able to think clearly.

Quickly pull down, securing your attacker's hand to your head. Press down tightly, so that your assailant is unable to pull your hair; i.e., their hand is pressed into your skull. This should take away much of their ability to move you—in a similar way that when someone grabs your lapels and starts throwing you around, you should pull their hand to your body and lock it to you. This is explained in *Krav Maga: Tactical Survival*, pp. 165-167.

Start to tilt your head down (make sure you are grabbing your attacker's hand (below the wrist, so that their wrist is free to move)...

...and step backward.

By ducking the head down as you step back, you will effectively apply a lock to your attacker's wrist, forcing them to bend over/down, or possibly kneel down, to relieve the pressure.

Once you have broken their posture/frame, and they are unable to move you, reach for a finger and start bending it backward to apply pressure on it, until your attacker is forced to release their grip. Once free, disengage to safety.

Identifying Potentially Abusive Partners

Few abusers identify this part of their personality at the beginning of a relationship—if they did, most people wouldn't go on the second or third date with them. However, there are warning signs, as most people will find it impossible to hide all sides of themselves—most abusers don't intend to engage in abuse, and in fact see themselves as the victim; e.g., their partner's actions, behaviors and interactions force them to behave in this way (blaming others and a failure to take responsibility), or that they are entitled to act in a certain way, and therefore it shouldn't be classed as abuse, etc. This is one of the reasons that many abusers don't respond well to therapy; they generally don't believe that they've done anything wrong.

If someone comes with a blueprint of what a relationship should look like, then they will be able to share their long-term plans for the relationship, very early on—usually too early on, and at an inappropriate stage in the relationship; e.g., talking about moving in together after a few weeks of dating may be flattering—especially if the person they are dating has had a problem with partners having commitment issues in the past—but in reality, it's too soon to be discussing such things. With this blueprint in hand, they are able to move the relationship along quickly without discussion or debate; in most relationships, the subject of moving in together is ventured, felt out and discussed as a possibility, rather than laid out as a certainty/inevitability. Many people are too polite to ask such partners to slow down, and are afraid of offending them, by not appearing to be as committed to the relationship as they are.

A narcissistic individual, will believe that they can, and are, meeting all of their partner's needs; i.e., you shouldn't need anyone else in your life. They also need, for their own ego, your undivided attention. Your friends, family members, and work colleagues are all seen as competition. As far as your partner is concerned, these are unnecessary people to have in your life, when they alone can provide everything you need. Their blueprint may also state that the relationship is fulfillment in itself, and you should commit all your time and energy to that, rather than be spending time with other people. If a partner questions why you should be spending time with others, rather than them, and you find that you start isolating yourself from others in your life, you may want to start reviewing your relationship.

If you find yourself in this type of relationship, you may feel that you need to do things secretly, to try to maintain your "old" lifestyle, such as spending time with friends and family members. Unfortunately, abusers are driven by a need to control your actions and behaviors—either because their ego requires it, or because they are working to a "relationship blueprint"—and this may see them start to gather information about you, and spy on what you are doing. They may note the mileage of your car, to see if you take "extra" trips, or call you to find out where you are, and who you are with. If they find out that you are doing something you haven't told them about, either because you forgot, or that you kept quiet to avoid a fight/confrontation, it is likely that they will explode emotionally.

A fight is a dynamic thing, often with movements that effect your balance, and that can prevent you from implementing standard and preferred solutions; e.g., in *Krav Maga: Real World Solutions to Real World Violence*, I detailed a solution for dealing with a side-headlock, where you are being pulled forward (pp. 187-190). Although this is a good and effective solution to such an attack, if an assailant is throwing you around like a ragdoll, rather than simply applying the headlock, you may find it difficult to implement. Still, your starting movement to deal with the headlock, should be to try and implement it; i.e., step forward as you are pulled down, strike the groin with your right hand, and bring your left arm over your attacker's shoulder to their eyes.

In a frenzied, highly emotional and angry attack, your aggressor may be looking to work out their anger, aggression, frustrations, and perceived lack of respect from the world on you. This puts you in a very dangerous place, because you will be dealing with a highly volatile individual who has no particular outcome in mind other than punishing you (and what they believe you represent)—this punishment may continue even after you are unconscious, in fact it will continue until they are emotionally spent. This "personal" violence is very different to a dispute in a bar, where as soon as one party has proved their physical dominance over the other, the incident will usually end.

If you are losing balance, and will be unable to execute your preferred solution, your first priority should be to stabilize yourself in some way, and slow down your attacker's ability to move you. To do this, quickly grab the back of their knee; if you can, grab their clothing, as this will give you a better grip. Pull firmly down and root your attacker's foot to the floor, so that they are unable to step with it. If you can prevent their movement, you will be able to prevent them from moving you. This is a similar tactic that is used when in a clinch, to prevent someone throwing knees at you (see *Krav Maga: Tactical Survival*, pp. 205-207.

Once you have their leg locked to the ground, release your grip, and bring both thumbs to the inside of your assailant's knee.

Start to push forward and down (at the same time) on the back of your aggressor's knee, driving your thumbs into the back of the joint.

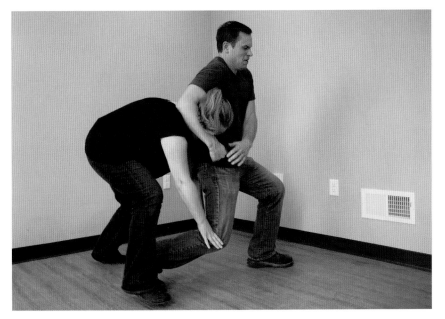

Drive their knee towards the ground. Be aggressive with this movement. If you can cause them to experience pain as their knee smashes into the ground, all the better. However, the main purpose of the knee drive is to break your assailant's posture and frame, so that they are unable to continue controlling your movement.

As your attacker is driven forward, they will start to lose control of your head, and you will be able to pull it out from under their arm. In many cases, they will release you in order to free their hands to help break their fall and slow their descent—often, their natural survival instinct will see them do this subconsciously, as the body will want to protect itself by putting the arms out.

Now that you are upright, you can stomp down on your attacker's ankle with the goal of rendering the joint inoperable—there is a good chance that you will rip/tear their Achilles tendon when you do this. Even if you do no serious damage to the ankle, your assailant will be reticent to put weight on their leg when they first get up, and this will buy you time as you disengage and make your escape.

Dealing with Kicks When on the Ground

In physically abusive relationships, the level of violence tends to increase over time. The first time an abuser assaults their partner, they may push or a slap them; the second time they may punch and/or choke them which may then escalate to repeatedly slamming their head into a wall, etc. Violence for abusers is addictive and results in them experiencing a physical/emotional high, as they enjoy physical dominance and control over their partner while they play out their frustrations and anger at the world. To keep experiencing this high, each incident will need to be more and more violent than the last. This may result in a level of normalization, where the victim becomes used to being assaulted, and accepts physical violence as an inevitability of being involved in a relationship. They may even discount what is happening to them, making the argument that all relationships experience this type of abuse to some degree, and theirs is no different from anyone else's. Nobody wants to see themselves as a victim, and so people will come up with reasons why they are to blame for the abuse and/or normalize the violence they experience. The danger in "accepting" violence is that there will eventually be an incident where the consequences are permanent and severe.

Incidents of physical abuse usually get worse with time. What may have started out with snatching objects, is likely to move on pushes and grabs, and then escalate to striking and punching. Many abusers "test" the boundaries, to see how far they can go, and what the extent of their power and control actually is.

If the ferocity and force of the blows are extreme, you may find that all you can do is to try and cover up and weather the storm, until you get an opportunity to disengage—or your partner calms down. In the course of this, you may lose your footing and fall to the floor; still try to protect your head.

Once you are on the floor, your attacker may take the opportunity to throw kicks at your head, rather than following you to the ground. Few attackers will give up a dominant position, when they have you at a disadvantage. As soon as you can, bring your right shin up, and push it against your attacker's supporting leg...

...by applying pressure against your attacker's shin, and pushing them back somewhat, you will lock the leg at the knee. This will both move their hip back—taking some of the forward driving force of the kick away—and compromise their balance. If your attacker was stepping forward from distance to kick you in this manner, you should propel yourself forward, and "crash" your shin into their supporting leg.

As you do this, bring both of your arms up. Your right leg should be pulled up so that there is no gap between it and your arms; i.e., you want there to be an "overlap" at your knee and elbow, so that your entire body is protected. In many ways, you are adopting a protective fetal position, which is extremely natural/instinctive in this type of situation; i.e., you are curling up to protect yourself. Make sure that you have your palms facing outwards, so that the fleshy parts of your arms can be used to absorb the kick.

As the kick comes toward you, push your arms out to connect with your attacker's leg. Keep your fingers together, and tense your hand, as it may be here that the kick connects, and you won't want individual fingers to be in the position of having to stop the kick as a) they won't be strong enough, and b) they'll get injured in the process. Although making a fist would protect the fingers, it would leave the thumbs vulnerable.

After you have stopped (or slowed) down the kick and your attacker starts to pull their leg back, "swim" your top arm over and around your attacker's kicking leg. Because these types of kicks recoil much more slowly than punches, you should have the time to catch and trap your assailant's leg. Keep your other arm in front of your face to protect it. If you miss catching their kicking leg, bring your arm back, ready to protect yourself and then attempt to catch it again when the next kick comes in. With these types of attack, it is likely that your attacker will not just throw one kick, but many.

Once you catch the leg, pull yourself over your assailant's kicking leg, pinning it to you...

...and continue rolling into them, so that their foot is locked to the floor, and their leg is pushed backward at the ankle, causing them to lose balance.

Most people will try to break their fall by putting their hand out to stop or slow their descent. This can put extreme pressure on both the wrist and the collarbone, often injuring or breaking these bones. This is one of the many advantages to throwing and/or taking down an aggressor who doesn't know how to break their fall properly.

As soon as you can, get up and disengage. Get to any exit you can and leave the apartment, making your way to a safe place.

The Difficulties of Leaving Abusive Relationships and Repeat Victimization

Often when people hear about a friend, an acquaintance, or somebody they know who is in an abusive relationship (physical or emotional, etc.), they are baffled as to why they don't leave—we all like to believe that we a.) wouldn't have gotten involved with such an abuser in the first place; and b.) would have left at the first sign of abuse. There are many, many reasons why an abused person may have difficulty leaving the relationship, and although the solution can seem simple and obvious to those of us looking in from the outside. When caught up in it—where there are emotions, responsibilities, fears and anxieties—things are much more complex.

Human beings are creatures who like familiarity—even if that which is familiar to us isn't always in our best interests. Leaving a relationship doesn't simply mean "leaving;" it means moving to something else, and this something else is an unknown. This can be scary and may cause us to stick with that which is familiar to us rather than head off into the unknown, even when there is a risk to our personal safety. This is one of the reasons that many victims of abuse keep ending up with abusive partners (secondary/repeavictimization); they are familiar and comfortable interacting with abusive individuals, and don't know how to relate to, or what to expect from, a non-abusive relationship. It is also worth noting that abusers are good at identifying and recognizing those they believe they will be able to control, and those who have weak boundaries, that can be exploited.

Many victims of abuse also genuinely love their partners, even though they cause them harm. They can often feel that their partner is a victim of their circumstances, and that they need help; and that they are the ones who can provide the necessary help. This is one way that the abused partner can feel some control, in a relationship where all the power is held by the other person. It should also be remembered that in most abusive relationships, the abuse isn't constant—that there are enjoyable moments, and times when their abuser may be generous, funny, and affectionate. An optimistic belief that the good times are just around the corner, and/or that their partner is working to control their issues (they are always repentant and sorry just after an abusive incident), will keep many abused partners staying to try and work it out.

Lack of resources—especially where children are involved—is another reason people will stay in an abusive relationship; and a good reason you should never entirely give up your financial independence. If you have dependents, who you are unable to provide for on your own, because your partner has control of the finances, leaving will be extremely difficult, and you may require help from a third party, such as a friend, family member, or professional organization.

When we consider that we are statistically most likely to experience aggression and violence at the hands of someone we know, rather than a stranger—regardless of our gender—we should as part of our risk assessments look at our particular vulnerabilities concerning abusive relationships; e.g., are we individuals who have difficulty setting boundaries, do we easily hand over control of situations to others, do we naturally take responsibility and blame for other people's actions and behaviors? Understanding who we are, and how we behave in relationships, can help us ascertain our level of risk when it comes to ending up in an abusive relationship.

Home Invasion—Stalkers and Stalking

Sometimes, when a relationship ends, one party has difficulty accepting their new reality—especially if they have invested heavily in the relationship, and believed that it was their role to be the controlling influence and decision maker; this is likely to be the case if they are suffering from a Narcissistic Personality Disorder. In such cases, they may try to entice their partner to enter back into the relationship, attempt to continue the relationship regardless of the other person's wishes, and/or engage in a series of activities and actions to punish them—possibly even to try to convince them through these punishments to re-enter the relationship. Stalking of an ex-intimate partner is often a mix of reconciliation and revenge. Depending on where you live, these behaviors and actions may be classed as either "Harassment" or "Stalking."

Both crimes are defined not so much by the actions themselves, but how these actions and incidents make you feel; e.g., if you break up with your partner and they start sending you gifts on an almost daily basis, you may interpret this to be a romantic gesture to get you back, which is touching but unwanted, however you may interpret it—based on the relationship you had with your partner—as being threatening, and giving you reason to fear for your safety. If this is the case, your ex-partner's action of repeatedly sending you gifts would constitute stalking (or harassment, depending on the state or country you live in). Each stalking action by itself may not be a criminal activity. It is not illegal to stand outside a person's place of work on a daily basis, or turn up to a fitness/yoga class they attend. However, when these activities are engaged in for the purposes of instilling fear, or forcing compliance/ acquiescence, then they become criminal activities. It is all these events, committed over a prolonged period of time, that defines stalking as stalking—an ex-partner who tries to make contact with you for a few weeks after the break-up of the relationship is not a stalker; if they consistently do this—and perhaps other similar activities—for several months, you are probably now dealing with a stalking campaign.

Many people who are being stalked are reluctant to classify what is happening to them as stalking —there is a default fear that they won't be believed, that they will be accused of overreacting and/or of trying to make themselves out to be important in some way. Many people still believe that stalking incidents are really only experienced by celebrities, and may see anyone who claims to have a stalker is somehow trying to make out that they enjoy some form of celebrity status, or think they deserve the full attention of another person. The truth is that most incidents of stalking are committed by partners and ex-partners (the 2011, CDC's "National Intimate Partner and Sexual Violence Survey" found that 61% of female, and 44% of male, victims of stalking were being stalked by a current or ex-partner), and while few turn violent, it can be difficult to predict which ones will, and which ones won't—especially if children and/or other third parties are involved in the relationship.

One of the easiest ways for someone to get into your home, is to wait until you return, and force you to let them in–if there are any burglar alarms, they can have you disable them, and if you have a dog, they can force you to lock it away, etc. An ex-partner is likely to know your routines pretty well, depending how long you have been together, and may have carried out some surveillance prior, to monitor your movements, and the times and days that you are likely to return home. It is not in your survival interests to go into your house with them. Once inside, they will be able to do whatever they want to do to you unseen, and if you live alone, will have all the time in the world to do this.

In many weapon threats and attacks–with knife as well as gun–the attacker will use their non-weapon hand to control you. They may grab the back of your neck to pull you in, while pushing the barrel of the gun up under your jaw/chin. Your head will now be clamped between their hand and the gun, restricting your movement. No attacker will make it easy for you, they will want to put you at a disadvantage. As they are doing this, they will likely be instructing you not to shout or scream, and to open the door for them.

In the moment, you may freeze, and struggle to make sense of what they are saying; this is a common response when you are put in extreme danger and become adrenalized. In a tight position, with the gun pushed up under your chin, there will be little space in which to work. It may seem counter-intuitive, but you should try to push down on the muzzle of the gun with your chin/jaw. Shrug your shoulders, and bring your hands up as close to the weapon as possible–it is the shrugging of the shoulders, which communicates your fear and submission; something that will help convince your assailant that you are not going to resist their demands.

Rapidly pull your head back to release the pressure on the gun, so it moves upwards and past your face—turn as you do this so that the gun can't easily be retrained on you. This turning motion, that sees you pull your left shoulder back, will create space for your right hand to come through and grab your attacker's wrist. Because this is such a tight maneuver, you will be more likely to gain control of the wrist/forearm, than the gun itself, as it offers a much larger target area. Move the arm across your body, so that the firearm is in front of your other hand. All of these things should happen as one movement.

Don't grab the gun, but instead "punch" it out of your attacker's hand, grabbing it as your hand makes contact. You are looking to disarm them in one movement, rather than grabbing and then trying to wrestle it out of their hand. Attackers will hold onto their weapons at all costs, which makes disarming extremely difficult. By punching the gun out of their hand, the first force they will feel, will be your hand travelling at high speed—this gives them less time to react and tense up.

Drive your punch through, until your arm is fully extended, while securing your attacker's wrist with your other hand.

Immediately follow up with combatives...

...and use the gun as a cold weapon, to deliver concussive strikes against your attacker. Keep the barrel directed towards them, to avoid muzzling yourself (this is also the strongest part of the weapon, and the part you can do most damage with). There are many issues with backing away and trying to control an assailant by threatening to shoot them, if they come towards you and/or move etc. If your attacker is someone you know, you may not be in an emotional place where you are ready to use potentially lethal force against them. You may not be legally justified, now that you have a firearm in your hand and they don't, i.e. although this may seem like the same incident to you, legally a "separation" may have occurred, taking away your justification to use lethal force, etc. For this reason, and many others, it is often preferable to use the weapon to deliver concussive force.

Dealing with Stalkers

Though stalkers are most often ex-partners, they can also develop from less serious relationships such as co-workers, roommates/neighbors, or acquaintances. Although there have been cases of strangers embarking on stalking campaigns these are much less common and are the sort that generally target celebrities and public figures. These types of stalkers are usually motivated by the need for intimacy with an individual they believe to be their "true love" (even though they may never have had an actual interaction with them). Many may have erotomanic delusions about their target, and in some rare—but headline grabbing—instances this may develop into a morbid fascination; as was the case with John Lennon's and Rebecca Schaeffer's stalkers who eventually assassinated their targets. Despite those occasions when intimacy-seeking stalkers kill, they tend not pose the same level of threat/danger as those who are motivated by rejection and resent; such as ex-partners.

Stalking is all about the stalker having a relationship with their target/victim, and it can be easy to forget this, and simply focus on each action, incident, or behavior; e.g., the 50th text message received that day, the last email in a chain of 40, etc. Stalkers want their targets to associate everything they do in life with them. The goal of continuously texting or emailing—55.3% of Stalking Victims reported unwanted electronic communication (CDC, 2011)—is to consume their targets life so that every time they get a text message, they think about them (even when it's someone else sending it). They want their target to think of them, each time they check their email—even when they haven't sent anything for a few hours. If you have a stalker and they sometimes stand outside the entrance to your building at work—never saying anything when you enter/exit. If they approach you as you enter/leave, they want you to associate arriving at, and leaving, work with them (61.7% of female stalking victims reported being approached outside their home or work by their stalker—CDC, 2011). If they leave hand-written messages under your car's wiper blades, you will soon start to think about them every time you approach your car. By doing these things, they can start to have control over you, something they seek.

All of these actions are also meant to demonstrate to you that you don't have the power to stop them; they can continue having a relationship with you, whether you want one or not; e.g., you can't stop them from sending you text messages or emails, or standing outside your place of work, or calling you on the phone. Neither one of these individual acts are criminal, and until you can prove that they form part of a coordinated and ongoing campaign against you, no laws are being broken. Your stalker will understand this; you may in fact not be their first victim—and there may be previous partners whom they have behaved this way with, before. The first thing you should start doing when you begin to feel fearful of an individual's actions, is to start logging them; each text, each email, each time they are outside your place of work, etc. Whatever evidence you can catalog to support your case, do so; e.g., If you can do so without them realizing, get a photograph of the person outside your place of work, or home. If you decide to get a Restraining Order against them, you will need to provide evidence that you are the target of a campaign—a Restraining Order, however, should be very much a last resort action, and not your initial solution.

The best way to deal with a stalker is to cut all communication with them. Recognize that you are not dealing with a rational person who can be reasoned with. Also, don't get caught up in what is right and wrong and feel that you must explain to your stalker/ex-partner that what they are doing is wrong and that they need to stop what they are doing; all this will do is confirm to them that their campaign is affecting you and that's a good enough reason for them to continue what they are doing. By communicating back to them, regardless of the context of that communication, you will be engaging in a relationship with them, and this is what they want. Some stalkers are what we refer to as "Incompetent Stalkers" who know that their attention is unwanted but believe they can wear their victims down—any response, whatever the content, acts as encouragement for them. Stalkers' motivations can change over time. What started out as a campaign to get you back (reconciliation), may just turn into a campaign where your stalker loses sight of any goals that they want to achieve as they literally become addicted to and absorbed by their campaign of revenge; fueled by the injustice and resentment of being rejected. The most successful way to end such activities, is to never communicate back however rational a request may seem; e.g., "please just meet me one last time," "I want to apologize for everything I've done and put you through," "I'm ready to move on" and "I'd just like to meet you to get some closure on the relationship," etc. Such a request may seem genuine and be met with relief; however, if they can get you to agree to this, they will have just found a way to control you. However much stress you are under and however much you hope and want to believe that this one last meeting could end their campaign, it is highly unlikely that it will—statistically, almost impossible.

We need to factor into our solutions the different ways that our assailant can respond to them. We should never assume that a technique should work. No technique deals with every possible response, and all techniques have strengths and weaknesses. It is always possible that an attacker will discover and exploit one of these—this is not necessarily the fault of the technique or the person performing it. No technique should lead you down a blind alley where no other options will be available to you if it doesn't work. If this is the case, you should question whether you want to risk everything on that technique or perhaps find better, more flexible solutions. In this situation, we'll look at what can be done if your attacker resists your disarm and starts to move/push the gun back.

As your attacker pushes back, don't try to resist them—if they are bigger/stronger than you, all you will be able to do is slow them down and delay the inevitable, which is to end with the gun pointed at you—instead, push down on the barrel of the gun. Even with a small frame, short-barrel pistol or revolver, the barrel length will give you a leverage advantage. As your attacker pushes back, their force will be redirected downwards, breaking their posture and frame.

Keep hold of their wrist and continue to push the barrel down. The more they resist, the more they will be forced towards the ground. If they release the pressure, you can once again try to disarm them of their weapon by "punching" it out of their hand.

Once their posture and frame has been broken, and their balance taken, you will now be able to take over their movement and start to pull them forward as you keep pressing down on the barrel of the gun. Once a person's head has moved past their shoulders, and their shoulders have moved past their hips, the natural direction of their movement is forward.

Keep moving backward and dragging them...

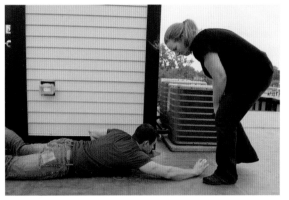

...until you have them sprawled out in front of you, and lying face-down.

At this point, you can simply rip the gun from their grasp and disengage as quickly as possible. When you move away, keep the gun close to your profile/silhouette so it is not easily identifiable; e.g., a concerned citizen with a concealed carry permit or a law enforcement officer may identify you as the aggressor if they see you waving the gun around in the air.

Although you shouldn't communicate with a stalker, it's a good idea to let them believe they still have access to you. A common response when you start getting inundated with text messages and phone calls from an ex-partner who is stalking you is to disconnect and stop using your number and get a new one. The problem with this is that your stalker will know that they are no longer reaching you and will try to find out your new number; they may get it from your friends/family members or find a way to access it through social media, etc. Stalkers can be extremely resourceful, and are adept at discovering information about you—they may have even done this in the early stages of your relationship; if you believe a partner knows more about you than you've presented to them, be suspicious—they could well be doing research on you, and this can be an indication of someone who is prone to developing obsessions. It is worth keeping your existing number active, and also getting a new one. On a weekly basis, go through the voicemails and texts of your "old" phone, and notify those people you want to stay in touch with of your new number, giving instructions for it not to be handed out and shared. This way, you can start to take back control of the communication between yourself and your stalker without them realizing. You will also be gathering evidence through their voicemails if you do end up having to go down a legal route.

You must be prepared to deal with any response that your attacker can make to your initial defense/movement; they may push back against your punch/drive to force the gun out of their hand or they may pull back in order to retain their weapon. In both cases, you shouldn't try to resist/work against their movement but instead work with it and use it to your advantage. If they pull back to keep hold of/retain their weapon, move with them...

...keeping hold of their wrist and lifting your elbow up...

...to bring it over their arm as they pull back. As you move forward, rotate the barrel of the gun so it is pointing away from you. If you just put your arm over your attacker's without doing this, you will end up muzzling yourself.

Once you have your arm over your assailant's weapon arm, pull their arm back in, squeezing it under your armpit and hugging it to your body. You will want to take away all space from the arm and isolate it. This will allow you to focus on the disarm without having to contend with any movement as you do so.

You may need to step forward as you move the elbow over and rotate the firearm in order to keep the weapon close to your body.

Once you have trapped the arm, restricting its movement, rotate the barrel of the gun away from you to release it from your assailant's grip.

Keep rotating the gun until it's released...

...and then follow up with striking/ combatives to create the opportunity/distance/time to disengage safely.

Most stalking campaigns fizzle out. It takes a lot of time and effort on the part of a stalker to run a campaign and the rewards of it often diminish over time, especially if they don't receive feedback or evidence of their actions getting the attention that they feel they deserve. It would certainly be difficult for them to devote the effort required for a stalking campaign if they became involved in another relationship; managing two "intense" relationships would take too much time. Even when a stalking campaign ends, safety and security precautions should still remain at a heightened level as a stalker's attention may return to a victim at a later date; e.g., after several failed relationships, they may once again start up a campaign against an "old" victim—often the first person they became obsessed with.

Although a stalker will often lose interest over time, there are times when campaigns may start to escalate, and the target's physical safety is put at risk. This may begin with property vandalism, and involve breaking and entering the target's home—not necessarily to steal anything, but to demonstrate that the target has no power to stop them doing whatever they want. They may even go so far as abducting, and taking hostage, their victim. If there are children involved, the risk of this goes up dramatically, especially if visitation rights have been denied, and they are prevented from seeing them —we have to be aware that certain things we do that are designed to keep us safe may actually end up increasing the risk of other threats and dangers; we may be solving one problem; i.e., ending an abusive relationship, only to replace it with another.

Rather than using a firearm to force compliance, an assailant may use a knife. Once again, if it is under your jaw, you will have very little room to maneuver. With their hand on the back of your head pulling you in, trying to pull your head directly back as part of your body defense is going to be difficult/impossible. It is worth noting that many assailants will use their free hand to control you even when they are intimidating you with a weapon.

Pivot and pull your head around (not back), as you push your attacker's weapon arm away. Just as you did with the firearm, look to feed the assailant's weapon hand to your free hand. Rather than "attack" the weapon itself, when it's a knife, you should attack their hand/grip to release the weapon.

Rather than placing your hand over theirs, make a palm strike against their hand to bend it back—you aren't pushing it, you're striking it. If your strike causes trauma to the tendons and ligaments of the wrist all the better, but don't rely on this happening. Aim your palm just below the knuckle-line, as this will give you the greatest leverage.

Once you have your attacker's weapon hand bent back, push directly down, bringing your weight down and over it. If done fast enough, you won't need to push down with much force as your attacker will instinctively bend their knees to prevent the wrist from getting damaged. As they drop their weight, continue to drive down, taking over their movement.

Once you have them moving downwards, with their frame/ posture broken, start to pull them forward...

...and towards the ground. Bringing them onto their front/ stomach and flattening them out means that all their "weapons;" e.g., hands and feet, will be pointed away from you and directed into the ground, something that wouldn't be the case if you pushed them backward. With your attacker face down, they will not have access to any secondary weapons they may be carrying at the front and you will easily be able to identify and counter any attempts they make to reach behind them.

If you wish to disarm, continue to push on the back of their hand below the knuckles, rather than at the fingers, until it opens up and you can slide your hand down and around their weapon...

...before "scraping" it out. Understand that, although you now have their knife, they may still continue to fight with you, so disengaging quickly will still be your best survival strategy. If you aren't prepared to use the knife against them, because you have a moral qualm about stabbing/cutting someone or simply lack the appropriate training, you may want to look at destroying their wrist so that they won't be able to use a second weapon with (what you can assume to be) their dominant hand.

If you're unable to scrape the knife out of their hand because of the strength of their grip, you will need a more forceful option. Keeping their elbow pinned, with their forearm vertical and at a 90 degree angle to the ground, keep hold of their wrist and release your top hand, bringing it up in preparation to smash it down onto the back of their hand.

Now bring it down with full force onto their knuckles, causing trauma to the hand and wrist to force your attacker to release/drop the knife. While this is one way to disarm the attacker of their weapon, "scraping" it out of their grip is generally quicker and more predictable; i.e., the knife will be in your hand at the end, rather than somewhere on the ground.

Restraining Orders

Many people have an over-inflated idea of what both the police and the legal system are able to accomplish for us; e.g., many people believe that the police will automatically be able to "deal" with a noise complaint; however, there are many factors at play in such incidents (the time of day, how the noise sounds from your property—which is subjective—and whether the noise comes from a commercial or residential area, etc.), and the police will not be able to intervene unless an ordinance has been broken—even if to you the noise seems intolerable. What is unfair, may not be illegal, or it may be very difficult to discern this legality. Believing that the police can always intervene on our behalf, where a perceived injustice has been committed, is to have an unfair expectation of what they are able to do in particular circumstances.

Unfortunately, a lot of people look on Restraining Orders (sometimes referred to as Orders of Protection) as a silver bullet for dealing with stalkers; i.e., you take out a Restraining Order against someone and they'll never bother you again. If someone has already engaged in a campaign of unreasonable and anti-social activities against their target, such as hanging around outside their place of work or their home, constantly emailing, texting and calling them, etc. it is unlikely that they will respect the boundaries that a Restraining Order places on them. If they believe that the person is their "true love," they will not let a piece of paper get in the way of their destiny to be with them. The value of the Restraining Order is that once it is broken, a criminal act has occurred, which can result in jail time and/or fines—if another act is committed alongside the breaking of the order, such as an assault, or an act of vandalism, the incident will be treated as more serious, and harsher sentencing is likely to be the result—in 1994, the U.S. Congress passed a law that gave state reciprocity regarding Restraining Orders so that a Restraining Order given in one state could still apply if a victim should move to another.

When you take out a Restraining Order, you should work from the premise that your stalker will break it. In fact, many stalkers will deliberately violate R.O.s to demonstrate to you, that you don't control them, and aren't able to influence or restrict their behaviors and actions. In certain cases, the response a stalker makes to a Restraining Order can be deadly. In 1988 when a temporary Restraining Order brought against Richard Farley, by his former co-worker Laura Black, was about to be made permanent, he responded by engaging in a shooting spree at her place of work, where he shot her through her office door (she survived). Laura Black, who had been urged by her employers to take out the R.O. against Farley had, privately feared he would respond in a violent fashion.

For a number of reasons, including stalking, violent partners and ex-partners, and working in industries/jobs which are predominately female—hospitality, customer facing, clinical jobs etc.—women make up the majority of the victims in incidents of workplace violence.

This doesn't mean that Restraining Orders don't have their place or worth, rather that if you take one out against an individual, you should expect, and prepare, for them to break it—and not trust it to be the solution that will end/finish your stalker's campaign.

Defending Third Parties

Sometimes our security is compromised by others. When we make our risk-assessments of a situation, we should acknowledge if other people—rather than ourselves—might be a vulnerability that a threat could exploit. This can include people we live with who might not be as vigilant or safety-conscious as we are. An ex-partner who is a stalker, may recognize that his target has started to take safety precautions that are making it difficult for them to gain access to them. However, it may be that their roommate or a family member whom they live with who is a much "softer" target, and who can be easily exploited. Instead of targeting their person they are stalking, they may turn their attention to them, using them to gain access to your property etc. They may execute a push-in of some kind and/or simply follow them into the apartment, when they fail to close the door before putting their shopping bags down, etc. They may now force the roommate at knife point to start providing information about their ex-partner; e.g., whether they are seeing someone else, if they've changed their phone number, etc.

This type of situation will see you having to defend a third party rather than yourself.

Approach the target from behind and place one hand on their shoulder. As you do this, grab the attacker's weapon arm and start to push it away from the victim's throat (this will form the hand-defense component of the solution), at the same time as you do this...

...start to pull on the target's shoulder so that their throat is turned away from the knife (this forms the body-defense component of the solution). Keep driving forward with your left arm to push the knife into the attacker's stomach. One of your first priorities when dealing with an edged weapon should be to take its movement away so it is unable to cut, stab or slash. As you pull the third party's shoulder back, pull/turn your body with theirs so that you are blading (turning your body to the side) your body to the attacker's —this will push your left shoulder forward and allow you to drive the knife further towards your attacker.

Once you have cleared the knife from the target's throat, and have pulled their throat clear of the knife, release your hand from their shoulder and get it into a position from which you can deliver a strike/punch.

When you are dealing with defending/protecting third parties, you may need to give them instructions and tell them what to do. Many will end up "freezing" and not react/respond to the situation. Shouting at them and telling them what to do can increase both of your survival chances. If you can get them to assist you in dealing with the attacker, and have them play an active role, then you will turn the situation into a multiple attacker scenario against your assailant.

Keep driving forward, forcing your attacker backward—you don't want to give them the opportunity to step back and make room to clear their knife. If you can, press them into something that restricts their movement so that the knife remains trapped. Using the environment to your advantage, and your attacker's detriment, is something you should try to do whenever possible.

Deliver concussive blows repeatedly at your assailant. Keep the arm that is pinning their knife locked throughout the entire process controlling their weapon arm. With the arm in this position, your assailant will find it extremely difficult to push the knife back towards you as they will be working against the joint—if your arm is bent, you'll need to use muscular force to prevent them doing this.

Keep striking while the third party gets hold of an improvised weapon that they can use to deliver concussive force against your assailant. You may need to instruct them to do this.

A solid object, such as a fire-extinguisher, will have both the weight and the structural integrity to deliver forceful blows. It will also be an object that, due to its size, will be difficult to defend against. Once your assailant is significantly stunned, both you and the third party should exit the environment. It will be easier for the two of you to leave a location than to force your attacker out.

It would also be possible for you to disarm your assailant from this position (see *Krav Maga: Tactical Survival*, pp. 101–103). When you perform techniques on behalf of a third party, you are effectively using the same movements you would use to defend yourself, and are merely modifying them so that you perform the hand and body defense on the other person's behalf. Another way to deal with the above situation is as follows.

If you are concerned about your hand sliding off the shoulder of the person you are trying to protect, grab their clothing instead, and use this to pull their shoulder back. You can also use your forearm, to move the knife away from their throat—you might use this alternative, if you feel your attacker's wrist/forearm is too big for you to be able to get an adequate grip on it, or if you don't trust your ability to control the weapon arm this way, due to sweat, etc.

Rather than simply "pushing" the weapon arm away, turn your torso and raise your elbow up. This will not only move the weapon arm away, it will also pull it past you.

You should always be aware of how your attacker may respond and be prepared for your defenses to work with their movements. It may be that you start to guide their movement or end up following it but either way, extend your arm and bring it over your assailant's forearm to start to push it back towards them. Start to bring your other arm/hand towards and over the upper part of the weapon arm. As you do all of this, start to move in towards them.

"Snake" your wrist/arm around your assailant's forearm, and take hold of their upper arm with your other hand.

Start to rotate their arm as you continue to move in towards them.

Keep moving into them as you rotate their arm (using the snaking action of your hand on the wrist and the pulling action on their upper arm/triceps). Pull their arm to your chest as you bring your chest to their arm. As you continue moving towards them, use your forward momentum to set up a knee strike.

As you deliver your knee strike and control the weapon arm, position your attacker so that the third party can use the fire extinguisher to deliver concussive blows without worrying about hitting you. If you have to choose between an improvised weapon that can potentially render an attacker unconscious or one that can cut/slash, go for the former. Knocking someone out is faster and more conclusive than waiting for them to bleed out from a wound.

If, when you snaked your left arm up your control ended up on the attacker's forearm rather than the wrist, you will need to slide down their arm to control the wrist. You will have a better chance of controlling the weapon arm here than further up the arm where it is stronger. Also, if your control is further up the arm, you may not be able to reach your attacker's hand to open it up to disarm them of the knife. Reach over, behind the knuckles, so your fingers are pressed into the back of their hand.

As the third party repeatedly strikes them with the fire extinguisher, pull on the back of your attacker's hand so that their grip starts to lessen and their hand opens up...

Keep pulling on their hand until the knife is loose, and then hook your little finger around it to pull it out of their grasp, wrapping the rest of your fingers around the handle, as you do so...

...and use it to cut the muscle and tendons of the upper arm so it can no longer mechanically function. Don't simply cut the muscle but instead drag the blade through and around the muscles and tendons of the arm in a continuous fashion in order to cause the most trauma and damage—your goal should be to completely disable the functioning of the arm. Once you can safely disengage, do so.

Stalking rarely involves extreme violence—most campaigns end after the victim stops communicating with their stalker; which is why this should be the initial and primary strategy for dealing with them. However, individuals who have committed time, effort, and resources to a relationship, may not be able to come to terms with it ending, and therefore begin to engage in behaviors and activities, that they eventually become addicted to. As each of their actions, fails to have the effect they believed it would, or the effect over time starts to lessen, they may adopt more and more extreme strategies that can come to include physical violence.

Our homes are places which we would should feel safe in; however, we often take this safety for granted and expect others to respect our right to both privacy and protection. Unfortunately, there are those individuals—be they strangers, acquaintances, friends, intimate partners, or family members —whose world view contradicts our own. These individuals may believe that they are entitled and justified to behave and act in a way that causes us harm and injury, or simply causes us to live a life in a continued state of fear and unease; because that's how they experience power and control.

Conclusion

Situations determine solutions. Concepts and principals can act as heuristics that guide us and help us fashion our solutions but at the end of the day, context is the determining factor as to what we should and shouldn't do; e.g., there are times we should control the weapon and times we should control the attacker, etc. We should avoid taking a prescriptive approach to dealing with violence that would see us decide on our strategies beforehand and doggedly adhere to them, however inappropriate they turned out to be. Instead, we should be looking to educate ourselves about what different types of violence look like and how we can identify instances of them before they occur, either to enable us to prepare for dealing with them or to give us a chance of avoiding them completely. Understanding the contextual and situational elements of violence will allow us to do this, and will also help us to be more aware of what is occurring in our environment.

Unfortunately, we have lost much of the curiosity we once had concerning what occurs around us. We rarely question things which are out of place and not the norm and instead ignore or discount them,\ rather than taking a closer look and investigating them. Klebold and Harris planted two significantly large bombs in Columbine's school's cafeteria, which were investigated and left—it was easier and less awkward to categorize them as a practical joke rather than raise the alarm (fortunately neither one went off; however, a third that they'd used as a "decoy" at another location, did). When we first came down from the trees and started walking on the Savannah Plains, we'd have been curious about everything and not just about that which affected our safety. Our environment was a new one and we needed to educate ourselves about it. This type of curiosity has been lost and we need to get it back. We need to question those things around us which our fear system brings to our attention and be far more curious about them than we are.

We need to plan more. We need to have our escape routes defined ahead of time, and have safe places where we can go should we need to. We need to think about our safety and be prepared to deal with those things that threaten it. This should not lead us to become fearful or paranoid but instead allow us to relax because we know what we should start doing when threatened. Our plans should be open and flexible and account for the context of the danger.

Above all, we need to develop and build on our own sense of worth—we need to believe that survival is our right and that nobody has the right to question it. We should develop an understanding that we are worth fighting for, and protecting, and be prepared to respond with all of our being and with every emotion when somebody believes that this is not the case. No killer has the right to take life and when responding to an incident of extreme violence, we should have no doubts about this and be prepared to do whatever is necessary to survive.

Acknowledgments

I am fortunate in the books I write to have a strong team behind me and the support of my school. There are, though, specific individuals who deserve a mention for their stellar and important contributions in making this book possible. First mention must go to our photographer Colin O'Reilly, whose generosity with his expertise and time allows us to have such excellent photos which both illustrate the techniques and demonstrate the situations so perfectly. I'm always amazed at his energy and enthusiasm for these projects and I really can't thank him enough or express how lucky we are to have him involved. I must also extend my thanks to Dave Matteo who helped us out with many of the locations where we filmed—his time and commitment to this project was more than I could have hoped for and I'm indebted to his continuous and tireless work to make sure everything ran smoothly on the shoots. Likewise, a big thank you must be given to Stephen Wroblenski, his drama students, and Wellesley High School for their help with the school shooting scenes and sharing their school with us, and to Joe Kislo, for allowing us to use his offices to shoot the section on workplace violence. I would also like to thank Nick Zagami for his help with other locations that we used, for his illustrative abilities and for his support in this and other projects which we value so highly.

This book would not have been possible without the help of those who played active parts in the scenes, either by performing techniques, acting as aggressors, or being supporting members of the cast. The scenes we shot required large groups to work effectively together on tight timelines, and in often uncomfortable and imperfect settings. Such is the nature of these things. Still, everyone involved threw themselves into it and I am grateful to those individuals who played the roles the book required, and did so with full commitment and in good spirits: Liz Berrien, Justin Brown, Scott Campeau, Griffin Coombs, Brett Fedigan, Pat Gagnon, Frederic Gay, Caroline Magnain, Jason Mantagos, Valia Markaki, Dave Matteo, Elizabeth Matteo, Kris Ni, Jim Rottman, Dave Schaffner, Jon Yee and Nick Zagami.

As always, a special thanks to Liz Berrien, who edits my writing so that it is understandable, and who on numerous occasions has burnt the midnight oil in order to meet tight deadlines, and to Allen Berrien for his professional guidance and and his love of the written word. Writing such a book is not a one-person endeavor, and while my name may go on the cover, it's a collaborative work and my thanks goes out to all involved.

About Tuttle "Books to Span the East and West"

Our core mission at Tuttle Publishing is to create books which bring people together one page at a time. Tuttle was founded in 1832 in the small New England town of Rutland, Vermont (USA). Our fundamental values remain as strong today as they were then—to publish best-in-class books informing the English-speaking world about the countries and peoples of Asia. The world has become a smaller place today and Asia's economic, cultural and political influence has expanded, yet the need for meaningful dialogue and information about this diverse region has never been greater. Since 1948, Tuttle has been a leader in publishing books on the cultures, arts, cuisines, languages and literatures of Asia. Our authors and photographers have won numerous awards and Tuttle has published thousands of books on subjects ranging from martial arts to paper crafts. We welcome you to explore the wealth of information available on Asia at **www.tuttlepublishing.com.**